The Girl with the Suitcase

The Girl
with the Suitcase

A Girl Without a Home and the Foster Carer Who
Changes her Life Forever

ANGELA HART

bluebird
books for life

First published 2020 by Bluebird
an imprint of Pan Macmillan
The Smithson, 6 Briset Street, London EC1M 5NR
Associated companies throughout the world
www.panmacmillan.com

ISBN 978-1-5290-2442-5

1 3 5 7 9 8 6 4 2

A CIP catalogue record for this book is available from the British Library.

Typeset by Palimpsest Book Production Ltd, Falkirk, Stirlingshire
Printed and bound by CPI Group (UK) Ltd, Croydon, CR0 4YY

Visit **www.panmacmillan.com** to read more about all our books
and to buy them. You will also find features, author interviews and
news of any author events, and you can sign up for e-newsletters
so that you're always first to hear about our new releases.

The Girl with the Suitcase

1

'She's been in several other foster homes'

'Back to reality,' my husband Jonathan remarked, as we carried our bags into the house. We'd managed to snatch a couple of nights away together by the sea, after unexpectedly finding ourselves with an empty house. A teenage boy we'd been looking after had moved on sooner than we'd anticipated and, by coincidence, the two other children we were fostering were both spending a few days with their relatives during the school summer holidays.

'Do you think it's OK for us to go away?' I'd said to my friend Joanne, who was also a foster carer. 'I mean, it's mid-week. Should we be doing this?'

'Don't be daft!' she laughed. 'Opportunities like this don't come around very often. It's not a long holiday or even a long weekend. When was the last time just the two of you managed to get away for a couple of days?'

Jonathan and I did take regular holidays whenever we could, and ever since we'd started fostering we'd taken whichever children we had staying with us on our annual week or fortnight away.

'Just us, with no kids? I honestly can't remember. Must be eight or nine years? Maybe longer.'

'I rest my case.' Joanne smiled. 'Just notify Social Services – book the B & B and tell them where you will be staying. As long as everyone has your contact details in case of an emergency, what's the problem? You're only going to be a few hours' drive away.'

I tentatively took my friend's advice, though I still felt uneasy about it and couldn't help fretting to Jonathan. 'What if a child needs us and we're not here? And what if Social Services urgently need our help and we have to say no? And there's the shop. Do you really think we can . . .?'

Jonathan reassured me that our assistant Barbara could easily run our florist shop for a couple of days, especially as my mum had offered to help out too. It had been my parents' business before my father died, and my mum had run the shop on her own for a while before handing the reins to Jonathan and me. She wasn't getting any younger, of course, but Mum was still a very capable woman, and she was always willing to roll up her sleeves if we needed any help. As luck would have it, we only had one small wedding in the diary that weekend, which was unusual for July. This meant Mum and Barbara could easily deal with the preparations for the church flowers, bouquets and corsages. We'd be back on the Thursday evening, when there would be plenty of time for us to take over and organise our regular deliveries too.

'There's absolutely nothing to worry about,' Jonathan told me. 'Everything is manageable.'

'I know you're right,' I sighed. 'But we're always needed here. I feel kind of selfish going away on our own.'

A few years after we started fostering, Jonathan and I began specialist training so we could take in children, and particularly teenagers, with complex needs. Now the majority of the children who came to us – often from another placement that had broken down, and frequently in an emergency situation – needed specialist care of some description. Demand for specialist carers always outstripped supply in our part of the country and I felt a huge burden of responsibility towards the social workers who struggled on a daily basis to find homes for kids in crisis.

It was Jonathan's turn to sigh. 'Look, what you say is true and part of me feels the same. I know we're needed here, but we need a break like everybody else. We haven't had an easy time of it lately, and every holiday we've taken for years has been with the kids.'

I couldn't argue.

'Anyhow,' he went on, 'I bet you a pound to a penny the phone will ring the minute we step foot back in the house. And guess what? It'll be Social Services and we'll be plunged straight back into the thick of a new challenge. We'll be ready for it, because we'll have recharged our batteries.'

I had to agree. The change of scene would do us both good, and I knew Jonathan was tired out and needed to relax. More often than not he was the one who opened up the shop, went to the wholesalers, ran around making the deliveries and closed up at the end of the day. He never grumbled; in fact it was the opposite. He would tell anyone who would listen what a good team we made, and how lucky we were to work together and combine the running of the shop with fostering. Whenever we'd had broken sleep or had been up half the night dealing with one of the kids, Jonathan was the one who sprang out of bed at the crack of dawn without a word of complaint. Disturbed nights had been happening often lately. The two girls who were living with us both had a lot of problems, and in recent times we'd also looked after a succession of children who came to us for short stays, or respite care, as it's known. Most proved incredibly challenging; for example, the teenage boy who'd just moved on had been in trouble with the police for stealing cars and joyriding. He never came home on time, and sometimes not at all. We'd lost so much sleep during his stay I felt wiped out.

Needless to say, I was very pleased I had finally agreed to go to the seaside. Jonathan and I had a wonderful time, soaking up some lovely sunshine, strolling along the coast and eating fish and chips out of paper trays. With the sea breeze in my hair I felt like I didn't have a care in the world – well, apart from knowing I had to face the dreaded scales at my slimming club the following week!

'We're so lucky,' I said as we watched the sun set. 'I feel blessed. We have a privileged life, don't we?'

Jonathan put his arm around me. 'We do. We certainly

do.' I didn't have to spell it out for Jonathan to know exactly what I meant by 'privileged'. We didn't have fancy cars or designer clothes and we didn't live a lavish lifestyle in any way at all. It was the old estate car and a caravan for us; my wardrobe was full of comfy jeans, 'flatties' and bargains from my favourite outlet store and catalogues; and the restaurant we ate at the most was Pizza Hut, because all the kids loved it.

But we *were* privileged. We were trusted to look after kids who had fallen through the cracks of society. Social Services may have picked them up, but they were still in desperate need of rescuing. When we first began fostering, Jonathan and I naively thought we could save these children by simply loving them and giving them a safe, warm home. For this we thought they would be grateful, and that they'd want to live with us. We soon saw that there was a lot more to it than that, and that dealing with the families they pined for would be a big part of the job.

We learned quickly that one of the keys to fostering success is to show each child you *believe* in them. Kids in care have most likely been rejected and neglected rather than championed and cherished, as children ought to be. Often, nobody has *ever* believed in them, throughout their lifetime. With their life in our hands, for however long that may be, it's our job to show the most damaged and dejected kids we believe in them wholeheartedly, and that their future does not have to be dictated by their past. Once they trust us and believe in us too, fantastic things can happen. It's such an honour to be given the chance to change a life; I can't imagine any other job could be so rewarding.

We had a good journey back from the coast and even managed to catch up with some old friends who lived en route and had invited us to drop in. I felt thoroughly relaxed as we sat on their patio, catching up on all their news. We didn't stay long; time was moving on and, despite having had such a good break, I was ready to go home. As soon as we'd left the seaside I'd started planning what needed to be done. The washing was the priority. There were our clothes from the trip and I wanted to strip all the beds and have the spare room ready for the next child to move into, whoever it may be. That's always a priority; if a child arrives at short notice, I want them to feel as welcome as possible, and having a clean, fresh bedroom is very important. The only thing I don't do is choose the bedding, as I like to give them the opportunity to pick whichever duvet set they like.

Back home, the phone rang before we had even unpacked the car. I was in the kitchen, reaching for the kettle, and Jonathan was bringing in our picnic rug and cool box. 'What was it you said before we went away?' I smiled, raising my eyebrows and nodding towards the phone.

'I bet you a pound to a penny the phone will ring the minute we step foot back in the house . . .' Jonathan replied.

'And guess what?'

'We'll be plunged straight back into the thick of it!' we said in unison.

Jonathan held out his hand, as if for his imaginary prize winnings, and I answered the call. Sure enough, it was a social worker asking if we could take in a child at short notice.

'I hope we can,' I said. Jonathan nodded his head in approval and gave me an encouraging smile. We'd been passed to take in up to three children, and if we had a spare room we always did our best to help.

Normally it would be our support social worker, Jess, who contacted us, as all our placements went through her. There was invariably a list of children who were waiting for specialist placements pinned up on a board in her office. However, she wasn't working that day and it was another supervising social worker I'd never met before who called. Mrs Chambers was very well spoken and she talked quickly and in quite a brisk, business-like tone, explaining that the child who needed a placement was from a neighbouring authority.

'You and your husband sound perfect for this young girl. There's nobody available in her region. Can I give your number to the social worker in charge of the case? I've heard tremendous things about you and I really hope you can help.'

The compliment was unexpected and I felt a rush of pride. It's always a boost to receive praise, though on this occasion I also found myself feeling slightly anxious. I'd learned from experience that kind words from a social worker you don't know might mean you're about to be talked into taking on a particularly tough challenge.

'Yes, of course, and we'll do our best to help,' I said. 'What are the child's circumstances?'

I found myself wishing I was talking to Jess as usual, because I knew I could trust her to be frank and realistic when discussing a possible newcomer. Jess would always share as much information as she possibly could but, unfortunately, this is not the case with all social workers. We'd heard some disturbing tales over the years. For instance, my friend Joanne had told us of one occasion when Social Services had claimed they had no background information available on a particular child they were desperate to place at very short notice. Joanne took the young boy in that same night, only to discover there was no shortage of notes at all. His paperwork, had anyone taken the trouble to share it, spelled out a set of severe problems that meant he was extremely difficult to manage alongside the other children she already had living with her.

Of course, it's not that social workers don't care about how foster carers are going to cope. It's simply a case of 'needs must' in an urgent situation. When it's late in the day and a child still has no bed for the night, social workers are under great pressure to place them with a foster carer. The child is the priority, and the sad truth is that if Joanne hadn't taken that young boy in, he probably would have ended up in a children's home that night, or even a secure unit. This was something we'd encountered earlier on in our specialist fostering career, when we took in a young girl, called Melissa, who was locked up in a secure unit as there was nowhere else for her to go. (I told her story in *The Girl in the Dark*.)

With bated breath, I waited for Mrs Chambers to give me some more information about the young girl. I checked the time. It was almost five o'clock.

'I'm afraid I have very little information. I'll get her social worker to call you, he's waiting for me to get back to him. I'll get him to ring you as soon as possible.' She thanked me very much and ended the call briskly and efficiently.

I felt anxious as I waited for the phone to ring. The social worker who was phoning was called Barry. I realised I didn't even know the name of the girl, or anything else for that matter.

I picked up the phone almost immediately when it rang. Barry sounded like a very affable chap. Like nearly every social worker I've met, he also sounded very busy and somewhat stressed, but he had an engaging manner. He told me the 'young lady' was called Grace. She was ten years old and her current placement was breaking down. He explained that her carers had given the usual twenty-eight days' notice to find her a new home, but unfortunately, due to an acute shortage of specialist carers, time was now running out.

'How long has she been in foster care?' I asked.

'Quite a number of years. She's been in several other foster homes.' Barry added that he had only recently taken over as Grace's social worker, I think by way of apology for not knowing the details of these facts off the top of his head. I could hear him rustling paperwork as we spoke. 'If you bear with me, I'll tell you more.'

I already wanted to give Grace a home. She was only

ten years old and she must have been in care from a young age. My heart went out to her, but I told myself not to rush in. I knew I needed to find out as much as I possibly could before agreeing to take in a third child; after all, we already had two challenging children living with us and I had to consider their needs before making a commitment.

'Can I ask, why is the placement breaking down?'

There was a pause while, I assume, Barry searched through Grace's file. 'Apparently Grace "winds other children up the wrong way". Her "aggravating and disruptive behaviour" has led to the breakdown of previous placements too, it seems. Let me see how many previous placements there have been.'

There was more rustling of paper and then an even longer pause. Barry tutted and began to count. I could hear him thumbing through lots of paperwork.

'Thanks for your patience. Grace's file is not the smallest one I've seen, unfortunately.' It's times like this that I feel a brief, chronological summary of a child's background and previous placements would be useful for any new social worker to get to know about their caseloads. I wish this was kept at the front of each file.

Finally, and rather reluctantly, Barry told me that Grace had lived in a total of eight different foster homes, including her current one, from the age of three. My heart sank. *No wonder the poor child was 'aggravating'*, I thought. *What ten-year-old child wouldn't be, if they'd been rehoused eight times in – what – seven years? Bless her little heart.*

Barry explained that, if we were happy to have her, he would bring Grace to our house the following day, which was a Friday, for a trial visit over the weekend. He apologised for the short notice but said that her current carers wanted her to move out as quickly as possible, as the placement had been breaking down for a few weeks by now. If we were in agreement, Grace would stay with us until Monday morning. She was on a full care order but had contact with her family and regularly went home for visits.

'If it works out and the trial period is a success – and I'm sure it will be, as I've heard nothing but praise for you and your good husband – then Grace will spend a week with her mother before moving in full time with you. She'll also go back to her current carers for a short stay, to say goodbye, before the move.' The plan was for this to be a six-month placement initially, with a view to extending it longer term.

'I'm hoping you and your husband will make all the difference. I'm told you have helped turn around so many other young lives. If only we had more like you, that's all I can say.'

I wondered why Grace couldn't live with her mother and why she would go and spend a week with her if her trial visit worked out and she was moving in with us. It seemed like a lot of disruption for her, especially as she would also be going back to her current carer to say goodbye. It was a set-up I'd never come across before but I didn't question it. Experience had taught me to let Social Services take the lead at times like this. At the end of the day, Barry was up against it and the priority right now was to find Grace a new home. The clock was ticking – it was almost five thirty – and we needed to make a decision.

Quickly, I asked Barry about what seemed to be the most pressing issue. 'When you say "aggravating and disruptive behaviour", do you know what that means, exactly?'

'Not entirely, no. I've found her to be a lovely young girl, friendly, lively, chatty. She's not statemented. No medical conditions. Aggravating others – adults and children, from what I can gather – is the thing that crops up time and time again in the paperwork.'

A statement of special needs is a formal document that spells out a child's learning difficulties and the help needed at school, beyond what their regular teachers can provide. I knew that not being 'statemented' did not necessarily mean a child had no learning difficulties. We've dealt with several kids over the years who we felt ought to have had a statement but, for whatever reason, had not.

The process of having a child statemented is quite complex and time-consuming and, with the backing of experts, we've fought for several children in our care over the years, to give them the help they need. Unfortunately, when kids with learning difficulties are being moved from one foster home to the next sometimes they slip through the net, as by the time their needs are picked up on by the carer or the school the child is on the move again and back to square one. I know of a case where a child in care had waited many months for an appointment with CAMHS – Child and Adolescent Mental Health Services – but just as the appointment came through he was moved out of county. Very frustratingly, the neighbouring county's CAMHS department said the boy would have to start again at the bottom of their list. After more than thirty years of fostering, I have to say that the lack of support for children with mental health issues is one of my biggest bugbears. The service is crying out for more staff and resources, because kids with mental health problems need help straight away, not at some indeterminate date in the future.

I waited for Barry to continue giving me information. He said he had the notes from the last review meeting with Grace's mother. 'Mum said, "Grace doesn't listen on purpose, to wind me up",' he read.

I considered this and asked if a single placement had been sought for Grace, as this would seem to be a logical strategy, given her apparent difficulties in getting along with others. Barry agreed with me. He said that that would have been ideal, but there was simply nobody available.

'The problem we have is that there are no specialist carers available at all in our area to take on Grace. There's nobody with your expertise and training, that's the issue. That's why this has become as urgent as it is. Time is running out. We didn't want to have to go out of county but we have no choice, because this young lady needs a fresh start in a new home.'

I asked Barry to hold the line while I consulted Jonathan, as I always do. We both agreed instantly that Grace should come for the weekend, arriving the next day. I shuddered to think how a little girl's tendency to annoy people around her could have led to such a devastating chain of events. Eight foster placements in seven years, and a mother who had access to her child but was not bringing her up? My heart ached just thinking about it.

2

'They call me Little Miss Trouble'

'Hello, I'm Grace.'

I looked down at the petite young girl standing on my doorstep. She appeared dwarfed by the burly middle-aged man standing on one side, who cheerfully told me he was Barry, and a large grey suitcase that was bulging at the seams on the other. Everything about Grace seemed small, from her heart-shaped little face and tiny hands to her soft, whispering voice. Everything, that is, except for her eye-catching explosion of strawberry blonde curls.

Grace looked slightly dazed as I told her I was pleased to see her, invited her to call me Angela and asked her to come inside. 'What about my scooter?' she said shyly, turning her head towards Barry but not looking at him.

'I'll fetch that for you, little lady,' he said kindly. 'Let me worry about bringing all your things inside. I trust you have room for a scooter, Angela?' Addressing Grace he added, 'There's a pogo stick as well, if I'm not mistaken? Aren't you the lucky one? I'd have sold my granny for a pogo stick when I was your age!'

Grace looked a bit confused and nodded at nobody in particular while I said that yes, of course we had room for her scooter and the pogo stick. I took to Barry straight away. He was less stressed than he had been on the phone, and I liked his friendly manner and the engaging way he talked to Grace.

Normally, a child coming for a short weekend stay would not bring so many belongings, but I didn't question it. Instead, I explained that we liked to get out in the fresh air whenever we could, and that there were plenty of places to go with the scooter. I also said we enjoyed cycling and liked to go on rides with all the children who stayed with us, and that we had a bike she could use, if she wanted to. 'My husband will be here in a minute and he'll show you where we can lock the scooter up, in the garage,' I said to Grace. 'The pogo stick will be fine in there too. My husband's called Jonathan, by the way. He'll also show you where we keep all our spare helmets and things.'

Barry caught my eye and gave me an encouraging smile and, unexpectedly, a wink. Having this conversation in front of Grace was basic good practice. Our training had taught us that when a child comes to stay they need to be reassured that their possessions are safe and secure, particularly when they are stored out of sight. I imagined that Grace, more than anyone, needed to have her mind put at rest; I couldn't imagine how unsettling and worrying it must have been for her to have moved house so many times.

I invited Grace to sit at the kitchen table while Barry went back to the car. I'd only expected her to have a weekend bag and I wondered why she had brought so much.

'Would you like a drink, Grace? It's very warm today. I'm having a glass of water.'

'Have you got any Coke?' she asked quietly, pushing some stray curls out of her eyes and fishing in the pockets of her jeans for something.

I avoided having fizzy drinks in the house, having seen how some children went a bit 'hyper' on them, as we used to say. In that day and age – more than twenty years ago – we didn't have half as much information as we have now about how bad fizzy drinks can be for kids, but it seemed common sense to avoid them; life was challenging enough without kids bouncing off the walls!

'I'm afraid not. I've got squash. Let me see – orange, lemon or forest fruits?'

Grace looked around blankly as she pulled a thick, white cotton headband out of her back pocket. In one swift movement she pulled it down over her curls until it was around her neck, then pushed the front of it up and over her forehead, revealing a shiny ring of sweat at her hairline. She'd clearly done that many times before. The wide, elasticated headband had the effect of flattening and taming the spiral curls on top of her head and creating two thick curtains of ringlets that cascaded down either side of her little face.

Grace was extremely pretty. She had lovely hazel green eyes and, under the last drops of evening sun that beamed through our kitchen window, her hair shimmered with copper and blonde highlights. I'd paid fortunes over the years to put highlights of all shades in my naturally mousy brown hair. I wanted to tell this to Grace and compliment her on her natural colour, but it wasn't the right time. Kids often feel incredibly self-conscious when they first arrive, and focusing on their looks, however positively, can increase their shyness and anxiety and make them feel uncomfortable.

Grace didn't seem to be able to make up her mind about which drink to have. She continued to look rather bemused and she screwed up her eyes, as if she was trying to concentrate hard. To fill the silence, I told her I could also offer her some fresh pineapple juice. Opening the fridge door to check, I added, 'We have some apple cordial too, if you'd like that?'

Grace blinked several times and looked around the room. Her skin was naturally very fair but was quite pink in the heat. I expected she really needed a cold drink.

'Erm, I don't mind. What have you got?'

I wasn't sure if Grace wanted me to repeat the list or remind her that I was drinking a glass of water, so I thought I'd make it easy for her.

'I've got a nice glass of cold water. Do you want water?' She didn't reply. 'Or maybe orange squash?'

'Orange squash,' she whispered.

The poor mite, I thought. She was probably feeling very nervous, and no doubt all her concentration was going into simply coping with being in a different house, yet again. She was probably tired too; the foster home she had come from was more than an hour away and Barry must have hit rush hour traffic, which was typically heavier on a Friday evening.

I prepared a tumbler of orange squash and asked Grace if she wanted ice.

'Ice?'

'Yes, sweetheart. Do you want ice in your squash? Like I have ice in my water? I've got a tray of ice cubes in the freezer. It's no trouble. It'll make your drink nice and cold and might help cool you down if you're feeling hot.'

'No thanks.'

Jonathan came through from our florist shop next door and introduced himself to Grace. He said he'd met Barry on the way and had suggested he take the scooter and pogo stick straight round to the garden, ready to go in the garage.

'What d'you think of these?' Jonathan was carrying a couple of bunches of flowers that were past their sell-by date. He explained to Grace that we ran the shop that was attached to our house. 'I thought these would brighten up our kitchen for the weekend,' he added cheerfully. 'Shame to throw them away.' Grace didn't speak. Jonathan then asked her if she liked flowers – I imagined that's one of the reasons he thought to fetch them in, to use them as an ice-breaker – and she nodded and said she did.

'But I like trees best.'

'Trees? I love trees too. We've got some trees in our back garden. Do you want me to show you, and we can lock your scooter and pogo stick in the garage at the same time?'

Grace picked up her beaker of orange squash, downed

the drink in one, wiped her lips with the back of her hand and got up to follow Jonathan.

'What's your favourite type of tree?'

'Any.'

'What about the mighty oak? I love oak trees. And conker trees, of course.'

'Any tree I can climb,' I heard Grace say as they headed outside. Her voice had grown a little louder, I was pleased to note.

I watched them from the window. Barry was in the back garden with the scooter and pogo stick, and he stayed chatting to Grace and Jonathan for a minute or two before coming into the kitchen to talk to me about the arrangements.

'She seems such a sweet little thing,' he said, nodding in Grace's direction and frowning slightly, as if he couldn't really understand her situation. 'Let's hope things start to turn around for her.'

Barry told me once again that he had not been Grace's social worker for very long. In fact, he was so new to the job he had only taken over when her last placement was already breaking down. He would continue as Grace's social worker even if she moved out of her local authority, and he told me that in the next week or so he would take charge of all her lifts, to and from her previous carer's home, and back and forth to her mother's home, both of which were about an hour away by car.

In normal circumstances, our support social worker would have been present for this drop-off, but as Jess was on leave it was left to Barry to do the handover on his own. He told me everybody involved was hoping this trial period would work, and that afterwards Grace could come to us for at least six months, and hopefully more.

'Is that why you let her bring so much stuff?' I asked, smiling.

'Ah, yes! I did try to encourage her to leave the scooter and pogo stick behind and not bring that big suitcase, but she wasn't having it. Lucky I've got muscles, hey?' He raised his fist and flexed his biceps jokingly. 'Seriously, though, I've got a big boot and it was no bother; I didn't see the point in arguing. I hope you don't mind.'

I said I didn't at all; we had plenty of space. 'What else can you tell me?'

Barry pulled a file from his briefcase and placed it on the table as I fixed him a glass of water.

'OK. Here goes,' he said, picking out several sheets of paper. 'Grace has been in care since she was three and has had eight placements. I told you that on the phone?'

I nodded. Barry shuffled through the files, pulled out more notes and continued.

'Dad was an alcoholic. Dad was in sole charge of Grace and her sister Lily after splitting from their mother. He left the two girls home alone. Lily, aged six, phoned a relative – paternal grandfather, now deceased. Said she and Grace were "frightened and hungry". Grandfather called Social Services. Mum was contacted. Didn't want to have the girls living with her. No other family members in a position to help. Both girls taken into care. Emergency order, placed in separate foster homes on the same day. Lily eventually went home to Mum – looks like the following year – yes, that's right. But Grace didn't. Since then Mum has consistently refused to take Grace back. Mum is now remarried and has two older stepsons living with her and her husband. Lily is now thirteen, still with Mum. Mum is on record repeatedly saying she can't have Grace back because of her "aggravating and disruptive behaviour". States she "never listens", "deliberately winds everyone up" and is "impossible to live with".

Barry cleared his throat and took a drink of water before reading from the most recent notes in Grace's file. He spoke quietly. 'This is what Colette – that's Grace's mother – said last week: "She is the same difficult child she always has been. It would be impossible to have her living with me. Nothing has changed and we also have no room in our house for her."' He said he had not met Colette in person; they had only spoken on the phone. We both took a moment to consider what Grace's mother had said. Neither of us commented, but there was a note of sadness hanging in the air.

Though Barry wasn't stressed, he did seem to be in quite a rush. He gathered together all the paperwork he was leaving with us, including the standard new placement form, complete with emergency contact details. This had Colette's address and phone number clearly written on it, in bold black pen. I stared at the information.

I'd cared for children whose parents had died or were in prison. Though Grace was on a full care order, meaning the courts had decided neither of her parents could have her living with them full time, Colette was very much alive and had her freedom. She had access to her daughter and Barry had told me that Grace was allowed to stay in the family home for weekend visits, and he reiterated that she was going home the following week, after her trial with us. *What exactly is the problem?* I thought. I didn't know the full circumstances, but I thought how desperately sad it was that Colette couldn't raise Grace herself. I wanted to know more, but at the same time I was happy to wait and find out, all in good time. Usually that's the best way, so you can make your own mind up about a given situation.

As is often the case, when I thought about Grace's predicament I found my mind wandering back to my own childhood. I thought about how lucky I was to have been brought up by two parents who loved and cherished me. We had our ups and downs and life was not perfect – my dad had struggled with alcoholism when I was a young girl – but fundamentally I had a happy, stable childhood. I knew I was wanted. I was safe and well cared for, and I was praised and encouraged and taught to expand my mind. Mum always told me the world was my oyster and I never forgot that. In fact, it's one of the things that helped me follow my dream and go into fostering. My attitude was, why not give it a go? If it doesn't work, at least you will have tried. I'd grown up with high self-esteem and developed a pragmatic, optimistic outlook on life that I'm still grateful for to this day.

Jonathan had a tougher time. He was smaller than his three older brothers, and short-sighted too. His father, a farmer, treated him like the runt of the family and hit him with a belt when he made clumsy mistakes on their farm. Despite this Jonathan knew his father was not all bad; rather, he was the product of another era, when boys were expected to match up to old-fashioned male stereotypes. Ultimately, Jonathan forgave his dad and looked for the good in him. He worked hard at school so he could leave home and get himself a good job, and he was fortunate to have had a loving mother, whose support carried him through the hard times.

What is Colette's story? I thought as I looked at her name and address. I had no idea how Grace had ended up being in care for so many years while her sister went home to Mum. I desperately wanted to find out more, and I wanted to help the family as much as I could. I simply couldn't imagine the trauma a child like Grace would go through, knowing their own mother can't, or won't, have them living at home. The fact Colette was raising Lily and her two step-sons must have been so confusing for Grace, and incredibly painful, I imagined.

I asked Barry for more details about the fact Grace would go back to the family home after her stay with us. He explained that Grace had always had fairly regular contact visits with her family, and typically spent a weekend at home once every six weeks or so; it was always a loose arrangement, depending on what was happening in the family, and in Grace's placement. In the summer holidays she usually spent a full week at home. I considered this. At ten years old, Grace was old enough to question her situation, and no doubt her sense of self. What went through her mind when she left the family home behind each time, seeing her sister staying there with Mum?

On the face of it, her circumstances seemed difficult to fathom, but of course I knew next to nothing about the family's background. If fostering had taught me anything, it was that you never really know what goes on in other people's lives, and therefore you can't jump to conclusions and need to stay open-minded. I mustn't judge Colette. All I could do was give Grace a safe and comfortable home for as long as necessary, make her feel as cared for and wanted as possible and show her that I believed in her as a lovely young person.

As he was leaving I noticed that Barry had a ring of perspiration in each armpit from the effort of moving Grace's belongings into the garden and hallway.

'Let's hope the trial is successful for all our sakes,' I said, smiling.

As well as the suitcase, Barry had brought in a holdall and a couple of over-stuffed carrier bags.

'Yes, let's hope!' he said. 'Best of luck. I'll be back on Monday. About ten o'clock OK for you?'

'Yes, that's fine.'

'Great. You have my details if anything changes or you need to get hold of me.'

Grace ran in from the garden and asked if she could have another drink. She was red in the face and out of breath.

'Goodness! What have you been up to?' I asked, as I made her another orange squash.

'Pogo-ing.'

Jonathan was right behind her. 'You'll have to show Angela how good you are,' he said. 'I've never seen anyone stay on for as long as that. Very impressive!'

'Fantastic! We'll have to call you Little Miss Bounce,' I said.

'It's not Little Miss Bounce,' she said quietly. 'It's *Mr* Bounce.'

'Oh, you're right,' I laughed. 'There isn't a Little Miss Bounce, is there? Silly me.'

Jonathan teasingly told me I needed to do my homework on the Mr Men and Little Miss books. The atmosphere was warm and friendly. I laughed, Barry gave me another little wink – that was clearly his signature move when he wanted to show approval – and even Grace giggled a little. Jonathan had obviously managed to engage with her, which was great to see.

'I'll leave you to it,' Barry said approvingly. 'Is that all right with you, Little Miss . . . what shall we call you then? Which character do you want to be?'

'They call me Little Miss Trouble,' Grace said, deadpan, before downing her squash at record speed and immediately asking if she could go back outside.

'Right,' Barry cut in, before Jonathan or I could respond. 'I'll be off then. I hope everything goes well. You've got all the numbers you need. Bye!'

Barry shot off. We heard the roar of his engine and he was gone in a flash.

'Little Miss Trouble, eh?' Jonathan said, raising his

eyebrows and scratching his head in an exaggerated way. 'I can't believe you are any trouble at all!'

Grace gave a shy smile. 'I try not to be,' she said. 'But it's, like, sometimes I can't help it. So, can I go back outside?'

3

'I don't like taking my clothes to my mum's'

Once she'd come in from playing in the garden, Grace took off the thin cotton hoodie she was wearing over her Spice Girls T-shirt. I realised then that she wasn't just petite but so slender she looked underweight for her height. Her arms were stick thin and her waist so narrow she looked doll-like. We'd waited for Grace to arrive before we ate, and Jonathan and I were hungry. When we finally sat down at the table I found myself desperately hoping Grace was ready for a good meal too, and that she wasn't going to push the food around her plate.

To my relief, I need not have worried. Grace enthusiastically had a second helping of the pasta bake I'd prepared and she even ate some tomatoes and cucumber from the mixed salad, which I'm well used to kids turning their noses up at. She also devoured a generous bowl of ice cream and asked for extra wafers and chocolate sauce, although of course that was something I was not so surprised about!

Often, children are feeling too shy and anxious on their

first night to eat very much at all. I never make a fuss, as I appreciate that eating with strangers under any circumstances can be stressful for a child. Dining with your possible new foster carers, in a home where everything is alien to you, must be quite a daunting prospect. I know I'd have struggled to deal with it when I was a child; I was a real home bird as a young girl and I sometimes felt homesick when I simply visited relatives or stayed with a friend for a day.

I always try to make an appetising but simple meal when a child first arrives, so as to encourage them to at least try a little something. Jonathan and I always make an effort to keep the conversation ticking along gently too, so the child feels included and welcome but not under the spotlight.

'That was nice,' Grace said, wiping her mouth with her hand before I could offer her a paper napkin. 'What is there for breakfast?'

I told her we had cereal, toast, crumpets, fruit and eggs. 'I could even do you a bacon butty if you like, seeing as it's Saturday morning. Or egg dippie.'

'That's not fair,' Jonathan joked. 'She never offers me a bacon butty! Or egg dippie!'

'That's not true at all,' I replied. Smiling at Grace I added, 'But Jonathan would eat bacon and eggs every day if I let him, and that's not good for him. So would I, to tell the truth. Anyhow, what do you normally eat?'

Grace bit her lip and looked thoughtful. 'Erm, crunchy cornflakes if the people have it. What's egg dippie? Have you got crunchy cornflakes?'

I couldn't help feeling a pang of sorrow. *If the people have it.* I thought again how sad it was that Grace had moved foster homes so many times. She'd had no consistency in her life and referring to her succession of foster carers as 'the people' was so impersonal it made it sound like she'd stayed in random B & Bs instead of foster homes.

I explained that egg dippie is sometimes called French toast, and that you make it by beating an egg with a splash of milk, dipping a slice of bread in the mixture then frying it. She didn't seem to know what I was talking about.

'I might have some crunchy cornflakes,' I told her, 'and if not we can go and buy some tomorrow. I'll check the cupboard in a moment and show you where things are. Then I'll give you a tour of the rest of the house and show you your bedroom and bathroom, so you know your way around.'

She frowned. 'How long am I on trial?'

Once again I winced at her turn of phrase. 'You're not on trial, sweetheart. These few days are for us *all* to get to know one another, so we can all see if you'd be happy staying with us longer term, and if we all think it would work. I hope it does work out. I think you're a lovely girl.' I added that ultimately it was her decision. This is always the case when a child is moving from one county to another, and I wanted to make sure she knew this.

She looked puzzled. 'So how long am I here for?'

'You are here for three nights. I think Barry explained it to you? So that's today, Saturday and Sunday. The plan is that he will come and pick you up on Monday morning at about ten o'clock and he's the one who will take you home.'

Grace furrowed her brow and stared absent-mindedly around the room. Meanwhile Jonathan gave me a subtle sideways glance, or should I say a wince. For a moment I wondered what I'd said, but then I realised it had been careless of me to call her mother's house 'home', just in case she didn't call it home any more. Thankfully, I didn't think Grace had registered this; she now looked like she was lost in a daydream.

It wouldn't have surprised me, in fact, if Grace did still consider her mother's house as her home, even after seven years in care. Many children cling on to a rose-tinted view of their former family life and refuse to give up on the dream of moving back in full time, even when they have been shut out for years and it is clear to everyone else they are not welcome and a reunion is extremely unlikely. When I first started fostering, I was shocked to learn that even children who have suffered terrible abuse at the hands of their parents, and have been removed from them by the courts, sometimes still long to return to them, often throughout their childhood.

'So do you know what's happening now, Grace?' Jonathan interjected. 'Monday's the day Barry will collect you from here in the morning, at around ten o'clock. He's the one who will take you to your mum's for a stay, and you will also see your other foster carers.' We didn't know the details of this so Jonathan didn't elaborate. He also avoided specifying that she would be staying at her mother's house for a week, as we'd been told, and he didn't go into what would happen next, as we didn't know if the trial visit with us would be successful or whether Grace would want to come and live with us. Also, we could not be certain her mother would keep her for a whole week, even if that's what she'd agreed with Social Services. Plans change and it's always best to assume nothing is written in stone.

I stood up and began clearing the plates from the kitchen table. We often eat in the kitchen rather than the dining room, and as it was Grace's first night I thought it would be more relaxed and informal if we sat in there. She sprang to her feet as soon as I began clearing plates and, without being asked, helped me stack the dirty dishes next to the dishwasher. Jonathan told me he'd do the rest of the clearing up, while I gave Grace the 'grand tour'.

'But leave your luggage to me. I'll carry it upstairs for you, before I do the kitchen.'

'Thanks,' I said, acknowledging I would have struggled to carry the heavy suitcase up the two flights of stairs that led to the bedroom Grace would occupy on the top floor of the house. It had fleetingly crossed my mind to ask her if it might be an idea to leave some of her belongings downstairs, as she clearly wouldn't need everything during this initial visit, but I immediately thought better of it. I'm a naturally practical person, but over the years fostering has taught me that being practical is not necessarily the best way forward. What's important is to focus on the child's emotional wellbeing. I didn't know what she'd brought with her, but Grace would no doubt be happier surrounded by all her familiar bits and pieces. Hopefully, having so many things of her own would help her feel more comfortable and settled, and perhaps increase the chances of this weekend visit being a success.

I began the tour by showing Grace what was what in the kitchen, as I'd promised. I didn't have any crunchy cornflakes but she seemed pleased by the wide variety of cereals I did have; I always have a good selection, including plenty of those miniature variety packs, as we never know what the new children who come to stay will prefer. I pointed out where we kept the juice and the snacks and told Grace to let me know if she was hungry or thirsty, and said that I would always get something for her. I explained our basic house rules, which included always asking before taking anything from the kitchen, but I encouraged her to help herself to water if she needed it. It may sound as if I was stating the obvious, but when children first arrive they can feel very intimidated and don't always speak up, even about their most basic needs. We had one child staying with us in the very early days of our fostering who didn't realise we would routinely replace toiletries like toothpaste and shampoo, and she even worried about toilet roll. She asked her social worker what was going to happen when she ran out, since then we've always made a point of explaining all these things very clearly.

'Shall we help Jonathan?' Grace asked, already heading to the hallway.

'Well, yes, why not? Let's take a bag each, shall we?'

With that, Grace picked up a carrier bag and started running up the stairs. I heard her talking to Jonathan on the top floor before I even got to the first floor.

'I'll let Angela show you into your room,' I heard him say. 'She's in charge of duvets and pillows and all that sort of thing, and you can choose what you want on your bed. I'm afraid I don't have much of an eye for design and if I was in charge of bedding you might well end up with a purple spotted pillow and a green striped duvet!'

Grace giggled and I smiled to myself. I knew exactly what Jonathan was doing: he was stalling for time, because he prefers not to be alone in a room, and particularly a bedroom, with any of the children who stay with us, and especially the girls. We've been told countless times on our training courses that children can make false accusations against their carers. Generally speaking, male foster carers are considered more likely to become victims of malicious allegations, although of course no carer is immune. Jonathan's caution is not just for his own benefit; the girls themselves – and boys – may not feel comfortable being alone with a man, for any number of reasons. That may sound sexist, but that is the reality. Exercising sensible caution is all part of the 'safe caring' policies all foster carers are taught.

We still didn't know a great deal about Grace's background, but we did know that she and her sister had been left home alone by their father, and that he was an alcoholic. When the little girls had phoned their grandfather they were frightened and hungry. Naturally, the last thing Jonathan wanted to do was alarm Grace in any way at all. For the time being he was her temporary carer, and she needed to feel as comfortable as possible in his presence, and in our home.

'Here she is!' Jonathan exclaimed when I reached the top floor landing. 'What kept you?'

I was a little out of breath, to tell the truth. I was heavier than I wanted to be and was trying to lose weight, both by dieting and stepping up my exercise. I never passed up the chance to go cycling or swimming or walking in the countryside with the kids, and I was doing my best to do a fitness video once a week, though I think I'd missed a few weeks, what with one thing and another.

'Cheeky!' I said. 'Let's go in. Jonathan, would you mind taking the suitcase in? We can manage the rest, and there's only the holdall left downstairs.'

I showed Grace into the bedroom. 'This is your room. Shall I help you unpack?'

She walked straight to the window and looked outside. From this vantage point, at the top of the house, you could see right over the playing field beyond our garden. 'Can I go and play out there?'

'I think we might just have time for a play before bed. Shall we unpack first, get you settled in here?'

She didn't reply and showed no interest at all in the bedroom. Most of the kids we'd fostered before had been very pleased with their room, and typically they said something positive about it. All three of the children's bedrooms were a good size, smartly decorated and kitted out with everything a child would need, including a desk, dressing table, toy box or wardrobe and a well-stocked bookcase. We were well aware that some children came from houses where they shared rooms or lived in poor conditions. Making their bedroom as welcoming and comfortable as possible while they stay with us is something I pride myself on, and I always love it when I get an enthusiastic response.

'Grace, do you know which bag your nightie's in, or your pyjamas? And what about your toothbrush?'

When a child comes directly from their own home or arrives as an emergency placement I never assume they have nightwear or a toothbrush, but I was confident Grace's foster carer would have made sure she brought these things with her.

'What?'

'Pyjamas? Nightie? Toothbrush? Any idea where they are?'

'No.' She shook her head and looked at her belongings. She seemed quite overwhelmed.

'Shall I have a look? Or do you want to look, while I make your bed?'

'Erm, what?'

'Why don't you have a look for your pyjamas?'

'OK.'

'And I will make your bed.'

'Yes.'

I usually let a new child take their time selecting their duvet cover and pillows from the large bedding collection I've accumulated and added to over the years, but instinct told me to keep this simple. It was getting late, Grace was itching to explore the playing field before it got dark and I didn't want to overwhelm her any more.

I presented her with a choice of two sets – one plain white

with silver stars, the other with a rainbow on a sky-blue background. She pointed at the latter, and while I made the bed she carefully unzipped the suitcase. It was brimming with clothes and underwear and I could see there were shoes wedged around the sides and a few soft toys stuffed into the corners. Heavy winter jumpers were piled alongside summer shorts and T-shirts, and on the very top was a lime-green drawstring bag. She looked at it for a moment, and then her face lit up.

'This is it,' she said, taking the bag out of the suitcase and opening it up. She pulled out a pair of short pyjamas with Take That on the front. I smiled. It was the mid-nineties, when Take That were at the peak of their boy-band success, and it seemed that every girl who stayed with us owned Take That clothes, bags, pencil cases, you name it. Grace's toothbrush and toothpaste were neatly packed in a small clear toiletry bag, alongside a folded flannel, and I could see a little hairbrush and a few headbands were in there too.

Grace looked visibly relieved to have found what I'd asked her to look for, and I was silently thankful to the foster carer whose home she'd come from for making sure these essentials were to hand.

'That's great! I'll show you the bathroom before we go back downstairs. Would you like me to help you put some of your summer clothes in the chest of drawers and the wardrobe?'

'No, thanks, I'll be OK.' That was a shame. I knew she would feel more at home if she wasn't living out of bags, but as she was only staying for a few days I wouldn't force it.

'But,' Grace started, sounding nervous, 'when I go home, can I leave some of my stuff here?'

This sounded promising. I was already feeling quietly confident that Grace's trial stay with us would go well, but of course I didn't want to jump the gun. 'That's an idea – I guess that's something we can decide on later,' I said, giving her an encouraging smile.

'OK, good. I don't like taking my clothes to my mum's.'

She said this in a quiet, worried voice. Her words sounded a little ominous, I thought. I repeated back what she'd said to me, with a questioning tone in my voice. 'So you don't like taking your clothes to your mum's?'

'No.' She looked at the rug, as if mesmerised by it.

I had another go at prompting her. Though I was feeling quite concerned by what Grace had said, I tried to speak in a soft, even tone, so as not to let my voice belie my concerns. This has become second nature whenever I sense a child may be about to disclose something. Kids who have suffered trauma in their lives, or perhaps haven't been shown enough attention, can exaggerate facts or invent details to draw you in further. It's best to show you are interested and that you care, but I've learned that you must never express shock or outrage. You can never be sure if the child is telling the truth or if they are genuinely confused about events.

I busied myself, opening a new box of tissues I'd put on her dressing table. Sometimes kids find it easier to talk if they don't have to give you eye contact. I hoped Grace would tell me more, but she didn't. Instead, she stood rocking from one foot to the other while she fidgeted and looked out the window.

'Can I go out and play now? Can I? Can I?'

'Yes, sweetheart,' I said, getting to my feet. I hadn't shown her the bathroom but that could wait. 'I think some fresh air will do us both good, and there's still a drop of sunshine out there. Aren't we lucky?'

Grace didn't reply. She was already running down the landing.

4

'I always have ants in my pants!'

Grace was up early. She said she slept very well and that her bed was comfy.

'I'm pleased to hear it,' I said. She looked bright-eyed and bushy-tailed. Her hair looked exactly as it had the night before, with her headband neatly in place, and I told her I wished my hair looked that good when I'd just got out of bed. She looked pleased by the compliment and gave me a smile.

I explained that Jonathan was already at work in the florists and that she could walk into town with me later that morning. I had a bit of shopping to do, and afterwards I needed to call in on my mum, who lived nearby. I didn't normally introduce the children to Mum so soon, as I felt they had enough to deal with in getting used to Jonathan and me and any other kids we were fostering. However, I'd arranged to see my mum before I knew Grace was coming to stay, thinking I had some time to myself. Mum was looking forward to it, and I wanted to give her a present I'd brought back from our trip as a thank you for helping Barbara in the shop.

'I'll show you around the town first and then we can have a cup of tea with my mum,' I said to Grace. 'If we're lucky, we might get a piece of cake. She told me she was baking this morning, and she always makes lovely things. Her name is Thelma, by the way.'

'OK,' Grace said politely, although she didn't sound particularly interested in cake or anything I'd just said, to tell the truth. 'Can we play frisbee?'

The night before, when she was looking from her bedroom window, Grace had seen some children playing frisbee on the field behind our house. They'd gone in by the time we got out there, but I'd told her we had a frisbee in the garage and could fetch it out and have a game some time.

'Of course. That's a good idea. Let's have breakfast, and I have a couple of jobs I'd like to do first, then we'll go out onto the playing field.'

'What jobs?'

I explained I had washing to hang out and that I wanted to quickly polish the shower unit in the children's bathroom. The two other girls we had living with us would be back the following day, and I wanted everything to be as spick and span as possible. I'd cleaned the bathroom in preparation for Grace's arrival, but I'd run out of time and the shower cubicle was still streaky and needed a quick buffing up with shower-shine spray and a soft cloth. This was always the last job I got around to, because the sides of the cubicle were awkward to reach and I never seemed to get them shining as well as I hoped.

Grace tucked in to a large bowl of cereal and devoured two thick pieces of toast and honey. She washed her breakfast down with a glass of orange juice and even asked for a cup of tea with two sugars. During breakfast she'd started to chat to me, unbidden, about her other foster placements. She spoke about them in no particular order, from what I could gather, and regaled me with details about some of their rules, particularly surrounding food.

'The one before last – or was it the one before that? – I didn't like it there. The people wouldn't let me have sugar in my tea and you could only have one biscuit from the tin. And the other people – when I was in Year 4, I think it was – they said I couldn't eat the sweets I got for Halloween. The man took them off me and said they were bad for my teeth.'

I listened attentively and tried to look as interested and sympathetic as possible without actually saying anything. I didn't want to interrupt, as sometimes when children start to unload about relatively minor niggles and grievances they end up disclosing something potentially very important.

Grace carried on talking, listing a few other complaints she had. Predictably, she mentioned how crisps and fizzy drinks had been limited in lots of the houses she stayed in. 'My mum lets me have whatever I want but other people don't. It's not fair. Some people don't even have orange squash! That's, like, weird. And once I had to live with a girl who was algeric to *everything*. Her mum was, like, completely crazy. She flipped out all the time about food. We couldn't have crisps, not even one single packet. Cameron gave me a packet of cheese and onion crisps once and she totally freaked out when she saw the packet. It was like they were poison, or something. What's wrong with crisps?'

Cameron was the older stepbrother, I'd found out. He was 'about sixteen' and his brother Lee was fourteen. Grace had mentioned Cameron several times and had told me he was 'nice to me'. However, she pulled a face on the one occasion when she mentioned Lee. She told me he was a 'pain' because he stole her clothes, but she clammed up when I tried to get her to elaborate on this. So far, she had said nothing about her sister Lily.

'Allergic to everything?' I said, wanting to correct Grace's mistake without drawing attention to it. 'What a pity, but you can't be too careful, you know. Allergies are serious. It's tough when you're allergic to any food.'

I explained to Grace how some children really could become very ill, or even die, if they had a severe nut allergy and accidentally ate something containing even a very small amount of nuts. I also chatted about how important it was to eat a healthy balanced diet, and I said that even though I did allow all the children who stayed to have sugar in tea, and to have the occasional slice of cake, bag of crisps or packet of sweets, there was a limit to how many sugary treats and junk food we all should eat.

She looked at me blankly, as she had a habit of doing, but I kept the conversation going as I thought it was an important one to have. I've cared for a lot of kids who confuse an unlimited supply of junk food – often provided by their parents or relatives – with a sign of generosity, or even love.

'I try to stick to healthy limits myself,' I went on. 'We'd all like to eat more sweet things, I expect, but it's important to get the balance right. After all, you want to be fit and healthy so you can go pogo-ing and running round the field with a frisbee, don't you?'

'I am fit and healthy,' Grace said cheerfully. 'I always have ants in my pants!'

I smiled. I guessed she was repeating a phrase she'd heard somebody else use to describe her, and I wasn't at all surprised. Grace *did* have ants in her pants. Not only did she want to play out all the time, but she ran every-where, even if she was just going from the kitchen to the utility room next door, or to the downstairs loo. I'd already had to remind her several times to slow down and be careful on the stairs, and even when she was simply standing or sitting, Grace had a habit of fidgeting and never being still.

'It's good to be active,' I said. 'And when you're burning up lots of energy I think it's fine to have a treat.'

'Can I have a biscuit? And can I have some orange squash?'

I told her she could later, as we'd just had breakfast, but reminded her that if she needed a drink she could always help herself to water. She did, glugging down a large glass.

'Everything in moderation. That's the rule Jonathan lives by, and I agree with him.'

'In mod-er-a-tion?' she intoned, giving me a quizzical look.

'In moderation, yes, that's right. It means limited, but in a good way, so there's a good balance. Not too much and not too little. Just right.'

'Like the three Goldilocks?'

'I know what you mean. Kind of like *Goldilocks and the Three Bears*, yes.'

'My dad called me Goldilocks.'

'He did?'

'Yes, because my hair was, like, loads blonder when I was little.'

'Was it?'

'Yes. He always called me Goldilocks.'

I didn't know if Grace still saw her father or not. I nodded expectantly and hoped she'd elaborate, but she said no more and started staring into space, rocking back and forth in her chair as she did so.

'Grace sweetheart, please can you stop rocking on the chair? Remember what I said? You might fall and hurt yourself.'

I'd already stopped her rocking on the chair several times that morning, pointing out that she might well slip backwards if she didn't keep all four legs on the floor. However, when I reminded her of this once again she looked at me as if all this was news to her. Thankfully she did stop rocking, though, and she got to her feet and started skipping around the kitchen.

'What's this?' she said, looking at a fridge magnet a friend had brought me back from her holiday in Ireland. It had an image of a laughing leprechaun on it and read: 'Murphy's Law: Nothing is as easy as it looks. Everything takes longer than you expect. And if anything can go wrong it will, at the worst possible moment.'

I explained where it came from. 'It's only a joke, really. The friend who gave it to me is the most positive person you could meet. Not everything that can go wrong does go wrong, of course. But I suppose it's a reminder to be careful. Keep your four chair legs on the floor, for instance, because the chances are you'll fall if you don't!'

Grace laughed. 'I've got the message,' she said cheekily. *Progress*, I thought.

I told Grace that the following day we were invited to a barbecue with one of our neighbours who had a large, extended family. There would be lots of children there and Grace would meet the two girls we had staying with us, as they were being dropped off at the barbecue after their weekend visits with relatives.

'Will there be crisps and fizzy drinks and am I allowed a burger?'

'I'm sure there will be,' I said. 'And of course you can. In moderation!'

Grace rolled her eyes and repeated the word moderation, spitting it out mischievously as if it were the worst word she'd ever heard. I asked her to go and clean her teeth and get dressed. 'Please do your teeth first,' I said. 'Then when I've hung out the washing I can get in the bathroom and polish the shower unit, while you get dressed.'

Grace sprinted off and returned just a few minutes later. She was still wearing her pyjamas but told me she had cleaned her teeth.

'Did you forget to get dressed?' I said gently.

'What?'

'Remember, I asked you to clean your teeth and get dressed?'

'Do I have to have a shower?'

'No, sweetheart. You had one last night and you can have a shower tonight before you go to bed. You just need to get dressed. Then when my jobs are done we can go out and play frisbee before we walk into town.'

Grace ran off again. I heard her chanting 'get dressed, get dressed' as she went. My heart went out to her. There was so much to take in and she was clearly trying hard to behave herself. I hadn't seen any hint of the disruptive or aggravating behaviour I'd been warned about, but of course it was very early days. Kids generally go through a 'honeymoon period' when they first arrive in foster care. They typically start off on their best behaviour and it's only when they feel comfortable that they start to display their true colours. I could see that Grace was putting all her energies into doing her best and the fact she needed reminding about a few things was not a problem.

I started to quickly hang out the washing while Grace was upstairs. Within just a few minutes she dashed outside to join me, dressed in grey leggings and another Spice Girls top. She was panting for breath. 'Can I help you?'

Plenty of ten-year-olds have no idea how to hang out

washing, but Grace needed no instructions at all. She pinned the T-shirts by their hems and even hung the socks up in neat pairs. The washing was blowing in the breeze in no time at all and I told her I was very impressed. I carried the peg basket over to the garden table, and as I did so I noticed Grace running up and down the length of the clothes line, eyes scouring the grass.

'What are you looking for, sweetheart?'

'Checking there are no pegs dropped. Can I play on my pogo stick now I've done that?'

I told her she could have a turn on it later, when I came back down from cleaning the bathroom, as long as she stayed on the springy grass. I didn't want her to fall and hurt herself, and certainly not while I was inside the house.

'Cool.'

'For now, why don't you have a go on the Swingball?' I pointed to the game, which was already set up at the end of the garden.

'Swingball? I love that!' Grace grinned and ran down to it. She picked up a bat and began whacking the tennis ball enthusiastically, making it dance on its string in all directions. I don't think I'd ever seen a child put so much energy into a game of Swingball, and certainly not a solo game. Her hair was fizzing in the sun; already she looked like a happier, more confident little girl than the one who'd arrived at our door the night before.

With Grace occupied, I quickly nipped up to the top floor of the house. The garden was secure and I'd told Grace I'd be able to keep an eye on her from the upstairs window and to come inside and find me if she needed to.

I swiftly buffed up the shower cubicle, squirted some bleach down the loo and gave the toilet seat a swift clean with a disinfectant wipe. This routine had become second nature to me during my years as a foster carer; I'm sure I could do it in my sleep, and at record speed. I was well aware that when children shared a bathroom you needed to do a daily inspection and make sure everything was at least hygienic, if not sparkling clean. (Annoyingly, the shower unit was still streaky after I'd polished it – that thing was the bane of my life!)

I looked out of the window and was happy to see Grace still playing energetically with the Swingball. Before I left the bathroom I checked the pedal bin, to see if it needed emptying. Again, this was a job I did daily, almost on autopilot. When the lid popped up I was surprised to see several chocolate biscuit wrappers. They were the brand I always bought and I knew they hadn't been there the day before, as I'd emptied the bin before Grace had arrived. I'm always very careful not to jump to conclusions, but in this case the only explanation could have been that Grace had helped herself to the biscuits from the kitchen and eaten them secretly. I wondered when she'd done that. She'd eaten such a good meal the night before and I didn't remember leaving her alone in the kitchen. This morning she'd eaten a hearty breakfast and again had not been alone in the kitchen.

I went into Grace's bedroom to check her waste paper basket and found it empty. I didn't want to snoop and I never root through a child's belongings unnecessarily, but I did take a moment to cast my eyes around the room. I was surprised and felt a bit sad, as it looked like she hadn't been there at all. Everything was exactly as it had been before she moved in, apart from the fact her suitcase and holdall were standing in the corner. They were both zipped up and her carrier bags were placed neatly beside them. She was staying with us for another two nights, but it seemed she was already set to move out at a moment's notice.

I scanned the room, hoping to see the pyjamas she'd taken off that morning, but couldn't see them. Her toothbrush wasn't visible either, even though I'd made a point of telling her to keep it in her bedroom, as I do with all children who stay with us. This is always the best policy when kids share a bathroom, to avoid any mix-ups, intentional or otherwise. On occasion we'd had cases of girls and boys sabotaging each other's toothbrushes, either for revenge after an argument or just as a prank. I've dealt with toothbrushes being smothered in shampoo, rubbed in soap or worse. Jonathan and I always keep our toiletries out of sight in our own, separate bathroom, next to our bedroom on the floor below, and I always make a point of telling the kids to keep theirs in their bedroom.

I looked at Grace's dressing table; there was nothing on it apart from the box of tissues I'd put there the day before. There was no hairbrush or comb, no sign of any of her headbands or flannel and certainly not the clear toiletry bag or toothbrush. I could see that the laundry basket was empty and her bedside table was bare too. At bedtime,

Grace had taken a copy of a book about zoo animals from the shelf in her room. I said she could read it before she went to sleep, but I guess she must have put it back. When I'd said goodnight I saw that she'd taken her own cuddly toy to bed with her – a floppy-necked swan that was a grubby grey instead of white – but that was nowhere to be seen either.

Bless her, I thought. I sighed as my eyes finally rested on her luggage. The large, grey suitcase, like the cuddly swan, looked as if it had seen better days. I wondered if it had been on Grace's fostering journey from the start, right from when she was the blonde-haired little tot her dad had nicknamed Goldilocks.

The suitcase was one of those slightly stretchy nylon ones, the sort people liked to use in the days before airlines started charging us all a small fortune for hold luggage. It was designed to expand slightly, so you could cram more into it than one of the old-fashioned, hard-shelled cases, and that's what Grace had done. The sides were bulging and the zips were fit to burst open, just as they had been when Grace arrived on our doorstep. It must have been quite an effort for her to zip it back up on her own.

She probably can't wait to get to her mum's house, I reasoned. I was confident we'd done our best to make Grace feel welcome. She'd even talked herself about coming back, but now I felt more uncertain about how things would work out. Perhaps Grace wouldn't want to return to us?

I could see from her window that Grace was still playing happily in the garden. She'd obviously tired of Swingball and was now darting all around the lawn, kicking a foam ball with all her might. Before I left her room, I lifted her pillow and looked underneath it. The vast majority of children never fold up their nightwear and place it neatly under their pillow, but I wondered if that's where her Take That pyjamas might be. It was wishful thinking, I suppose, and they weren't there. My heart sank, not only because Grace had obviously packed her pyjamas in her suitcase, but because there was something else under her pillow: a miniature packet of breakfast cereal and some cheese crackers wrapped in kitchen roll.

I sighed. I'd told Grace that she only had to ask me if she needed something to eat or drink. There was certainly no need for her to smuggle food upstairs like this, and my initial reaction was to wonder if perhaps she was too shy to ask me for snacks. I didn't think that was the case; she'd asked me for a biscuit straight after breakfast, hadn't she?

Inevitably, I had to consider if there might be a deeper or more serious explanation for Grace's behaviour, especially considering the fact she appeared underweight. It wasn't long before this that Princess Diana's struggle with bulimia had made headlines around the world, and I was well aware that even ten-year-old girls were at risk of developing eating disorders. I'd have been naive not to question whether Grace might have an unhealthy relationship with food. Thinking about it, I realised we'd talked an awful lot about food in the short time she'd been here. Perhaps she was hung up about it in some way, or was I overthinking things?

I can remember smuggling food, as a young girl myself, into my friend's bedroom during a sleepover party. We'd intended to have a midnight feast but we all fell asleep before twelve o'clock, and when we woke the next morning we were dismayed to find the room smelled awful. Our haul had included some fish fingers we managed to swipe from the dinner table, not thinking about how cold and smelly they would be hours later. I had a little laugh at the memory and told myself not to get carried away with hypothetical theories. Hopefully, the truth about Grace's food haul wouldn't be as bad as I feared.

I left the cereal and crackers where I'd found them and decided I would talk to Grace about this later on, when I felt the time was right.

5

'It's as if the paperwork has been muddled up!'

Back in the garden, I let Grace play on her pogo stick as I'd promised. She appeared to have completely forgotten what I'd said earlier about staying on the soft grass and immediately started bouncing on the patio. I asked her to move to the lawn and reminded her why.

'Sorry,' she said, 'I forgot.' Lots of kids forget things 'on purpose' when it suits them, but this didn't appear to be the case with Grace; I think she genuinely forgot.

'I'm sorry,' she repeated solemnly. 'I didn't mean to wind you up.'

'I know, sweetheart, and you didn't wind me up. You just forgot what I said earlier, that's all. There's a lot to remember in a new place, isn't there? I just don't want you to hurt yourself. I wouldn't let any child bounce on the patio. It's dangerous.'

'I didn't mean to wind you up, honest,' she said anxiously. She was staring all around, her eyes wide and unblinking and her front teeth biting into her bottom lip so hard it went white.

'Sweetheart, it's fine. I know that. You didn't wind me up at all. Now, let's see what you can do on your pogo stick!'

I sat in a garden chair and watched Grace step on her pogo stick and launch herself on the grass. I was glad of an excuse to take the weight off my feet for a few minutes, but I soon found myself feeling anything but relaxed. It was exhausting to watch Grace. She bounced so frenetically, a look of deep concentration on her face as she earnestly counted how many bounces she could stay up for. Every time she faltered she diligently went back to zero and started counting again. She was relentless. After five minutes or so Grace was red and panting, and her curls were clinging to her sticky little face. The sun was already full of heat and I suggested we should both have a cool drink and then go over to the playing field with the frisbee. Thankfully, she readily agreed.

'Will the people at that barbecue tomorrow like me?' she asked quietly as we headed out of the garden gate. She suddenly seemed quite subdued after all her exertion; her voice reminded me of the little whisper she'd used when she first arrived. She was also looking away from me, into the distance, although I'd noticed that she avoided eye contact a lot of the time. That's not uncommon in children who are settling in and are feeling shy. I don't ever mention it, but I do make a point of giving eye contact back, in the hope they will mirror my actions. Saying 'Look at me when I'm talking' is never advisable. We've been told this in training many times, because although the child is not looking at you, for whatever reason, he or she can still hear what you are saying, and the majority of the time they are taking in what you are saying to them.

'Will the people at the barbecue tomorrow like you?' I repeated back cheerfully, focusing all my attention on Grace. 'I'm *sure* they will! You're such a lovely girl. I think everyone will be very pleased to meet you.' I reminded her that the barbecue was taking place at the home of a good friend of mine who had lots of children, and that she would also meet the two girls who were living with us at that time.

'I hope they all like me,' she said meekly. 'But if they don't, what can you do?' She shrugged and bravely flashed me a half-smile. Once again, I had the feeling she was mimicking a phrase she'd heard someone else use. 'What can you do?' It sounded like something an older person would say, not a ten-year-old girl. I wondered who she'd picked it up from.

We had a great game on the playing field. Grace raced around like an excited pup, retrieving the frisbee even when it fell closer to me than her. When she'd had enough we walked over to the play area, where two young girls, roughly the same age as Grace, were taking it in turns to idly launch their dolls down the slide. They looked slightly bored. Grace immediately went up to them and asked if she could play. I was pleased she'd done this all by herself. I saw the girls exchange uncertain glances but then the older-looking of the two shrugged and said OK. Grace smiled and set herself up as the 'catcher' at the bottom of the slide, running the dolls back to the girls at the top of the steps after each turn.

I sat down on a nearby bench, from where I could keep an eye on things without cramping Grace's style. I noticed that the first time she scooped up their dolls the girls didn't look entirely comfortable, but when she quickly handed them straight back after each slide, the two girls relaxed. Very quickly, they seemed to be having a lot more fun than before Grace joined in, which was good to see. I heard Grace say nice things about the outfits the dolls were dressed in, which was also heartening.

'Why don't you give them a race?' Grace suggested excitedly.

The girls liked this idea and they both lay on their tummies on the wooden platform at the top of the slide, ready to launch the dolls when the race began. Grace gave the 'starting orders', and as the dolls careered down the slide she provided a lively commentary that made the two girls giggle. 'Sindy's giving her a run for her money, but it's Barbie in the silver skirt by a nose!' Grace had the patter down to a tee; I reckoned she must have watched horseracing on the telly.

'We have to go home now,' one girl said eventually.

'Can you play with us again?' the other asked Grace. 'Do you live here? When do you come out to play?'

The two girls looked like they'd had a great time.

'I'm not sure,' Grace muttered. 'I'm just here for a few days. Then I'm going home, to my mum's.'

'OK then. Bye! Thanks for the game.'

The girls linked arms and walked off together, chattering animatedly. When I told Jonathan about this later, I remarked that Grace had lit up the girls' morning. 'They really enjoyed her company,' I said. 'Isn't that great?'

'Yes,' he replied, looking impressed. 'No winding up?'

'No.'

'No aggravating?'

'No.'

'Isn't it odd?' he said, scratching his head. 'This doesn't tally at all with the sort of behaviour we expected from Grace. I know we've barely got started, but . . .'

We'd had cases like this in the past, where the notes from Social Services didn't seem to describe the child we had staying with us at all. I finished Jonathan's sentence with him, knowing exactly what he was about to say: 'It's as if the paperwork has been muddled up!'

We were forever saying the same thing at the same time, and we still do. Lots of children have asked us if we're telepathic, which always makes us smile. Often a child asks one of us if, for instance, they can stay up late, and when they don't get the answer they want they ask the other. They're always dismayed when they get exactly the same response from both of us, despite the fact we haven't consulted one another.

My trip with Grace to the shops and to my mum's house was really enjoyable, and incident-free. She helped me pick out a few bits and bobs to take to the barbecue the following day, we got a packet of the crunchy cornflakes she liked, and Grace even insisted on carrying one of the shopping bags. At my mum's she was very polite and well behaved.

'What a little poppet,' Mum commented. Grace had shown great interest in my mum's knitting and patiently listened when my mum explained how she made all the separate panels of a baby's cardigan then sewed them all together. At Mum's suggestion, Grace explored the garden and delighted in filling an old margarine tub with some blackberries that were ripe and juicy.

'Can I eat them, Thelma?'

I was impressed by Grace's social poise. Mum always told the kids to call her Thelma, but I noticed that many of them avoided using her name to her face, or they said it but looked self-conscious, as if they'd accidentally addressed their head teacher by their Christian name.

'Yes, of course you can, dear, but let's give them a wash first. Bring them through to the kitchen. That's it. This way, dear.'

By the time we reached the kitchen sink Grace already had purple stains around her lips, though I hadn't spotted her popping any berries into her mouth. 'They look yummy,' she said as Mum washed the fruit. 'I can't wait to eat them!'

'They do,' I agreed. 'I think they're going to be delicious.' Mum caught my eye and gave me a knowing smile; she'd spotted the giveaway stains on Grace's lips too.

We had a generous slice of Mum's homemade lemon cake and a cup of tea before we left, and on the way home I decided to talk to Grace about the chocolate biscuit wrappers I'd found in the bathroom bin. She was in such a chatty mood and we'd had a lovely morning. I hoped that if I approached the subject gently she'd be open to discussing it.

'Oh yes, there's something I'd like to talk to you about,' I said casually. 'When I cleaned the bathroom this morning I found some biscuit wrappers in the bin.' Grace didn't look fazed at all, and she waited for me to carry on. 'I just wanted to remind you that if you want anything to eat or drink, please just ask. I know there are lots of things to learn, but in our house we don't allow children to help themselves without asking, and we don't allow food upstairs.'

'Oh,' she said, unperturbed. 'So I'm not allowed chocolate biscuits?'

I was relieved she hadn't denied it, as there was nobody else who could have put the wrappers in the bin, and of course I'd seen the stash under her pillow. I gently explained that of course she *was* allowed to have a chocolate biscuit or a snack if she was hungry between meals, but that she needed to ask me first. This was one of the rules we had for all the children, I reminded her.

'Nobody told me,' she said. She narrowed her eyes, as if she was thinking hard. 'I'm not lying, you know. Did you tell me that?'

'Yes I did, but as I've said, I understand you've had a lot to take in.'

'Sorry. It's hard to remember all the different rules and stuff. Every house is different, isn't it?'

'Of course, and I know it can't have been easy for you to move house lots of times. I'm not cross, but now you know what the rule is in our house, please just ask next time you want a snack or anything from the kitchen. You can help yourself to water but please ask about anything else. This is for your benefit, by the way. The rule is there so all the children who live with us eat healthily. Do you remember that phrase we talked about?'

'No, sorry.'

'Everything in moderation. It's not that you can't have treats, but you can't have too many, and that's why you need to ask first.'

'OK. Sorry.'

'It's OK, there's no need to apologise again. Have you taken anything else you want to tell me about, or is it just the biscuits? I'm not cross, I just need to know if there is anything missing from the cupboards, in case I need to replace it.'

She thought for a minute and told me about the crackers and 'something else I can't remember'. She added that she hadn't eaten the other stuff but just had it there 'in case I needed it'. I think she genuinely had forgotten what the other item – the mini cereal pack – was.

'That's all right, sweetheart. Thanks for telling me. If you remember what the other thing is, please let me know, and when we get home you can put them back in the kitchen and ask me if you want them.'

I felt some relief. I was no expert on eating disorders but I did know that, typically, those with issues were likely to feel ashamed and cover up their habits. I was confident Grace was telling the truth, and I was relieved she didn't lie or look embarrassed or guilty. Also, I'd seen her enjoy the slice of lemon cake at Mum's house in a very normal way, just as my mum and I did. She didn't pick at it or disappear to the toilet afterwards; she simply enjoyed it, as any child would. My instincts were telling me Grace's food smuggling had more to do with her unsettled background and unstable predicament than with any kind of eating disorder, but I'd still keep my eyes peeled. I've always lived by the motto 'you can never be too careful', and one fact was undeniable: Grace was very thin for a child who enjoyed her food so much. *Mind you, as she said herself, she does have ants in her pants.* That thought collided with all the others in my head as I tried to work Grace out.

I'm always on particularly high alert at the start of a placement, trying to assess a child from all angles. Not only am I aware that you rarely, if ever, get the full picture from Social Services – sometimes with good reason – but I've also learned that the longer a child has been in care, the sketchier the handover information can be, simply because of the volume of notes in a child's file. I've never met a social worker who hasn't been snowed under with work and, as I've said before, when a child urgently needs a new home there is rarely enough time to fully digest and summarise a child's full history in order to pass this on to a new foster carer. Often, we have to make do with notes that only scratch the surface of the child's background and circumstances, and in some cases information of a confidential nature is deliberately held back for data protection reasons, or only handed over on a 'need to know' basis. I don't object to this; a child in care, and their family, has the same rights to privacy as everybody else. However, this often means that when I start to look after a new child – and particularly one who has been in multiple placements – I feel like I've been given a jigsaw puzzle with pieces missing. I don't even know how many pieces there are to find or if they have been lost forever. Grace was definitely a puzzle, but I welcomed the challenge. I liked her a lot already, and I wanted to understand her and help her as best I could.

Our conversation about the chocolate biscuit wrappers prompted me to ask Grace if she would like me to write down a set of our house rules for her to keep in her room. She said she would like that and repeated that she couldn't remember me telling her the rules in the first place. I knew I had, because I always run through the house rules with every child who comes to stay with us as soon as I possibly can.

When I first started fostering I didn't like the idea of imposing rules, especially on the day a child moved in. It seemed unwelcoming, but I soon learned that it's beneficial to children to know exactly what to expect, and what's expected of them. Having rules, sticking to them and being consistent are all keys to happy fostering. When children know where they are, and what the boundaries are, it makes them feel more stable and secure in their new environment, and helps them settle in and feel more confident in themselves.

'Look at it like this,' a social worker once explained, when Jonathan and I began attending our ongoing training sessions for specialist carers. 'Do you remember going to a school friend's house for tea for the very first time, or starting a new job?' she asked the group. We all nodded knowingly, and were urged to recall how we felt, being out of our familiar routines and comfort zones. I thought about when I moved away from home to take a job in the city. I was eighteen years old and eager to spread my wings, yet I was still homesick and had moments of feeling lost and lonely. 'Now imagine that the first thing you do, in this new situation, is sit in someone else's chair unwittingly. You are immediately asked, or told, to move. It might be your friend's father who politely tells you that you've sat in his place at the dinner table, or a work colleague who rudely tells you to get out of his seat. Either way, how do you feel?' The dozen or so foster carers in the class all agreed they would feel embarrassed and also annoyed, because nobody had explained to them which chairs were taken. 'Precisely,' said the social worker. 'And that's how children feel when they break rules they don't even know exist. Let them know your house rules. Photocopy them and pin them on the walls if need be, but whatever you do make the children aware of what those rules are.'

Once Grace and I were back home I took a piece of card from the collection of art material I kept in a cupboard in the dining room and carefully wrote out a set of house rules for her. The first time I ever compiled a list of house rules I typed it up on my old Olivetti typewriter. These basic rules were pinned up on the noticeboard in the kitchen and had been for years. I knew them off by heart. However, with each new child I always make an effort to consider if any additional rules need to be put in place, and with Grace I decided to start from scratch and customise a list for her. I'd recognised that she often needed things to be told to her twice, and that she had a habit of forgetting things. I thought a simple, personalised set of rules would help her. Some of our general rules, such as 'no smoking in the house' and 'always come in on time' were aimed at older kids and teenagers, in any case.

This was the list I wrote out for Grace:

<u>House Rules</u>

1. No shoes indoors.
2. Ask permission before borrowing anything.
3. Check first before taking food or drinks from the kitchen.
4. No food or drink upstairs.
5. Put dirty washing in the laundry bin in your room.
6. Everyone helps with chores.
7. Keep your toothbrush, towel and wash bag in your bedroom.
8. Say please and thank you.
9. Have a shower/wash every day.
10. Be kind and treat others the way you want to be treated.

I signed my name at the bottom and asked Grace to sign hers. I didn't normally do that, but she had sat beside me the whole time, asking if she could use my pen when I'd finished with it. I reckoned signing her name would appeal to her, and it seemed to work. Grace asked if she could stick the list on her bedroom wall, and she darted upstairs with a lump of Blu Tack in her hand before the ink was dry.

That evening, Grace again ate a good meal and she thanked me for a nice day. 'I'm tired,' she announced. 'Can I go to bed straight after my shower?' It was before her bedtime but of course I said yes, that was fine. It had been a busy day, and children are often exhausted when they first arrive. Grace went upstairs and reappeared about ten minutes later in her pyjamas.

'What do I do next?' she asked.

'Have you cleaned your teeth?'

'No. I'll do that.'

She dashed off and then ran back a few minutes later. 'Do I need to put my shoes outside?'

'Your shoes? No, your trainers are fine in the hall cupboard. Oh, do you mean the ones still in your suitcase?'

'Yes, all of them. It says "no shoes indoors".'

'Ah, the rules!' I said, smiling. 'I should have written "shoes off indoors". That's what I normally write. Sorry, Grace. That was confusing. The rule is that nobody walks around the house in shoes. It's to help keep the house clean, for all of us. Your trainers and your other shoes are fine where they are, you don't need to put them outside. Where are your slippers?'

'In my case.'

I told her she should take them out and wear them around the house. 'OK,' she said, and ran off again.

When she reappeared she was still barefoot and was holding the mini packet of cereal I'd seen under her pillow and the crackers wrapped in kitchen roll. 'Shall I put these back in the kitchen? I only put them in my room when, like, I didn't know all the rules and stuff.'

'Yes, sweetheart. That would be great. Is there any other food in your room that we need to take out?'

She thought long and hard. 'No, I don't think so.'

I thanked her again and told her I'd be up to say good-night shortly. 'Did you remember to do your teeth?'

'No, I forgot.'

'OK, then go and do your teeth and get into bed. I'll be up in a few minutes.'

When I went in to say goodnight Grace was grappling with the zip on her large suitcase. Once again, it appeared she'd packed everything away.

'There's no need to do that,' I said gently. 'You can leave some of your things out. It'll be easier for you.'

Reluctantly, she took out the clothes she'd worn that day and put them in the laundry bin and placed her toiletry bag on the carpet beside the case before rezipping it. I left it there, thinking, *One step at a time.*

'I'm really, really tired,' Grace said, climbing into bed.

'I'm not surprised. I am too – we've had a busy day. Sleep tight. Do you want a hug?'

'No thanks. You're nice but no thanks. Night night.'

I wasn't in the slightest bit offended. I always ask the kids before giving them a hug or a cuddle and they often decline, but that's preferable to not asking, in case they need one.

'You're nice too, Grace. I'm very glad you've come to stay with us. Night night.'

6

'Somebody call an ambulance!'

Grace was excited on the day of the barbecue. She was up very early, even though it was Sunday, and she was in a bright, chatty mood. Despite her initial shyness, it was already apparent that Grace was a naturally friendly little girl, and resilient with it. It takes most kids longer than a couple of nights to start finding their feet, or to even give the thinnest of smiles, but Grace seemed in remarkably good spirits. I wondered if that was because she was going to her mum's the next day – I imagined it probably was.

'Are the other two girls *your* kids?' she asked chirpily.

I explained that no, they weren't. 'Both girls are living with us on foster placements, like you.'

I'd already told Grace that the two girls were visiting their relatives and would be returned to us at the barbecue later that day. When I'd explained this, I thought it was obvious we were fostering them too, but perhaps I hadn't made it clear. I couldn't remember the exact words I'd used, but it didn't matter. I took the opportunity to tell Grace a little bit about the two girls, such as their ages, their hobbies and which clubs they attended. I told her they were both good-hearted girls, which they were. Grace seemed satisfied with my brief descriptions and said she was looking forward to meeting them.

Of course, I omitted to tell Grace about the various problems the girls had; they'd both come to us because we were specialist carers. Jonathan and I never discuss the reason a child is in care with anyone bar the professionals we deal with, and the other foster carers we talk to in confidence at our regular training or support groups. I would never even tell my mum about any of the kids' backgrounds or issues, despite the fact she'd been passed by Social Services to babysit for us and had been for a number of years.

Perhaps surprisingly, it's rare for children to ask each other personal questions about why they are in care, or to put us on the spot by quizzing us about other foster children in our home. Occasionally a child might ask us what is 'wrong' with another child, or why they are 'naughty' or 'bad', for example. My response generally goes something like this: 'There is nothing wrong with them and they are not bad. Sometimes people behave badly, but that doesn't make them a bad person.' This is something I believe in very strongly. Children are not born bad. Unfortunately, bad things happen to them as they grow up, and this impacts on their behaviour. It's a lesson I learned very early on in fostering, and it's helped me deal with so many situations, Grace's included. Even before I met her I wanted to know what had *caused* the aggravating and disruptive behaviour she had apparently displayed for so many years. Whatever she did – and I was expecting to see some of this behaviour at any moment – I was never going to blame her. She was a vulnerable little girl who appeared to want to please. Clearly, something had derailed her best efforts, and I saw it as my job to help find out what that something was.

'So where are *your* children?' Grace asked me, after we'd briefly discussed the other girls. 'Are they all grown up?'

I guessed it was a reasonable question. Jonathan and I had recently entered our forties and Grace probably viewed us as being plenty old enough to have had children who'd flown the nest. In fact, we'd never had our own children. It was something that simply never happened for us and we accepted that was the way it was, just as many other couples did before IVF was available as it is today.

'No, sweetheart,' I said to Grace. 'We haven't got any children of our own.'

'Oh. Is that why you are a foster mum?'

Nowadays we're trained to avoid using the words 'foster mum' or 'foster dad' and to stick to 'foster carer' instead, given that the vast majority of children in care already have a mum or dad, or both. Jonathan and I have always been sensitive to the fact that we don't want to step on the toes of any parent whose child is living with us, and we've always suggested to kids it's best to call us their foster carers, particularly in front of their mum, dad and other close family relatives. I'd mention this to Grace at the right time, but for now I was happy to explain to her that we didn't become foster carers because we didn't have children ourselves. It's a common assumption that many people have made over the years.

'We decided to become foster carers long before we even thought about having a family of our own,' I told her. 'It was something I wanted to do from when I was a very young girl.'

'Why?' Grace looked confused. 'Kids are nothing but hard work.' She began to look blankly into the distance and once again I had a feeling she was repeating something she had heard from an adult. I waited a moment in case she wanted to say any more, but she simply asked 'why?' again, this time with more purpose.

'There was a family in my neighbourhood who fostered children. I loved going to their house when it was full of kids to play with. I thought it was great that they fostered and I nagged my mum to do the same, but she said she was too busy and didn't have the patience. I've always thought she was wrong about that, but she was adamant.'

'Haven't you got any brothers or sisters?'

'I only had one brother and he was much older than me, so he was already an adult when I was still a little girl. It was like I grew up as an only child, really.'

'I wish I was an only child.'

'Do you, Grace? You wish you were an only child?'

'Yes. It's not fair. Mum can only keep one of us, and my sister is mean and she tells lies! It's not fair she gets to live with my mum.'

'Your mum can only keep one of you?'

'Yes. She would have me back home forever if she could

but, like, she can't yet because of Lily, that's all. But soon I think I *will* go back, she's told me I will. Can I play out now? Can I go to the field? Can I, Angela?'

Grace was now gazing out of the kitchen window, and she was fidgeting with her hair. Absentmindedly, she was pulling her ringlets down to full stretch and letting them ping back up to their usual length, bobbing just below her jawline. I gently reminded her that she would be seeing her mum very soon, as her social worker Barry was collecting her at ten o'clock the next morning to take her back to her home town.

'I know,' she said vacantly. 'Maybe she will let me stay but I don't know. Where am I staying after that?'

A look of worry crossed her little face and she began to chew the end of a stray ringlet that was now dangling over one cheek. Again, I was aware we'd had a version of this conversation already. If everybody else was in agreement, it would ultimately be Grace's decision as to whether she wanted to move away from her home county to live with us. I knew I'd explained this to her already, but I understood that Grace might need several attempts to process it. I wished I could tell her she was coming back to us after she'd stayed with her mum for a week, but I couldn't. Nothing was confirmed and I didn't want Grace to suffer any unnecessary uncertainty and upheaval. She'd had far too much of that in her short lifetime already.

I smiled at her and told her we'd both find out soon enough. As I spoke, out of the corner of my eye I saw the Murphy's Law fridge magnet. 'Nothing is as easy as it looks.

Everything takes longer than you expect. And if anything can go wrong it will, at the worst possible moment.' I'm not a superstitious person at all and we'd enjoyed the joke while it lasted, but in that moment something told me to get rid of this magnet. Discreetly, I took it off the fridge and shoved it in a drawer. Hopefully Grace would never notice, as the fridge was covered in dozens of other magnets, collected on our travels and given as small gifts from friends and children we fostered who knew we collected them.

I told Grace I'd happily take her over to the field to play. I also told her she could talk to me some more about her family, or about anything else if she wanted to, but she shrugged and said it was all right. I felt sorry for her, as she looked very small and defeated and sad for a few moments. However, as soon as we put our shoes on to go out, she appeared recharged. Her hunched shoulders sprang up and she was suddenly raring to go once more. I had a job keeping up with her as she zoomed across our back garden and over to the playing field, where she launched herself onto the monkey bars and chatted easily to the other kids she encountered in the play area.

'Isn't she a gorgeous little thing?' one of my neighbours commented.

'She is,' I said, feeling proud of her.

When I had a few minutes to myself, I made a note of what Grace had said about her mother apparently stating she would have her 'back home forever if she could'. Clearly, that was at odds with the version of events presented by the family and relayed to me by Social Services. I went over what we knew. We had been told that Grace's older sister Lily had gone to live with their mother, Colette, around a year after both girls were taken into care. Grace's mum had 'consistently refused to take Grace back' because of her 'aggravating and disruptive behaviour' and the fact she 'never listens', 'deliberately winds everyone up' and was 'impossible to live with'. There was no mistake about that; Barry had read the notes straight from Grace's Social Services file, in my kitchen. Grace's story about her mum only being able to keep one child didn't fit either, as Colette was raising two older stepsons as well as thirteen-year-old Lily. Why would a mother only be able to keep one daughter, but raise two teenage stepsons? Was this an excuse Colette had given to Grace for not having her back home, or had Grace invented this, to help her deal with the painful reality? Sadly, it seemed to me that pretending her mum had promised to have her back was exactly what a rejected young girl might do, to try to make an unbearable situation a little easier to cope with. My heart bled for Grace, it really did.

The sun was beating down as we got ready for the barbecue later that day. Grace's skin was milky white and I was pleased when she allowed me to put sunblock on her without the fuss a lot of children make. 'I've got some of my own but I don't know where it is,' she told me. I hadn't checked her bedroom that day but I had a feeling that all of Grace's belongings would be packed up again, just like the day before.

'No problem, I've got plenty. And it's a high factor, just right for your fair skin.'

75

'Good. I don't like getting sunburned. Blisters hurt, don't they?'

'Blisters?' I said, unable to hide my concern.

'Isn't that what they're called? The big, like, bubbly things?'

'Yes, sweetheart, that's blisters.'

'So that's, like, what I had. Lots and lots of blisters. All over. Yuk!'

'I'm sorry to hear that, Grace. You got sunburned and had lots of blisters? I got sunburned as a child too.'

I wanted to hear more. During my childhood it was commonplace for kids to get badly burned in the sun, because far less was known about the harmful effects of sun damage. In this era, however, cases of severe sunburn were much rarer; in fact, it was virtually unheard of for young kids to get so badly burned they were blistered all over. It could have been accidental in Grace's case, of course, especially given how fair she was, or it could have been the result of negligence. If she were older, I might have been more persuaded that it was accidental, because I'd already learned that you can't rely on a teenager to put sunblock on. Once, we left two teenage girls on the beach on holiday. They both promised us faithfully they would apply their cream but neither did, and both got burned and blistered. They had difficulty sleeping that night, and never forgot their experience. However, I would never leave a child of Grace's age or younger on a beach, of course, and I wouldn't expect a ten-year-old to be responsible for applying her sun cream properly, on her own.

Not wanting to put words in Grace's mouth, I repeated back what she had said, with a quizzical tone in my voice.

'Lots and lots of blisters, all over?'

As was often the case, just when I wanted to hear more, she quickly moved on to another topic. I made a mental note to write this down later, to pass on to Social Services.

'Angela, did you say you had a brother?'

'Yes.' This question took me by surprise. My brother Andrew had died of cancer several years earlier. His death had been completely unexpected and came as a terrible shock, and I think I was still coming to terms with it.

'What's his name?'

'His name was Andrew. I'm afraid he passed away.'

'Died, you mean?'

'Yes, sweetheart. He was poorly and he died. It was a very sad time for all of us.'

'Was he nice?'

'Yes, he was a lovely person.'

Unexpectedly, Grace took hold of my hand and gave it a squeeze. 'Never mind, these things happen,' she said very seriously. 'We all have our crosses to bear.' That struck me as yet another turn of phrase she'd picked up from an adult in her life. She then commented that I was lucky I'd had a 'nice' brother.

'I know. I miss Andrew. It was very sad when he died.'

'I miss my dad.'

'You miss your dad?'

'Yes, I do.'

'I remember you told me he called you Goldilocks.'

For a moment I thought I'd misremembered, because Grace looked completely taken aback and frowned at me, but then she said, 'Oh, yeah. That's right. It was a long, long time ago. When I was a little girl. When he was my daddy.'

She said this in a babyish voice and looked up at me, squinting shyly through a bundle of curls. She was still such a little girl, I thought. I wasn't sure what she meant by the phrase 'when he was my daddy', but I assumed she meant when she lived with her father, or perhaps she was referring to a time when she simply had more contact with him than she did now? I left a pause, hoping Grace would tell me some more about him, but she didn't. There was no rush, and I certainly didn't want to push her. She'd had such a terrible start in life and her situation was still very precarious. The damage that had been done by her long journey through the care system was incalculable, but I told myself it wasn't too late to make positive changes. I was willing to do anything in my power to help turn her life around. Jonathan felt the same.

The barbecue was already in full swing when we arrived and, although she was very quiet to begin with, Grace quickly settled in and started enjoying herself. There were kids of all ages to play with and Grace also chatted to several of the adults. Gail, our neighbour who was hosting the barbecue, remarked what a lovely, friendly girl she was, and when Grace offered to help with the food Gail was impressed.

'Thanks Grace, that's very kind of you. How about

bringing some more hotdog rolls out? They're on the breakfast bar.'

Grace started running towards the kitchen. 'OK. Hotdog rolls. Where are they?'

'They're on the breakfast bar,' Gail called after her. 'Oh, and while you're in there, can you fetch a new packet of paper cups, please. They're next to the fridge.'

Moments later, Grace ran back out with the bread rolls.

'Thanks. Sorry, love. Can you pop back for the cups?' Gail asked, taking the packet of rolls off Grace.

'Cups? Where are they?'

'Next to the fridge.'

'OK!'

Grace ran off again, only to return empty-handed.

'What cups? Do you mean, like, mugs?'

'No, love. Sorry, I wanted a new packet of paper cups. They're by the fridge. Thanks ever so much!'

This time Grace returned with the cups. Gail thanked her again and asked her if she'd like to tell the other children there was a fresh jug of juice and some lemonade and they could come and get a drink if they wanted one. Grace nodded and raced around the garden, delivering the message to all the children. Whenever she was being praised, and particularly when she felt useful, she seemed to be in her element. She was also very pleased when I said she could have some lemonade, and I thanked her for asking me so politely.

When the other two girls who were living with us arrived at the barbecue during the course of the afternoon, Grace made a big effort to be friendly towards them. Neither seemed to be in a very good mood, although it's perfectly normal for kids to be a bit out of sorts when they're returned to us after staying with their families. Shifting between two diverse worlds is unsettling for any child. Not only do they have to switch between homes with completely different rules and boundaries – or, in some cases, no rules or boundaries at all – but afterwards they typically pine for family members more than ever and experience fresh waves of resentment about being in our care. With these two girls, it usually felt like we took several steps back each time they visited their relatives.

Grace didn't seem fazed by the girls' lukewarm response to her and she did her utmost to be kind and friendly. In fact, of all the children at the barbecue, Grace was the one who was making the most effort to please everybody else. She sat down next to Jonathan and me and ate a good meal, and afterwards she went over to Gail's niece Lena, who was dressed in a Disney princess outfit and playing on a rug with a collection of Barbie dolls.

'You look pretty,' Grace said. 'I like your dress.'

'Thanks, I got it for my birthday.'

'How old are you?'

'Eight.'

'I'm ten. Can I play with you?'

'Er, OK. What d'you want to do?'

Grace scanned the large garden.

'Let's take the Barbies on the trampoline!'

Lena smiled and gathered up the dolls, and both girls

charged to the end of the garden, where there was a mini trampoline in place. It was designed for younger kids and had a handrail on one side. I kept an eye on them as they knelt beside it, took hold of two dolls each and made them spring into the air and do somersaults. The girls were laughing their heads off, and then they must have had a bright idea. They piled all the dolls in the middle of the trampoline and then took it in turns to bounce as high as possible and see how many dolls fell off. They were roaring with laughter as the dolls were catapulted in different directions. Together, they retrieved the Barbies from the grass and repeated the process again and again, shouting, 'Boing, boing, boing!' and pulling silly faces and poses as they jumped. The grass was dry and the dolls were unscathed; it all looked like good, innocent fun.

I nipped inside to use the toilet. 'Keep an eye on them all, will you?' I said to Jonathan. He nodded. He was sitting on the raised patio and had a good view of Grace and Lena and our other two girls.

The downstairs toilet was occupied and Gail had told me to help myself to the main bathroom upstairs if I needed to, which I did. It was at the back of the house and the window overlooking the garden was open. I was just washing my hands when I heard a child's piercing scream.

Adrenalin flooded my body. It doesn't matter whose child it is; whenever I hear or see a little one in pain I have this instinctive reaction and immediately go into fight mode. I charged back downstairs as quickly as I could, my heart pounding and my nerves feeling like live electric wires.

Ominously, it felt like all eyes turned to me as I burst out of the patio doors.

'What's happened?' I shouted. Nobody answered. There was already a melee around the mini trampoline and everyone else was heading there. Hysterical wailing and panic-stricken cries filled the air.

'It's one of the girls . . .'

I couldn't see Grace or Lena through the circle of people but I felt sick to the pit of my stomach.

'Somebody call an ambulance!' a woman screamed. 'Call an ambulance. Oh my God, Quickly, please! My baby! Call an ambulance!'

I realised it was Lena's mum. I could see her now. She was on her knees, cradling her dumbstruck daughter. Lena's face was white and frozen in fear and her princess dress was soaked with blood.

7

'Why does this always happen to me?'

There was a large gash in Lena's forearm, and so much blood had been spilt I felt nauseous. Jonathan had been the first on the scene – he was a lightning fast runner – and it seemed he'd taken charge. Calmly, he was explaining to Lena's mum, Shannon, that they should use her cardigan as a tourniquet, as it would help to stem the flow of blood. 'Everything's going to be all right,' he was telling Lena, who had now started to sob quietly, soaking her mum's already blood-spattered summer dress with tears. Shannon was still frantic and panic-stricken, and her hands were trembling uncontrollably.

'What happened, Lena? What happened, baby? Please tell Mummy what happened!'

Lena didn't answer; her sobs grew louder.

Shannon let Jonathan secure the makeshift bandage. He worked as gently as he possibly could, but Lena was emitting pitiful moans, in between which she desperately gasped for air.

'Do we need an ambulance?' It was Gail, who was breathless and holding a cordless phone.

Shannon seemed in no fit state to make any decision. 'Maybe it would be best to take her to A & E ourselves?' Jonathan suggested. The bandage was doing its job now, and there was no more blood flowing. Thankfully, Lena was starting to calm down, ever so slightly, but her mum was still distraught.

'How did it happen, baby?' Shannon begged.

Someone said there was broken glass in the greenhouse, and a few people went to inspect.

'Did you fall, Lena? Tell Mummy. We need to know what happened, baby.'

Lena nodded and then she suddenly looked frightened, as if she'd just had a flashback.

Fortunately, one of the other guests turned out to be a nurse, and she knew Shannon. She'd been pulling up outside when the accident happened, and as soon as she'd heard the commotion she'd let herself in through the back gate and dashed to help. The nurse approved of the cardigan bandage, checked Lena over and offered to take her to A & E herself. 'No need to bother the ambulance service,' she said positively. 'My car's already warmed up! Let's get going now. OK, Shannon, love?'

Shannon nodded but didn't seem to attempt to move; she must have been in shock and was staring at her daughter.

'OK, Shannon? Shall we get going? Can you get to your feet and help me with Lena?' The nurse had a firm but friendly way about her and was completely unflustered.

'How about you, Lena? Can you stand up, darling?'

Lena struggled out of her mum's arms. She looked a bit wobbly, but she got to her feet, and Shannon then pushed herself up off the grass.

'So how did you do this to yourself, poppet?' The nurse kept up a dialogue, chivvying mum and daughter along. She also thanked Jonathan and told Gail she'd ring from the hospital. 'Save me a burger.' she smiled. 'I'll be back!'

I don't think there was a person at the barbecue who wasn't in admiration of the nurse; she was brilliant.

'That's it, let's go to my car. We'll be at the hospital soon. They'll fix you up, Lena, don't worry. And I'm sure your dress will come up clean after a good wash. I love that Disney film . . .'

Shannon was still asking what had happened, and as they headed to the back gate I heard Lena blurt out, 'Where is she?'

'Who, baby?'

'That girl!'

'What girl?'

I knew exactly who Lena meant. It had to be Grace. They'd been playing together minutes earlier, yet Grace was now nowhere to be seen. While Lena was being tended to, I'd been scanning the garden, wondering where on earth she'd got to.

'It . . . was . . . her! It . . . was . . . that . . . girl. Grace! She did it!'

After the nurse and Lena had left it took us several minutes – it felt like hours – to find Grace. She'd hidden herself in a very narrow gap between the back wall and the garden shed, which stood in the opposite corner of the garden to the greenhouse. She was crying when Gail's husband spotted her and encouraged her to come out.

'I didn't mean to do it,' she told him. 'I didn't mean to do it. It's not my fault. It just, like, happened.'

Grace looked forlorn and dishevelled. Her clothes were covered in green-coloured dirty smudges; there must have been moss growing in the cranny at the back of the shed. I led her to a quiet spot, where I could talk to her in private, while Gail did her best to get her barbecue back on track.

'Do you want to tell me what happened, sweetheart?'

Grace shook her head and refused to look at me. She hung her head so low all I could see was an unruly mop of curls, sprinkled with bits of old twig and dead leaves.

'It was an accident. I didn't mean it. Why does this always happen to me? I'm not a wind-up merchant, honest I'm not. I'm *not* a wind-up merchant.'

Grace was red in the face and looked angry as well as upset. 'Stupid old greenhouse! I was only trying to play nicely! I hate it here! Nobody likes me! Why do I always get the blame? I didn't know her stupid arm would go through. How could I know? It's not fair!'

Jonathan and I decided to take Grace home; she was creating another scene now and I didn't want to spoil the barbecue any further. Our other two girls weren't bothered about staying and so the five of us left together, having apologised profusely to Gail and offering to pay for any damage to the greenhouse that Grace may have been responsible for. I say 'may have been' because we didn't have the full story yet, and I didn't want Grace to be blamed unfairly. I asked Gail to give my number to Shannon, with a message explaining I was Grace's foster carer and asking her to call me when convenient.

Before we left the garden, Jonathan and I had a good look at the greenhouse. It was old and apparently unused, standing in a corner at the very end of the garden, behind where the girls had been playing on the mini trampoline. Two of the panels were smashed. From the snippets we'd managed to pick up, it seemed likely that Lena's arm had gone through one of those panels, but how, exactly?

Grace was very moody for the rest of the afternoon, and she had to be coaxed down from her room for some food later. However, once she was at the table she ate well, even having seconds of strawberry blancmange. She also tried hard to make conversation. The other girls were polite enough but didn't make much of an effort with her. This saddened me, but it was understandable, I suppose. Both girls were tired, and Grace hadn't exactly made a good first impression on them, what with all the drama of the accident and our hasty retreat from the barbecue. Grace had also forgotten both their names, which I could tell irritated them, though they didn't say anything.

After dinner, Grace buzzed around helping Jonathan and me clear up and then she ran upstairs for a shower when I asked her to. The phone rang while Grace was in the bathroom. I half expected it to be Lena's mother, and I braced myself.

'Angela? Hi.' It was a man's voice and I didn't immediately recognise it. 'It's Grace's social worker.'

'Barry? Hello. Is everything all right for tomorrow?'

'Yes, just a quick call. Sorry to disturb. Change of plan for tomorrow morning. Grace's mum is picking her up. Same time.'

'Oh, I see. I'll let Grace know.'

'Thanks. Oh, and can Grace phone her mum tonight please?'

'Yes, I'll ask her, I've got the number, and I expect Grace knows it anyhow.'

'Great. Thanks. I'll be in touch again soon. I'll leave you in peace. Enjoy the rest of your evening.'

Barry had hung up before I had a chance to say anything else. I wasn't very impressed that he hadn't asked how the weekend had gone; we'd had no contact since Grace had arrived. However, I gave him the benefit of the doubt. He was working late on a Sunday and, as my mother never failed to remind me, 'you never know what goes on in somebody else's life'. My guess was he was doing his stint as a duty social worker, which meant he was probably run off his feet, and we'd talk about Grace's trial visit when he had more time.

To my dismay, Grace came down from her shower with a face like thunder. She had put her clothes back on, and not her pyjamas as I'd asked her to.

'What's wrong, sweetheart?'

'Nothing.'

'Are you sure?'

'It's my stupid case. I can't do it!'

As I'd suspected, Grace had been repacking her bags every time she used anything. I told her I'd help and that I was sure we'd manage to sort it out. I then explained that her mum and not her social worker was collecting her the next day. Grace immediately perked up.

'Really? Are you joking with me, Angela? Are you, Angela?'

'No, Grace,' I smiled. 'It's your mum collecting you, not Barry. She's asked if you can phone her tonight.'

'Really? OK. OK, good. I'll ring now. What's the number?'

I wrote it down on a piece of paper so she could take it to the phone. 'Use the phone in the lounge if you like. I'll show you how it works.'

I started up the stairs – our lounge was on the middle floor of our town house – and Grace followed, right behind me. 'Steady on! It's not a race!' Grace was rushing and was far too close to me, so I told her to slow down or overtake, otherwise she'd step on my heels or trip herself up. She overtook me, and then I had to remind her not to run on the stairs.

'Sorry!' she puffed. I could see she was over the moon at the prospect of calling her mum. Her eyes were shining and when I followed her into the lounge she was already hovering over the phone expectantly. 'What do I do? How does it work? Can you show me, Angela? Can you?'

'Right, first you press this button here, to start the call. Then you dial the number.'

Grace looked worried about these simple instructions.

'Shall I stay here until you get through?'

'Yes,' she said, adding 'please' as an afterthought. I'd had a gentle word with her about remembering to say please and thank you, and she was trying her best.

Grace pressed the wrong button to activate the phone and I had to remind her which one it was. As I did this she was looking at her mum's phone number and not paying attention. This was a common problem with Grace. Though she'd only been with us for the weekend, it wasn't difficult to spot that she had a habit of letting her mind, as well as her body, race ahead. I imagined that was why she had forgotten the other girls' names; no doubt when she was told she was already thinking of something else.

Once again, Grace pressed the wrong button. 'Can you do it, Angela? Can you? Can you, Angela?'

She was so excited about phoning her mum, and she was getting more impatient.

'Look, it's easy when you know how, Grace. Watch. It's this button here, in the top left-hand corner. The one with the little picture of a phone handset on it. See?'

She sighed, finally pressed the correct button and then made a hash of dialling the phone number. In the end I had to show her again which button to press and then slowly read out the number, keeping a close eye on the keypad to make sure she didn't make any mistakes. I always try to give children privacy when using the phone – unless I'm instructed by Social Services to monitor the call, as I some-times am – but I asked Grace if she wanted me to stay in the lounge, in case we needed to write down anything about the arrangements for the next day. I thought it was wise, as I could see that a mistake could easily be made. Thankfully Grace said she'd like me to stay.

Her call was answered after several rings.

'Mum! Mum! It's Gracie.'

She was flushed in the face and was bouncing in her seat as she listened to whatever her mum had to say.

'OK. Angela! Angela! It's ten for half ten. Angela, is ten for half ten OK? Angela?'

'Yes, perfect. Thanks, Grace. I've got that.'

'Write it down! What? Mum? What did you say? What? What?'

Another of Grace's habits was talking over you. I guess this was linked to the same issue she had with mentally jumping ahead to the next thing before you were finished with the last. I imagined holding a phone conversation with her would be very difficult; it didn't sound relaxed, that's for sure! Though I couldn't hear what her mum was saying, the way Grace was talking reminded me of when I used to make transatlantic calls to a relative in Canada, in the days when there was an annoying delay on the line.

I busied myself by tidying up a pile of magazines I kept by my favourite armchair. I've always been a big reader and I like nothing better than getting my teeth into a good book. I love women's magazines too, and I always have plenty on the go. Barbara, who worked in our shop, was the same. We shared what we bought and kept a stash in the shop, to fill quiet moments. Often, I completed a word search that

Barbara had started and given up on, and vice versa, or I'd read half an article, only to find she'd torn out a page to enter a competition or to keep a recipe!

One of the magazines had a headline that caught my eye: 'E numbers turn my angel into a little devil!' I put it to one side to read when the children were in bed. Like most people in those days, I had a lot to learn about links between kids' diets and behaviour. New research was coming out all the time. I'd seen for myself that fizzy drinks made some kids go a bit hyperactive, and I made a point of reading everything I could get my hands on that might be useful. It hadn't escaped my notice that Grace had drunk lemonade at the barbecue before everything unravelled. Was she one of those kids who should avoid fizzy drinks altogether, or was she just a naturally exuberant child? And what was all this about E numbers?

After the call Grace was on a huge high. She looked completely wired, in fact, as she talked nineteen to the dozen about how her mum was coming in the morning, and how she was going to spend a whole week with her.

'She's coming at ten for ten thirty,' she told me. 'Angela, she said ten for ten thirty. Does that mean she's coming at ten but she might be late, or what?'

'It means we need to be ready for ten, but she might not arrive until about half ten. It's hard to give an exact time when you're driving. I expect it'll depend on the traffic.'

'I hope it's ten. How long is that? How many hours until ten in the morning?' She went up to our grandfather clock and tried to count the hours but got in a bit of a tangle. I helped her, and she said she was going to go to bed early, as 'the sooner I get to sleep, the sooner it will be tomorrow'. I smiled; it's not often a child tells *me* that!

I hadn't yet heard from Shannon, or Gail, and had not spoken to Grace about the incident since we came home from the barbecue. I didn't want to bring it up now, because as a rule I always try to avoid having difficult conversations just before bedtime. I know how things can play on the mind overnight – and that goes for me as well as the kids – and I didn't want to put Grace back into a bad mood. However, given that her mum was coming in the morning, and I might well get a call from Barry too, I needed to ask Grace what had happened.

I spoke to her gently before she went back upstairs.

'Grace, I'll come and help you sort out your case and find your pyjamas in a minute,' I ventured. 'But first, I just need to ask you about what happened today, with Lena.'

'Oh.' Her little face fell and she flushed red. 'I bet everyone is blaming me, but it wasn't my fault! It wasn't me! It's not—'

'Grace, sweetheart. I'm not blaming anyone. Please don't get yourself upset. I just want you to tell me what happened.'

'What's the point? Everyone will blame me and not her!'

'That's not true, Grace. Now, come and sit down here and tell me about it. Lena's mum might well phone me later, and I'd like to make sure everyone knows the truth about what happened. OK?'

Grace nodded, took a deep breath and embarked on an agitated monologue.

'So, this is what happened. I'm telling you, Angela, this

is the truth, the whole truth. I swear! This is it. This is what happened. So, you know that girl? What was her name? Lena, yeah, Lena. Right, me and that girl decided to play tag. She had to count to five before she could chase me. I ran around the back of that greenhouse and she followed me. She nearly caught me so I ran into the greenhouse and tried to, like, shut the door. Lena put her arm up to stop me and there was a smash. Her arm went through the glass. I didn't see any blood. I don't think she cut herself then, I'm sure she didn't. But when she pulled it out, well, that's when I saw the blood. That's when she screamed. That's when she got the cut and all the blood started to . . . See? Do you see what I mean, Angela? Do you get it?'

'Yes, sweetheart. Thanks for telling me. That must have been a nasty shock for both of you. I'm sorry that happened.'

I believed Grace. By strange coincidence, this jogged my memory about something similar that had happened to my brother when he was a young boy, playing with our next-door neighbour on their allotment. My brother had been left with a line of stitches on his arm after play-fighting with his friend and crashing through a panel of glass. My father refused to accept it had been an accident and instead blamed the other boy for pushing my brother. It caused a rift with the neighbours, which wasn't resolved until a long time later, when someone else who'd witnessed the accident happened to bump into my dad and described exactly what had gone on. The truth was, it really was an unfortunate accident and neither boy was to blame. My mum told me this story years later and I'd heard her referring to it many times since, usually to illustrate a point about the fact you shouldn't jump to conclusions. She was always very fair and considerate, my mum. She had a sensible, measured approach to life and, whenever I was put on the spot, trying to work out what to do or say about a dilemma with one of the kids, I often tried to imagine how she would react if she were in my shoes.

'What time can I get up in the morning? Angela? What time? What time am I allowed to get up?'

Grace was in my face and she brought me crashing back to the present. As ever, she had moved on much quicker than me and was already thinking about the next thing. I told her I'd be getting up at about seven thirty, and that she should try to stay in bed until then, at least. She sighed.

'Tomorrow's going to be the best day ever!'

Before we turned in, I found myself saying to Jonathan something that was becoming quite obvious.

'I think Grace might have *something*.'

'What do you mean?'

'I'm not sure, some kind of condition? She's hyperactive, that's for sure, and not just physically. Her mind races and she has trouble focusing. Do you think we should suggest she gets checked out?'

'It's very early days, but I think you might be right.'

'I can't stop going over Lena's accident. I believe everything Grace said. I think she has a good heart, but she's so exuberant. And she can't control her energy levels. I can't help thinking that if she had some kind of medical explanation for what's going on it might make her life easier all round.'

Like most people in the mid-nineties, I had never heard of Attention Deficit Hyperactivity Disorder (ADHD). Of course, in this day and age, those would have been the first words on my lips, but back then the public was only just starting to hear about the disorder.

8

'You could find yourself in a children's home'

I looked out of the window and saw an old white jeep pull up outside the house. It had bright pink stripes down the sides and wheels with shiny white hubcaps. I'm not normally very observant about cars, but I could tell the stripes were stuck on, not painted, as one section was damaged and peeling off. As for the wheels, I think they were what our young joyrider – the boy who had recently moved on – would have called 'pimped up'.

Grace was at the front door before the bell stopped ringing and I joined her. I hadn't managed to glimpse her mother yet and, after seeing the car, I was now more intrigued than ever to meet her. Grace was jumping up and down with excitement as I opened the front door.

'Hello babe!' Colette trilled as her eyes fell on her daughter. As she spoke she pushed her huge sunglasses onto the top of her head and flicked her long, blonde hair flashily over her shoulders. 'Look at you! Aw, babe, it's good to see you! How have you been, Gracie?'

Grace said 'good' very meekly. She looked like she'd suddenly shrunk in her mother's imposing presence. Colette was a large and very striking woman. Tall and curvaceous, she stood with her shoulders back and her chin lifted forward at an angle, as if she were posing for a photo.

I introduced myself.

'Pleased to meet you, I'm sure, Angela,' Colette replied confidently. 'Thanks for having our Gracie over. Has she been all right?'

She made it sound like we'd invited her for a play date or a sleepover with one of the other children.

'She's been more than all right,' I said brightly. 'It's been a pleasure having her to stay.'

'Well *that's* a relief to hear. Thank God for that, seeing as she's got to come back, eh?'

Colette gave a hoot of laughter while I found myself wincing inside. Having Grace come back to live with us may well have been what Colette wanted for her daughter, but she was jumping the gun. I hadn't spoken to Social Services since Grace arrived, apart from the quick call from Barry when he changed the arrangements for her to be collected. In any case, it would be down to Grace to make the final decision about moving back in with us long term. Far more importantly, I wondered what Colette was thinking, talking like this the minute she arrived. She wasn't even over the doorstep yet! Was she nervous, or just not tuned in to how her daughter might be feeling? I glanced at Grace and was relieved to see she looked undaunted by her mum's remark.

In fact, she was gazing up at her in awe, as if Colette were standing on a pedestal.

I invited Colette in. She removed her denim jacket, commenting loudly that she'd been 'sweating like a pig' on the journey over, and complaining that her make-up was melting off her face.

I offered Colette a drink and she said she'd love a cuppa. When I asked if she'd like a biscuit she accepted and asked if she could put her chewing gum in the bin. I said yes and showed her where the pedal bin was. I was just about to offer her a tissue or a bit of paper to wrap the gum in, when I saw she had her own method of disposing of it. Colette swiftly put her foot on the pedal, and when the lid lifted she fired the gum at speed, straight from her mouth into the bin.

'Thanks for that,' she trilled. 'If I do it with my fingers it gets all stuck on my nails, know what I mean? And I've just had them done.' She waved her hands around to show me her false nails, which were very long and immaculately French manicured.

What manners! I thought. *Fancy spitting in the bin! And those nails would drive me mad.*

'Can I have a biscuit?' Grace asked.

'Manners!' Colette blurted out. 'Say please, Gracie!'

Jonathan had been delayed on his way back from the wholesalers, which was perhaps for the best. We'd have been unable to resist exchanging glances if he were here, as we would have both had the same thought about Colette: *How could she reprimand Grace for having bad manners after spitting gum into our pedal bin like that?*

'Please, Angela?' Grace said sweetly.

I gave her a reassuring smile and passed her the biscuit tin.

'So, babe, you all ready?'

Grace nodded at her mum and said yes. 'I'm leaving some stuff here,' she then announced, in a determined tone of voice. As she said this she looked her mum straight in the eye; it was almost what you'd describe as a steely gaze. It was news to me that she was leaving some of her things here. Though Grace had mentioned this was a possibility over the weekend, this morning she had asked Jonathan to help bring all her belongings down. She'd even reminded him to fetch her pogo stick and scooter from the garage. Everything was stacked in the hall, waiting to go with Grace.

'Whatever, babe,' her mum said absent-mindedly. 'We'll go when I've finished my tea, yeah?'

I'd have expected Colette to perhaps ask to see Grace's room – most visiting parents do – and to at least ask more about how the weekend had gone, and what we'd been doing since Friday. However, she seemed more focused on enjoying her tea and biscuits, and as soon as she'd finished she got to her feet.

'Thanks for that. Just the job. I love a good cuppa. Let's go then, babe. What are you bringing?'

I followed them to the hallway, where Grace pointed to her belongings. 'Just the suitcase, that's all. The rest can stay. Is that OK, Angela?'

I said it was fine.

'Thanks. I will see you again, won't I?'

Poor Grace, I thought once again. It was painful to see her so uncertain and unsettled, and I wished I could tell her exactly what was going to happen the following week, but it hadn't been decided yet and so I had to tread carefully. Grace needed to talk to her social worker before making any decision about coming back to live with us, and of course we would need to talk to Social Services too.

'I hope you'll be coming back to stay with us for longer,' I said, choosing my words carefully. 'We'd love to have you.'

She looked pleased, and then Colette said she'd suddenly remembered something.

'I can't bring her back myself. We're going away next week, see.'

Clearly, Colette was under the impression Grace would definitely be moving in with us because she talked as if this was already the plan.

'Where are you going, Mum?'

'Torremolinos, babe. Just the five of us. You'd like it there! One day you might be able to come, if you learn how to behave yourself properly, that is.'

Unbelievably, Colette delivered this killer line with a flourish, as if she were giving Grace some triumphant news. I felt myself bristle.

'I've been good.' Grace spoke the words very quietly, through shrivelling lips. Her face looked sapped of light, and for once her slender little body was very still, as if sucked of all energy. I wanted to scoop her into my arms, but I had to stay rooted to the spot.

'So, you've been good for a *weekend*, Gracie! But how

many times do I need to tell you? You've got to behave yourself properly *all* the time. It's not just about being good for a couple of days, you know. I need to be able to *trust* you, all the time, babe. Angela, here, may not be able to keep you here if you start getting up to your old tricks, you know that, don't you? Then what? You could find yourself in a children's home. You sure she's behaved herself, Angela? Is there anything I need to know, because if there is I'd rather hear it now, know what I mean?'

I was angry with Colette for speaking out so carelessly. It felt to me like Grace couldn't do right for doing wrong, and to use the family holiday as a carrot as well as a stick seemed unnecessarily cruel. I bit my tongue, of course. Falling out with Colette was not going to help Grace, and so I did my best to hide my annoyance and disapproval. It wasn't easy. This was something I'd had to keep practising over the years, as my face used to give away how I was feeling.

Poor Grace now looked so anxious and stressed I thought she might start hyperventilating. No doubt Lena's accident was at the forefront of her mind, and I desperately wanted to put her at ease.

'Really, Colette, it's been a pleasure to have Grace staying with us,' I said politely. 'She's very helpful and is good company. I've enjoyed having her to stay, very much. So has my husband.'

I'd wanted to find out more about Grace and I'd hoped Colette and I could at least have had a chat so I might be able to fill in some of the blanks about her past. I really didn't understand why Colette wouldn't have her living back at home. Ever since I met Grace, I'd had a nagging thought in the back of my mind. Her situation really didn't seem to add up; was there something important I didn't know about her that would explain why, out of the four children Colette was responsible for, Grace was the one who was excluded from the family home?

After this encounter, however, I began to wonder if the real problem lay with Colette herself. Was she the one with the issues, not Grace? I didn't know, but the seed of that idea had been planted in my head.

After I'd said my piece about how much we'd enjoyed having her to stay, Grace visibly relaxed and Colette said no more. The three of us pitched in to load her suitcase and a few other bits and pieces into the boot of the jeep. Her holdall, bike, pogo stick and a carrier bag and box of belongings were left behind in the hall.

'Bye, Grace. Take care. I'll look after your things, don't you worry.'

'Thanks,' she said. 'You have been nice to me. You're nice.' She went to give me a hug. It was a spontaneous move on her part, or at least it started out that way. But when Grace made contact with me, it was as if something suddenly made her change her mind part way through, and she ended up giving me an awkward half-hug. I reciprocated as best I could, not wanting to invade her space while still trying to show I cared.

Colette was already in the driving seat by the time Grace and I had said our goodbyes. She wound down the window and chivvied Grace along.

'Come on, Little Miss Trouble!' she called. She said this chirpily, as you would if it were an affectionate nickname, but in the circumstances it felt disingenuous. Colette really did think Grace was a troublemaker, didn't she?

Grace rushed obediently into the passenger seat and I waved them off as they drove away. Grace had no seat belt on and Colette sped off far too fast, black smoke puffing out of the jeep's noisy exhaust.

Jonathan returned within minutes.

'Sorry I missed them,' he said. 'Just as well I said goodbye to Grace earlier. What was her mum like?'

'Well,' I said. 'Quite a character. I'll fill you in, come on. The kettle's still warm.'

Barry phoned and I told him how the weekend had gone. I'd still not heard from Lena's mum but I filled in the social worker on what had happened. I explained that Grace maintained it was an accident and that I'd logged everything for Social Services. Barry listened and took note of this without asking me what I thought, but that's not uncommon. Foster carers are rarely asked for their opinion; by and large we simply pass on whatever facts we have and let the social workers make the decisions.

'Overall, we think Grace's trial visit has gone well,' I said. 'There are a few issues to flag up – hiding food, trouble focusing, complaints about her stepbrother Lee, who apparently steals her clothes – but the "aggravating behaviour" we were warned about hasn't been an issue. I've jotted everything down that may be useful. We've enjoyed having

104

her and we'd be happy to have her back, if that's what Grace wants.'

Barry said his other line was ringing, quickly thanked me and said he'd be back in touch. Our support social worker, Jess, also called. I relayed the same message to her, and also told her about Colette, and what she'd said about the children's home.

'Charming,' Jess sighed. 'Thanks for passing this on. I'll keep you posted.'

We heard nothing for days on end. Every morning I woke up thinking about Grace and wondering how she was getting on at home. We'd put her things safely away. Would Barry, or someone else, simply turn up to collect the rest of her belongings? Perhaps we'd never see Grace again? It seemed unlikely, all things considered, but we'd have to wait and see. I left her bed made up; there was no point in stripping it, in case she came back.

When I went in Grace's room to dust and vacuum, the day after she left, I spotted several empty cartons of orange juice pushed under the end of the bed. I hadn't missed them from the utility room cupboard where I usually stored them. I'd bought a large box in bulk from the local cash and carry, seeing as they were very handy for packed lunches and picnics, and we went through a lot of them, especially in the summer. Back then I assumed that drinks containing fruit juice and marketed for children were healthy and nutritious. Like a lot of people, I thought it was only fizzy drinks you had to be careful about. Incidentally, I also avoid buying individual cartons now, as I'm far more conscious of reducing waste. I encourage children to use refillable bottles, but in those days this was what we typically bought.

Before I threw the discarded cartons away, something told me to have a look at the packaging. The night before I'd finally got round to reading the magazine article with the headline that read, 'E numbers turn my angel into a little devil!' It had opened my eyes about 'hidden' additives in food and drinks, telling the story of how a child's behaviour spiralled out of control after he ate certain colourful sweets, fizzy drinks and processed food. To be honest I wasn't that surprised, and I didn't really think it affected us too much. It had always seemed common sense to me not to feed kids sugar-laden or heavily processed foods, and we already limited fizzy drinks, sweets and crisps. I enjoy cooking and pride myself on making meals from scratch and using fresh ingredients whenever possible. Nevertheless, after reading that article, I vowed to be more vigilant about 'hidden' additives, and that's why I read the side of the empty juice cartons that day.

I'd been buying this particular brand for ages, so imagine how my heart sank when I studied the ingredients. To my dismay, each carton contained only a very small percentage of fresh orange and the rest of the drink was made up of sugar, water, thickeners, flavourings and colourings that had names and numbers I'd never heard of, including some of these E numbers that apparently had a negative impact on kids' behaviour. Inevitably, I wondered if the additives had affected Grace. After all, she always had 'ants in her pants' and could never sit still. Was that just how she was built, or did her diet play a part?

'I'm throwing all those cartons away,' I told Jonathan.

'What? Don't do that, there's a huge box, dozens of them! I'll drink them. A few mouthfuls of juice aren't going to turn me into an energy bomb!'

Jonathan wasn't joking. We both hate waste of any kind and have always lived by the motto 'waste not, want not'; I guess that comes from being born in the fifties to parents who lived through the war. I agreed to put the cartons in the storeroom at the back of the shop, so that we could drink them ourselves, which we did over the course of that summer. It became a standing joke, as I remember, as often one of us would find the other taking a breather in the back, a carton of juice in hand.

'Oh look at you with your feet up! There's no ants in your pants, are there? Ha ha!'

We still laugh about that now.

On the Friday morning – four days after Grace had left us – we finally got the news we were waiting for. Social Services were very keen to place her with us and Grace had agreed to move in. Our support social worker Jess explained that, though the placement would initially be for six months, all being well it would run for longer.

The plan was that Colette would take Grace back to her current foster carers later that day. We weren't told why Grace had only stayed for five days with her family when originally we thought it was going to be for a week, but that was what was happening. She would spend the weekend with her foster carers before coming back to us on the Monday.

Even when a placement breaks down it's important to say goodbye and try to leave on good terms and with happy memories at the forefront of the child's mind. 'Good goodbyes' was one of the training courses we'd had to attend. Positive messages are so important and ending a placement on a happy note is what foster carers should always strive for.

Unfortunately, because of the timings, Grace was going to have quite a long goodbye. Barry didn't work weekends unless he was in the office as duty social worker, and as he was the one who would drive Grace from the other foster carer's to our home, she was going to be there for three nights. Barry would drive her to our house when he was back at work on the Monday and then we'd have a placement meeting with him and Jess. Colette had been invited to attend this meeting too, but she had informed Social Services she was going to Torremolinos early on that Monday morning so couldn't make it.

Jess told me that Barry had tried to fix it so that the handover could happen on another day, so that Colette could attend the meeting, but she had refused this offer. I thought this was a shame, and I also didn't think it was ideal that Grace was spending three nights with her soon-to-be former foster carers. They had wanted her to leave as soon as possible, and all Grace needed to do was say goodbye and collect anything she'd left behind. One day would have been preferable, I thought. I said nothing to

Social Services, as it wasn't my place to and my opinion would not have made any difference, but I complained about the arrangements to Jonathan.

'I don't know why Colette didn't organise it better, so Grace wasn't being messed around so much. Three nights with us, four nights with her family, three nights with the other foster carers. I feel sorry for Grace, I really do.'

Jonathan agreed with me but didn't join in with my grumbling as he didn't want to fuel my irritation. 'Look.' He sighed. 'The important thing is, Grace is coming to live with us. Let's focus on that. It's great news, isn't it?'

'Yes,' I said, smiling at my husband. This was one of those moments when I felt a surge of appreciation for the fact I have his support and we work as a team. I'm a better foster carer for working in partnership with him, and he says the same to me.

'It really is good news,' I said. 'I just hope she's not going to be even more unsettled after all this to-ing and fro-ing. Monday can't come soon enough.'

9

'You'll be a foster care kid forever'

Grace seemed very agitated when she arrived back at our door with Barry. It was hardly surprising, I guessed. As well as all the upheaval she'd gone through over the past week, returning home as well as to her former carers', I couldn't imagine what it must have been like seeing her sister and two stepbrothers preparing for their holiday to Torremolinos. No doubt they were packing their holiday bags while she was repacking her suitcase for the next leg of her foster care journey. In addition to that, Social Services would have been talking to her about her wishes, asking if she was happy to come and live with us. It must have been quite an ordeal for her, I thought.

Jonathan and I welcomed Grace back with open arms, of course, and told her how pleased we were that she was moving in with us, but she didn't look very happy at all. In fact, she scowled and could barely look at us when we first opened the front door, and as soon as she came into the house she tore her trainers off, threw them at the

110

skirting board in the hall and charged upstairs angrily.

Barry shrugged as he watched her run off. 'Have hardly been able to get two words out of her,' he said, shaking his head. 'It's a shame, as she was much chattier last week. She's like a different girl. I thought she might have perked up when she saw you. Sorry, it's not the best start, is it?'

'Don't worry, Barry. She's had a lot to contend with, and believe me we've had worse.'

Jonathan nodded as I spoke. We've met children who've stood on our doorstep and told us they didn't want to stay in our 'crappy house' with our 'rubbish rules', or screamed 'You're not my parents!' 'You only look after me because you get paid!' is another one we've heard many times, as is 'Why don't you give the money you get to my mum and then she'll be able to look after me herself!' It was tempting to tell them that the money we were paid from fostering rarely covered our costs and that we did it for love not money, and supported ourselves through the florists, but of course we never went down that road. Neither did we ever take anything personally. There were always lots of reasons – some we could have no idea of – for every child's behaviour, and Grace was no exception.

The placement meeting was held in our lounge, with Barry and Jess both in attendance, as planned. Despite arriving less than ten minutes after Barry and Grace, Jess apologised profusely for being late, explaining that she'd been held up at the magistrates' court, dealing with another child in her caseload.

'No problem,' I said. 'It gave me a chance to make a pot of tea. Everyone take milk? Sugar, anyone?'

The two social workers accepted the tea gratefully; they both looked glad of the chance to catch their breath and recharge their batteries. Jess was only in her mid-twenties but was one of the best support social workers we'd had, always striking just the right balance between being professional and friendly, and with a wonderfully perceptive and empathetic way about her that belied her years.

Jess talked briefly to Barry about an interesting case that had been in the news in his region, before asking us about how the florists was doing, as she'd noticed that the new petrol station on the bypass was now selling flowers and hoped it wasn't affecting our business. All of this she did swiftly and seamlessly, and when we went on to talk about Grace there was a warm atmosphere in the room, almost a team spirit. That was Jess's gift. She was in the perfect job, in my opinion, and she was a total natural at making everyone around her – kids included – feel they were valued and that their opinion mattered.

We had left Grace upstairs in her bedroom for the time being, and I hoped she'd calm down as she started to unpack her bags and finally find a home for all her familiar belongings.

The social workers talked to Jonathan and me about Grace's schooling. I was very pleased to hear that Jess was already on the ball with the education authority and was optimistic Grace would get a place at one of our best local primaries, where she'd enter in Year 6. I was not so pleased to hear that Grace had attended a total of nine schools since she was four years old – more than one for each year she had been in education. She'd also missed a lot of school because of her multiple moves. I found myself silently praying nothing would go wrong this time and that, whatever happened, she could complete Year 6 uninterrupted.

Grace eventually sat through some of the placement meeting. It's always best if the child can take part, or at least be present, in some of the discussions. This way they have an opportunity to share their views, which helps in decision-making and makes the child feel empowered, and hopefully less anxious, about what is happening in their life.

When I fetched her from her bedroom, Grace still looked irritated and distracted, and she was uncommunicative. She didn't even attempt to run down the stairs as she usually did; she walked reluctantly. In the living room she sat quietly and appeared uninterested when we chatted to her about school. She seemed equally indifferent when Barry talked to her about maintaining contact with her family.

'Just like you always have before, you can phone your family whenever you want to, and they will be able to ring you here.'

'Mmm.' She twizzled a section of her hair and I saw her eyes dart around the room.

Barry also told her that she would spend a weekend in the family home approximately every six weeks, as had always been the case. This could be fixed up directly with Colette. Jonathan and I would be able to help Grace organise the visits and we could phone the family home as and when we needed to.

'Are you happy with all that?' Barry asked Grace. 'Sound good to you?'

He was doing his best to sound upbeat and to drum up some enthusiasm.

'I suppose.' Defiantly, she added, 'I won't take my stuff.'

'Oh no,' Barry said, eyes widening. 'You don't need to take all your things! No, no. Just a small weekend bag will be absolutely fine!'

Grace gave him a quizzical look and then looked at me, and I realised there had been a bit of a misunderstanding. Understandably, Barry was focused on the fact he'd only just delivered the rest of Grace's belongings to our house. She'd returned with far more than she'd left us with, despite the fact we'd also kept hold of lots of her things while she was away for the week. As well as her large, overstuffed grey suitcase, Grace brought with her a box filled with toys and knick-knacks, a pair of roller skates and a plastic mic stand and toy microphone. Barry looked tired from the effort of lugging everything in from the car, and he clearly didn't want to carry stacks of luggage to and from her mother's house every time she went for a weekend contact visit.

'You won't take your stuff?' I said with a question in my voice. I put the emphasis on the word stuff, hoping she would expand on what she meant.

'No,' she said through gritted teeth. '*You* know why.'

I glanced at Barry, who had caught up by now, realising she was probably referring to the fact her stepbrother, allegedly, stole her clothes. Barry tried to backtrack and get Grace to talk about this, but she'd shut down. This was hardly surprising; kids find it hard enough to talk candidly to one adult, even when they know that person well. Having four grown-ups you hardly know as your audience does not make for flowing dialogue when sensitive topics are on the table.

As soon as it was appropriate, I checked it was OK with Barry to let Grace go back to her room.

'Yes, I must dash, in any case,' he said, adding with a chuckle, 'Sorry to mention *cases* again!'

Though Grace didn't seem to get the pun, Jonathan and I appreciated Barry's attempt at ending the conversation with her on a light note.

When Grace was out of the room I asked Barry about her father, and whether she was in touch with him at all.

'He's dead,' he said, as if surprised I didn't know. 'He was a drug dealer as well as an alcoholic. Died of an overdose, years ago. He was only a young fella.' I knew about his alcoholism, but this was news to me. I remembered Grace's comment about 'when he was my daddy' and thought how sad it was for her to have lost her father in this way. I didn't know how much she knew about the circumstances of her dad's death, but whatever she had been told it must have been a terrible shock to lose him when he was still a young man and she was such a little girl.

I went on to ask about the visit to Grace's previous foster carers. Barry said she hadn't wanted to talk about it, but the carers had reassured him the weekend had run as smoothly as it possibly could have done, and they had managed to end the placement well, enjoying a farewell meal together. I was pleased to hear that.

We talked about the routine appointments we would arrange for Grace, as we are required do for every child who comes to live with us. We would take her to the doctors, opticians and the dentist. I mentioned the fact we were wondering if Grace's hyperactivity and lack of ability to concentrate might mean she had some sort of disorder or condition that should be checked out, and that I would like to discuss this with the doctor. Jess and Barry agreed, although they both suggested it might be wise to let her settle in first and keep monitoring the situation, as the upheaval she'd been through would have had a considerable impact on her. This seemed sensible advice.

Everything was up in Grace's room now. I went to see her after the meeting ended, but instead of unpacking as I hoped she was doing, Grace was turfing her belongings all over the carpet, raking through the contents of her suitcase, bags and boxes and becoming increasingly agitated.

'Did I leave my Spice Girls top? Did I, Angela? Did you wash it? Did I leave it? The baggy one with the short sleeves? You know, the glittery one? Ginger Spice in the, like, flag dress? Did I? Did I leave it, Angela? Angela?'

'I don't remember seeing it, sweetheart. Let me go and check in my ironing pile, just in case it got mixed up in there.'

The top hadn't found its way into my ironing pile, and when I thought about it I was certain she hadn't left it at our house the week before. When a child is only staying for a short time, I'm always careful to keep tabs on their washing, and I separate it out to avoid dramas exactly like this one.

'Are you really sure, Angela? Can you look again?'

'I'm sorry, sweetheart. I really don't think you left it here. It would be in the ironing pile if it was anywhere. I know nobody else has it by accident, as the last time I ironed I sorted out all the clothes and handed them back to the other girls myself.'

Grace was only half listening. She was now clawing even more desperately through the contents of her big suitcase. The carpet was littered with clothes but the top she was looking for was still nowhere to be seen.

'Shit,' she spat. 'I knew it! Can I phone home?'

She was bright red in the face, and she wiped her sticky brow dramatically before planting her feet firmly on the carpet and standing with her arms folded tightly across her chest.

As tactfully as I could, I reminded Grace that there would be nobody at home, as her family had gone on holiday early that day. It was the first time I'd heard her swear and I also told her not to use bad language, though I could see she was extremely agitated and was not exactly in control of herself.

'My nightie's gone too!' she snapped, rummaging through the clothes once more. Then she spun her head around and fixed her eyes on me.

'No, they're *not* on holiday yet, they're still there.'

'No, Grace, I don't think that's right.'

'It is! They're going tomorrow, Lily told me. Can I call? Can I phone home?'

I was sure she'd got that wrong, as Colette had been clear about her holiday dates, saying she would be unable to attend today's placement meeting as she was going away early in the morning. Grace had told me before that Lily told lies, and I wondered if this might be a fib of hers. Either that, or maybe Colette had made a mistake? Or had she been economical with the truth because she didn't want to attend the placement meeting?

'Can I, Angela? Can I use the phone?'

I couldn't refuse. I would never stop a child attempting to call home, and I thought that if Grace got the answer-phone, at least she'd had the chance to try to speak to her family. We went down to the lounge, Grace running ahead. She looked wired, as if on high alert, and her eyes were shining as she snatched at the phone impatiently. I told her to try to be calm, saying that's the best way to be when you want to get answers, and to get your message across.

I helped her dial the number, as she couldn't remember it and had forgotten how our phone worked. Someone answered almost straight away. I busied myself at the other end of the room, so as to give her some privacy.

'Have you got my Spice Girls top?'

Grace was standing stiffly, with one hand on her hip, looking like she meant business.

'You're a liar! I'm telling Mum. Is she there? Can I speak to her? What? What d'you mean? I hate you!'

There was a pause and then she spoke to someone else,

mentioning the holiday and checking when they were going, before slamming the phone down. I wanted to ask who she had spoken to but I could see I needed to tread carefully. Grace looked so upset and her face was contorted, as if she were about to cry, but she didn't shed a single tear.

This response is something I've seen a lot. After a difficult start in life, many children suffer from what I now recognise as a symptom of attachment disorder. Again, back in the nineties I was only just learning about how the brain develops in babies and children, and I knew far less about this kind of thing than I do now. That said, I'd started to recognise a pattern and worked out that kids who hadn't had a nurturing, loving upbringing often didn't have the 'typical' reactions you'd expect to see in children who had been loved and cherished in the normal way. Long before I did research on different types of attachment disorders, I used to look at some of the children in our care and think it was as if their brain was wired up differently to other people's.

In a way, I was right. A child's brain doesn't develop how it should when it is starved of the basic nourishment it needs to grow. In other words, when there is a lack of bonding between the child and their caregiver, and when the child doesn't feel secure, and is not consistently nurtured, brain development is damaged. The consequences can be far-reaching. Some children lack self-esteem and the ability to self-regulate. They may be unable to empathise in a normal way, show compassion or even develop a normal conscience. In some cases kids lack healthy defences against, and reactions to, stress and trauma – crying being one of those – and they may struggle to make friends and form meaningful relationships.

We couldn't be sure how Grace's psychological development had been affected up until the age of three, when she was taken into care, but we did know she had been scared and hungry when her dad left her and her sister home alone. Neither could we know, or quantify, what damage had been done by her repeated moves to different foster homes; it was many years before I would start to see research highlighting the negative effects of multiple moves on a child in care. All I could do was look at the evidence in front of me and hope to God that Grace would be able to overcome any damage she had suffered. It broke my heart, because before me I saw a very angry, hurt and confused little girl. Grace was desperate to be loved by her mum and she tried hard to be friendly and popular with her peers. She seemed quite lost and desperate to me. It was an incredibly sad situation.

Silence fell on the room for a moment after Grace smashed the phone down. Then she kicked the edge of the sofa and spat the word 'liar!' again.

'Sweetheart, what is it?'

I asked her not to kick the furniture and she stopped dramatically, as if she'd frozen on the spot.

'Grace, do you want a hug?'

She didn't react immediately but then suddenly screamed, 'No! Leave me alone! You don't even like me! You hate me, like everyone else!'

With that Grace ran back up to her room and I heard the door slam.

'Honeymoon period over already?' Jonathan said despondently when I went down to the kitchen.

'Looks that way.'

I told him everything and he sympathised and gave me a hug.

'More tea?'

'Yes please. And chocolate.'

'Coming right up.'

I felt better already as I sipped my tea, ate a chocolate biscuit and chatted to Jonathan, and I found myself wishing that it would be as easy for Grace. Unfortunately, tea and sympathy were woefully inadequate. Grace would need a lot more help than that, and I imagined she would do for a long time to come.

After a short while I went up to check on Grace. There was no reply when I knocked on her door but I could hear her moving around. It sounded like she was dragging something across the floor and for a moment I was worried she was about to barricade the door.

'Sweetheart, can I come in?'

Still no reply.

'Grace, I'm going to open the door now, as I want to see you and make sure you're all right.'

I heard footsteps, and she flung open the door before I even reached for the handle.

To my surprise, there was nothing strewn across the

carpet as there had been earlier; not one single item. I saw that Grace's bags and belongings were stacked up neatly in the corner, and for a moment I was pleased, because I thought she'd tidied up, unpacked and found a home for everything. Of course, this turned out to be wishful thinking. Grace, I realised, had packed all her belongings back into her case and bags once again, just as she'd done during her trial visit. The room looked completely unlived in and, as before, there was not even her cuddly toy on the bed or her toothbrush on the dressing table.

'How are you feeling, sweetheart?'

'I'm fine,' Grace huffed, avoiding eye contact. 'Why? Can I just go and play outside?'

I said that she could but I also had a word about how she mustn't be rude to me, because it made me feel upset.

'OK. Sorry. It's just such a wind up!' She breathed out, as if expelling something nasty from her mouth. 'Can I play out now?'

'Yes. I'll come with you. Shall we go over to the playing field?'

'Yes. Can I take my scooter?'

I said that was fine. I had lots of jobs I wanted to do in the house, but they could wait. I could see that the priority was for Grace to get outside and let off a bit of steam. However, I didn't bargain for quite how much steam. As soon as she was through our back gate, she scooted around the pathways so energetically I had to run to keep up with her. Two of my neighbours commented on it.

'Wow! Speedy Gonzalez!' one remarked.

'Me or her?' I joked.

'Who have you got staying with you this time – Damon Hill?' another laughed, referring to one of the most successful British racing drivers at the time.

Everybody in the neighbourhood knew we fostered and most were very friendly and interested. I often got comments along the lines of 'I don't know how you do it!' and 'You must be a saint', to which I always replied that we were privileged to be able to do the job we did. That's truly how we felt; no matter what problems we had to deal with, it was an honour to be in a position of trust, and to be responsible for a precious child who needed more help than most.

One of the girls Grace had met at the play area on her trial visit was out on the field with her mum. I saw her recognise Grace. 'Mum, that's the girl I told you about!' she shouted out. I heard her explaining to her mum that Grace was the one who'd organised the Barbie race on the slide. The girl looked very animated and she began chasing after Grace along the winding path, her face full of excitement and expectation. I watched as Grace slowed down, lay her scooter on the grass and started smiling and talking to the girl. Then the two of them ran back over to the girl's mum and spoke to her. The woman looked over to where I was standing, not far away, and started making her way towards me.

'Hello,' she smiled. 'I'm Jill. It seems the girls met last week. Briony has asked me if your daughter could come over and play some time?'

'That would be lovely,' I said, telling Jill my name. 'Are you new to the neighbourhood?' I'm sure Grace was in hearing distance and she hadn't corrected Jill when she said 'daughter', so I said nothing either. That's always my policy; I take the lead from the child. Most foster children don't want to spell out that they are in care and I never volunteer the information unnecessarily.

Jill told me the family had only recently moved in, which made sense, as I tended to know all the neighbours. I explained that we ran the florists and had lived next to the shop for many years. We sat on a bench and chatted for a while, watching the girls play a skipping game. I warmed to Jill straight away. She seemed like a very gentle person, quite shy but keen to make friends. I was in no rush to have Grace go over to her house, though. It was her first day back with us and I wanted her to find her feet and settle down. Inevitably, the incident with Lena continued to niggle me. I still hadn't heard anything from her mum, and unresolved business like that always plays on my mind.

'Grace looks like she's got so much energy!' Jill said. 'She's exhausting to watch.'

'Tell me about it. She never stops! Something tells me we'll be out here quite a lot over the summer holidays!'

'That's good, as I'm sure we will be too. And if you're happy for Grace to come over to play – maybe when they've got to know each other a bit better – perhaps we can fix that up? We're only in that house there.' She pointed across the field.

'Great,' I said, feeling relieved Jill wasn't in a rush to arrange the play date. 'I'm sure she'd like that. Mind you, it looks like they're more than happy out here for now. We might as well make the most of it while the weather's so good.'

Briony looked quite heartbroken when Jill told her they had to go in and get changed very shortly, as they were going to visit her gran.

'When can Grace come to our house?'

'We'll fix that up soon,' Jill said, catching my eye. 'Don't worry, Bri. We've got lots of the summer left. There's plenty of time.'

Briony smiled at Grace, who was beaming and bright red from the exertion of playing.

'I need a drink, but can I go on my scooter again first?'

'Irrepressible!' Jill smiled. 'Lovely to meet you, Grace. I wish I had your energy.'

Grace smiled then sped off, panting and dashing and glowing with life.

Back home, she glugged down a large tumbler of water. She was wearing a top with three-quarter-length sleeves, and I suggested she might want to change into something cooler.

'OK!' she agreed, running upstairs. When she returned, wearing a vest top, I noticed her shoulders were badly sunburned.

'Grace, what happened?'

'Oh. I forgot about that. It's not sore, honest. It was just, like, well, Mum forgot to put cream on me the other day. She doesn't mean to forget things. It's not her fault. It's like with the holiday. She, like, gets muddled up with stuff. Dates and times and rules, I don't know. Just, like, stuff.'

'Muddled up, with the holiday dates?'

'Yes. That's what happened.'

Grace explained that when she had phoned home earlier, Lee had confirmed that the family wasn't going on holiday until the next day, which was Tuesday. This is what Lily had already told her too, though I'd definitely been told that the holiday started sooner, and that this was why Colette could not attend the placement meeting. It was all quite confusing.

'Lee said Mum lied about the dates on purpose, so I had to go back into care quicker, but that's not true. She must have just got muddled up with the dates. Lee tells lies. He does, you know. He's a liar, he tells lies, Angela. He does it all the time, like Lily. He does it to be nasty to me.' She called Lee a 'druggie' and a 'weirdo'. 'Lily said he takes drugs. He smokes cannabis. That's what Lily says.'

As she'd accused both Lee and Lily of telling lies I really didn't know what to believe.

'I heard you calling someone a liar on the phone,' I said. I left a pause after saying this, then added, 'You seemed very upset.'

'They all wind me up, but I'm the one who gets called a wind-up merchant!'

Grace was getting more and more agitated. 'Lee winds me up. He tells me, "Nobody will believe you. You'll be a foster care kid forever."' Grace paused for a moment, and her mind went off in another direction. 'I hate it when he goes in my room. He does it when nobody else is there! I don't have to go round to that girl Briony's if I don't want, do I?'

'Of course not, sweetheart. You certainly don't have to go to anybody's house you don't want to.' I added that we could maybe invite Briony to our house, as this is what I'd normally do if I didn't know the person.

At that time certain social workers asked for police checks on anyone the child visited, even if only for a few hours and even if they were members of our own family, so I'd have to check with Social Services before I made any arrangements. Eventually, 'delegated authority' was brought in, which made life easier. This meant a form was completed, usually at the initial placement meeting, spelling out exactly what we could and could not agree to. It saved us a lot of time and energy in trying to get hold of Social Services to ask permission for things on a case-by-case basis.

'Really, Briony can come here? OK, that's good, because I'm not sure about going to her house.' She squinted up at me suspiciously before saying, 'Because you never know what goes on behind closed doors, do you?'

'Well . . .'

Before I could answer, Grace was running off, saying she needed the toilet. My heart felt as heavy as a stone as I watched her disappear in a cloud of dancing curls. Needless to say, I was concerned about Lee. If what Grace had said was true, what did he mean when he said nobody would believe her? And why did he go in her room when nobody else was there?

I made notes and, later, I let Social Services know what Grace had said about Lee. I hoped that in time she'd tell me more.

10

'I love buying new shoes!'

As Grace was adjusting to living with us, she started to become increasingly moody and unpredictable. I told myself it was only to be expected. Starting again in a new foster home was an awful lot for a ten-year-old to deal with, and the fact she was used to moving and starting again didn't help in the slightest; in fact, I think it made it even harder for her to settle.

Grace refused to unpack. During her trial stay this was understandable as she knew she was going to visit her mum and was also returning to her previous carers. Nothing was set in stone about her future with us – the only certainty had been that she was staying with us for three nights. Though I'd have preferred it if she'd made herself more at home during that initial weekend, I could see why she didn't. She was a girl used to packing her bags and moving on.

Now it had been agreed that she was living with us things were different, and I was worried about why Grace continued to refuse to unpack. Was she in denial about the fact she was staying with us for six months, and hopefully longer? Was she refusing to accept this was now her home? Perhaps she was hoping her mum would have her back sooner rather than later? I hadn't forgotten that Grace had said her mum had made promises about having her back, but I wasn't sure how true this was, or exactly what Colette had said. I started to worry that perhaps more promises had been made, and Grace was living in hope of moving back home soon.

I decided it was Jonathan's theory that perhaps held the most water. He thought Grace didn't unpack because she was so used to being moved and, either consciously or subconsciously, she expected to be uprooted again at any minute. It was possible she thought we would decide the placement wasn't working and ask for her to be placed elsewhere, just as her previous carers had. I sincerely hoped that was not the case and I took every opportunity I could to tell her how pleased we were to have her living with us.

I gently tried to nudge Grace towards putting her clothes in the drawers and wardrobe and finding a home for the toys and knick-knacks still stacked in cardboard boxes. When that didn't work, I talked about the plans we'd made with Social Services, and with her social worker, Barry.

'You're staying with us for at least six months, Grace. Remember, that's what Barry explained?'

'Yes. So?'

'Hopefully it will be longer. We love having you here. We really want you to stay with us. It would be easier for you if you unpacked.'

'Right, yeah, OK.'

She pouted and tugged at her hair, as if she was deeply frustrated at something.

'How are you feeling about being here, Grace?'

'I like you and Jonathan. But . . .'

She buttoned her lips.

'But what? You can talk to me about anything you want, Grace. I'm here to help you.'

'I'll unpack,' she said hastily. 'There's no need to keep going on! I'll do it! It's not a big deal, is it?'

'That's good,' I said, not taking the bait. I reminded her she could keep her empty suitcase and bags in her bedroom. I'd already told her more than once that there was plenty of room in the wardrobe for them, as I didn't want her to worry about any of her luggage being out of sight, just in case that was a factor. She could put her big suitcase on top of the wardrobe, as there was space up there for it.

Unfortunately, nothing changed. Grace continued to repack her belongings every single day. Without fail, her cuddly swan, pyjamas and toiletry bag went back in her suitcase. She did put her dirty washing in the laundry bin, but every time I gave her back a pile of clean, ironed clothes, it went straight back in the case. I started to put everything I could on coat hangers to encourage her to put her clothes straight in the wardrobe, but she would take them off the hangers, fold them up and zip them back in her case.

I asked Grace if she had any life story books, which are a kind of scrapbook for kids in care into which you place photographs and mementos of their time in the foster home, such as concert and cinema tickets. It can also contain details about their family, where they were born, their first school, information about their religion and so on. We always help and encourage the children to record their memories and, in an ideal world, the same book travels with the child if they move from one foster home to the next. Some kids end up with several different books, and I expected Grace might have a few, given her various moves. I thought that if she showed me her books this might spark some conversation about all the different moves she'd had and would perhaps get her talking about why she didn't want to unpack. Also, I was interested to see if she had any pictures of her family. Obviously, I'd met her mother, but I couldn't picture her sister or her stepbrothers at all, and as for her stepfather, I didn't even know what he was called. I wanted to find out more, reckoning that the more information I had the better I would be able to understand Grace, and help her.

'No,' she frowned. 'What even is a life story book?'

I explained what it was and Grace shrugged and told me she'd never had one, not ever. I was very surprised at this, given that she'd been in eight other foster homes, but I didn't question her. In hindsight, I wonder if Grace left her life story books behind on purpose. None of her previous placements had worked out, so maybe she didn't want to remember them. She had said precious little about her former carers, and the only things she had gone into any detail about were negative, such as her criticism of the carer who wouldn't let her eat crisps.

*

131

I took Grace to the GP as planned, and was looking forward to picking the doctor's brains about whether or not he could offer any help in terms of her hyperactive behaviour. I explained that she continued to run everywhere, couldn't sit still, was accident-prone and could be clumsy and sometimes struggled to remember things or follow instructions. I could have said more but I was conscious that Grace was in the room and I didn't want to upset her in any way, even though she didn't appear to be listening. I also told the GP Grace would get very hot and red in the face and needed to drink a lot of fluids, which was something that had started concerning me.

'I've actually wondered if she may be diabetic, as she gets extremely thirsty. And it would be very helpful to hear your opinion on everything else, and whether we need to think about having Grace tested, perhaps.' I had gently explained to Grace, before the appointment, that I was going to mention all of these things and ask for advice so she might get some 'extra help' and she had shrugged and said she didn't mind.

'Diabetic and prone to hyperactivity, you say?' our elderly GP replied, raising his white eyebrows. 'I see.'

First, he ran through the basic health checks he had to perform on Grace, such as measuring her height and weighing her. She was officially underweight for her age, though only slightly, but the GP didn't seem too concerned about this and simply suggested that she put on a bit of weight. Then, reclining back in his chair, he told me that, all things considered, he felt that Grace was simply a very active, busy young girl. 'She gets hot because she's on the go all the time,' he said, 'and when you get hot you perspire more and need to drink more. It's as simple as that, I think. But do bring her back in if you have any more concerns, or if she starts to drink more, particularly when the weather begins to cool down.' He said this to me as if Grace wasn't in the room with us, which made me feel uncomfortable. She had already told me she hated going to the doctors and was in a grumpy, impatient mood that day; I can't imagine being talked about in this way helped her mood. Grace sat there fidgeting with her hair and looking distractedly out of the window. I had to remind her three times not to fiddle with the blood pressure monitor on the desk in front of her, and she only stopped when the GP himself asked her not to touch it again. That was the only time he addressed her directly, I noticed.

Before he dismissed us I asked the doctor about E numbers and food and drinks Grace should avoid, to help curb the high energy spikes she often had, which I explained sometimes lasted for days on end. I also repeated that her concentration often waned and said I was worried this might affect her education, stating that any help and advice he could offer would be very much appreciated.

'Ah, that's quite common in lively young girls,' he said kindly. 'Interested in everything; can't concentrate on anything!'

I had to prompt him for dietary advice, pointing out that I'd read something about the link between certain foods and kids' behaviour but, unfortunately, he wasn't very helpful on that score either. 'I can't tell you what to avoid as every individual is different, but if you have your suspicions that certain foods have a negative effect on Grace's behaviour, then I would cut them out and see if it makes a difference. If you think she may be allergic to certain foods, there are some tests we can do. Keeping a food diary may be useful.' In fact, I had just started to do this as I'd read a magazine article about food diaries, but it hadn't enlightened me so far and I had no idea which specific foods may have been having an impact on Grace, if any. In hindsight, I realise the GP himself wasn't very enlightened either, which was understandable, I suppose. The influx of artificial colourings, sweeteners, flavourings and preservatives in our foods was a relatively new phenomenon in the nineties, and something dieticians and nutrition experts were learning more about every day. Our GP was very close to retirement age and I guess this wasn't something he'd have learned about at medical school, when ready meals were unheard of and rationing would have still been in place!

A few weeks later, Grace had still not unpacked. This bothered me, as I wanted her to feel as settled and comfortable as possible in our home; it was *her* home now too. I gave her a little desktop calendar and put it on her dressing table, hoping it might help her understand that she was here to stay.

'This is for you,' I said. 'School starts soon. Here's the date – do you want to mark it on?'

Happily, Grace's place at the popular local primary

school we'd been hoping for was confirmed, and Jess had made all the arrangements. I knew the school well and was very pleased Grace had got a place there. She hadn't seemed very interested when I first gave her the news, but that didn't really surprise me. There were still a couple of weeks of the summer holiday left and, from a child's point of view, that might as well be a lifetime!

I was pleased when Grace patiently wrote 'start new school' on the calendar. By now I had started a life story book for her and I encouraged her to write some basic details in it, including the name of her new school. She concentrated very hard whenever she wrote. Her writing was neat and I'd noticed her spelling was generally good too.

'Well done, Grace. Lovely writing. By the way, I'll take you uniform shopping at the weekend.'

She seemed pleased about this and asked lots of questions about the colour of the uniform, when we would find out about the clubs they did, whether her new friend Briony would be at the same school and so on. I didn't know which school Briony was attending, but I hoped it was the same one. At least Grace would see one familiar face on her first day.

'You'll be able to write other dates on here too,' I said to her. 'The calendar will be useful for helping you remember things. I'm always checking dates on my calendar, and I like to know what's coming up.'

'Like, when I go home?'

'Like when you go home for a visit with your family? Yes.'

'When is that? Did Mum tell you? She didn't tell me. I asked her but she said she didn't know yet. Do you know, Angela? Do you?'

I had to tell her I didn't know either. The family had been back from their summer holiday for a while. By now I knew for sure that their departure date had not clashed with the placement meeting, as Colette had made us believe. They left on the Tuesday, as both Lee and Lily had told Grace. Since then, Colette had been keeping a very low profile. Grace had spoken to her mum briefly on the phone on a couple of occasions, but the calls sounded rushed. I'd spoken to Colette too. I had wanted to touch base and let her know how Grace was getting on, and I also wanted to find out when Grace was going on a weekend visit, but Colette had been elusive and fobbed me off, really quite rudely on one occasion.

'Didn't I tell you, I'll call *you*,' she'd said, somewhat indignantly. 'There's a lot of stuff going on at the moment, things you wouldn't believe! Nuts, it is. I'll be in touch, don't you worry. Gotta dash now.'

In my continuing efforts to try to help Grace settle in and unpack her bags, I also talked to her about the fact she would still be living with us at Christmas, and for her birthday in January, when she would turn eleven.

'Do I have to stay with you on Christmas Day? And on my birthday?'

Again, I had to tread carefully. I told her that even though the plan was that she would be living with us over Christmas and when it was her birthday, I wasn't sure if she'd be with her family or with us on those particular days.

'What if . . .?'

She stopped herself, as I'd seen her do before, and when I prompted her she still didn't finish her sentence.

'Grace, I want you to know that Jonathan and I love having you here,' I repeated. 'We hope you will stay for a long time.'

Grace started counting on her fingers, working out how many months it was until her birthday. She had first come to us in July and it was August now. The six months would have started around the middle of July.

'So, August, September, October, what's the next one?'

'It begins with N. Can you remember?'

'No.'

'Nov . . .'

'What?' she looked thoroughly confused.

'Remember, remember the fifth of . . .'

'What?'

'November!'

'Oh. What's on the fifth?'

I explained about it being the date of Bonfire Night but Grace looked nonplussed and started counting the months again, going back to the beginning and stopping when she'd reached January again.

'Five months from now, until my birthday.'

She gazed at the calendar. It had a section at the back where you could jot down upcoming dates for the following year, but she didn't mark her birthday, or the fact that's when she would have been with us for six months. I was pleased about this; I certainly didn't want her to start counting the days with us, and I definitely didn't want her to think that her life would be routinely turned upside down again in January. That was not how things worked. Generally speaking, when Social Services placed a child with us for an initial six months, the expectation was that the child would stay for longer, and possibly even right up until they were ready to move out and live independently. There would always be a review meeting, run by an IRO (independent reviewing officer) after the first six months, but so long as everything was running smoothly and there was no change in the birth family's circumstances, the placements typically just carried on indefinitely. I wouldn't spell this out, as it could be alarming for a child to think too far into the future, but I was desperate to somehow get Grace to acknowledge that she lived with us now, and she was not just a temporary visitor.

'Your birthday is a long way off,' I said. 'I want you to see our house as your home. It *is* your home. Is there anything you'd like to do to make your bedroom feel more like your room? Posters, maybe?'

There was a pause. Grace exhaled and began to speak in a meek, quiet voice.

'Mum said we are going to talk about me moving home next time I go on a contact visit.'

'Did she?'

'Yes.'

'OK, Grace. Thanks for telling me that.'

I stood up and pointed to a space on one wall. 'So, what about posters? This is a good place to put them?'

She shrugged.

'And, let's see. Are you going to make use of this lovely big wardrobe and chest of drawers?' I opened the doors of the wardrobe.

'What do you mean?'

'I mean, why don't you unpack your things, Grace? It'll be easier for you than living out of suitcases. You have all this space here.'

'OK. I will. I'll do it.'

'Do you want me to help?'

'I can do it by myself.'

Still nothing changed.

Grace was very excited when we went shopping for her school uniform. She was ready and waiting to go for about an hour before the time I'd said we'd leave, and when we started walking into town she was like a coiled spring, darting here and there and almost bouncing down the street.

'Stay with me,' I had to call a few times, as she sprang ahead of me. 'But not that close!' I had to add, because when she doubled back she walked too close to me, so much so that I caught her with my handbag several times, and she stepped so hard on the side of my shoe it came off at the pedestrian crossing.

Once in town, we saw several people we knew. Grace had helped me out in the shop once or twice. She loved watering the flowers and she was a very willing helper when it came to carrying the displays in from the street at the end of the day. She was also very chatty with any of the customers who talked to her.

'Aren't you a good helper,' they'd typically say. Or, 'I hope Angela and Jonathan are paying you!' We did give her some extra pocket money, as that was always the rule when any of the kids 'worked' in the shop, even when they were young like Grace and were really only pottering about and lending a hand because they wanted to.

Grace would tell the customers all about her pocket money, describing the magazine she was saving up for, or the new pens or hair accessories. A lot of the kids we cared for just smiled sweetly – or shied away in embarrassment – when customers spoke to them like that, but not Grace. She seemed intent on doing her best to please everyone who spoke to her, to the point where the customers often had to be the ones to excuse themselves from the conversation as Grace just wouldn't stop talking!

'Hello!' one of our older customers, Dot, exclaimed as we stepped off the zebra crossing in town. 'How are you?'

I'd known Dot for years and I assumed she was addressing me. I was looking down at my feet at the time, trying to put my shoe back on as Grace had stepped on my foot again. When I looked up I saw that Dot, who must have been well over eighty, was talking directly to Grace. Dot looked absolutely thrilled to bump into Grace, and I saw that her whole face lit up.

'I'm fine, thank you,' Grace responded merrily. 'I'm going to get my new school uniform!' She told Dot which school she was going to.

'Are you really? Well isn't that quite something? A brand-new uniform? And new shoes too, I shouldn't wonder?'

'Am I, Angela, am I having new shoes?'

'Yes, Grace.'

I looked at Dot and wanted to say something about the shoe shop we were going to, as I knew she used to work there when I was around the same age as Grace was now. I remembered her fitting my school shoes. However, I didn't get a look in. Dot was listening carefully to whatever it was Grace had to say next. Dot then burst out laughing, told Grace how lovely it was to see her and went on her way. Almost as an afterthought she said, 'Oh! Goodbye, Angela.'

I smiled to myself. Grace had a gift, that's for sure. I'd seen it with the kids in the play area as well as the customers who came into the shop. You couldn't teach a child to be like that, I thought. Grace was naturally gregarious and curious and she could be very friendly when she wanted to be. Generally speaking, I'd noticed she made even more of an effort with new people she met than with anyone else. I wondered why this was. Once, I suggested to Jonathan she might be protecting herself, in that she could afford to be friendly with strangers because they couldn't let her down like the people closer to her might.

'Be careful of amateur psychology!' he smiled.

Jonathan had a point; I found myself trying to psycho-analyse situations all the time and it was something I needed to treat with caution. But each new child always raised so many questions in my mind, and more often than not Jonathan and I were kept in the dark about so many elements of their life.

I hoped our shopping trip would be as enjoyable as the walk to town. I knew from experience that girls of Grace's age are typically becoming very self-aware and starting to worry about how they look. They want the most fashionable styles they can get away with and are prepared to scour every shop meticulously before making a final choice, even if they've found something they like on the very first rail. They also like to have long debates about what everybody else will be wearing instead of focusing on what they actually like themselves. I remember one girl cut designer labels out of one top to sew into another, as she said she would be laughed at if they saw she was wearing a top from a cheap shop! I had to allow it; I can remember going through a phase of being incredibly fashion conscious myself, though in my case it was all about having flares and tank tops like the Bay City Rollers!

Anyhow, needless to say I'd endured lots of frustrating clothes shopping trips over the years with girls who just couldn't decide what to buy and often ended up with nothing, despite trying on countless styles that looked good, fitted well and seemed perfect to me.

As we were shopping for school uniform, I hoped I

wouldn't have too much trouble with Grace. Of all the high street shops selling primary school uniforms, most of them stocked very similar items. Usually, it was simply the quality that altered from shop to shop, and after that the only choice you really had was whether to go for a skirt or trousers.

'What do you prefer, skirt or trousers?'

'Skirt. No, trousers. No, wait, what's the playground like? Are you, like, allowed on the field? Is there a yard, like, or is it grass?'

I could see where this was going, and I had visions of Grace racing round the school field like a demon. As she was so active, trousers would be better, I thought, but she was also quite a 'girly girl' too. She had lots of skirts, some of them shiny and glamorous, and she liked to dress up like the pop stars she idolised. I'd discovered she could really sing, and she'd belt out her favourite songs into her toy microphone.

'I thought she was going to be a tomboy when she first arrived with her pogo stick and talked about climbing trees,' Jonathan commented when he saw her performing a Spice Girls track. 'But I think I got that wrong!'

I agreed and said Grace was not a child you could easily put a label on. This was no bad thing at all, but it did mean you could never quite work out which way she'd jump in any given situation!

I reassured Grace I'd take her to have a good look around the school before term started. This had already been agreed with the head teacher, and I told Grace she'd be able to see everything for herself, including the playground and school field.

'Shall we get one of each to begin with? A skirt and a pair of trousers?' I asked. I thought that if she did choose to wear a skirt, I could always buy her a thick pair of tights, so it wouldn't matter if she did end up dashing around or even climbing.

'Am I allowed? Yes! One of each. Yes!'

'Good. Do you like this pair or that? And what about that skirt?'

Luckily, there were quite a few styles to choose from. The school was not particular about the cut of the trousers or the skirt, so long as the colour was the right shade of grey.

'That one!'

'Good choice. Trousers?'

'Those.'

Grace was decisive and, to my surprise and relief, both fitted well and the shop had everything else we needed in her size. The whole uniform was in the bag within about half an hour; I could hardly believe it.

'Shoes next?'

'Yes!'

I wanted to make sure Grace had a hard-wearing pair of school shoes as I'd noticed all her shoes had scuffed toes; she was obviously one of those kids who was heavy on her shoes. Despite our success with the uniform, I was expecting the shoes to be a harder sell, especially if I was going to succeed in steering her towards a good, sturdy pair.

'Let's go!' I said, optimistically adding, 'I love buying new shoes!' I told Grace the large shoe shop we were going to had been in the town for years and was where Dot used to work when I was at school. Dot had fitted my school shoes on many occasions. I assured Grace it was *the* place to go and she gave me a thumbs-up.

The shoe shop was packed out. We had to take a ticket from a little dispenser on the wall and wait our turn, which Grace found difficult.

'Why do we have to wait?' she moaned. 'Shall we come back?'

'No, Grace, we'll just have to wait our turn and be patient like everybody else.'

All the seats were occupied by children who were having their feet measured, or having shoes fitted, and so there was nowhere to sit.

'Let's have a look at the girls' section while we're waiting.' I pointed towards two racks of shoes suitable for girls of Grace's age and headed towards it. There were so many people in that part of the shop it wasn't easy getting through to the relevant racks, even though they were only a few feet away.

'Excuse me,' I said, squeezing past a couple with a baby in a buggy and a harassed father with a fed-up toddler who was grizzling and straining against his reins. The shop was hot and stuffy, and when I reached the girls' shoes I felt quite flustered. I took a deep breath.

'Phew! Which ones do you like the look of?'

I turned around, expecting Grace to be right behind me, but she was nowhere to be seen.

'Grace?'

A young boy was standing over my shoulder, where I had expected Grace to be. He looked at me in confusion and sidled away. I felt my stomach lurch as I quickly scanned the children's section. She can't have gone far. She'd been right behind me only moments before, but the shop was so busy and I couldn't spot her.

'Grace? Grace?'

In my panic, the shop looked twice as packed as it had before. My eyes were everywhere and nowhere. I was flicking my eyeballs from person to person so quickly everything became a blur, and I was seeing nothing and nobody in focus. I tried to breathe in deeply and calm myself down, but I didn't succeed. I felt incredibly stressed and anxious.

I started to walk very quickly around the shop, checking every section and looking repeatedly towards the entrance door. The worst thing would be if Grace had deliberately given me the slip and run off into town. Surely she wouldn't do that? I figured this wasn't beyond the realms of possibility and I couldn't rule it out. The thought made me shiver.

Unfortunately, the store had a large central island with seats around it, which meant you couldn't stand in one place and see the whole shop. There was also an archway on one side, leading to the adult section, and beyond that was a sports department. Having only ever used this shop for children's shoes, I'd never noticed before how huge it was, and I cursed its size.

'Grace? Grace?' I was calling her name louder now and people were starting to look at me.

'Is everything all right, love?' a woman asked me.

'No. I've lost a young girl. She was with me a moment ago and she's disappeared . . .'

'What does your daughter look like?' A teenage shop assistant was speaking to me now.

'Big, curly hair, strawberry blonde. Aged ten. Dressed in jeans and a white top. No, not white. Pale pink. White hairband. White trainers.'

'And your name?'

'Angela. Angela Hart.'

'OK, Mrs Hart.' The young shop assistant rushed off before I had a chance to say anything else to her.

'Grace? Grace?' I continued searching the store, dashing through the sports section and then men's shoes, but still she was nowhere to be seen.

An announcement rang out. It sounded like it was coming through a megaphone rather than a speaker.

'If Grace is in the shop, please come to the cash desk. That's Grace, aged ten. Your mum is waiting for you.'

The teenage assistant came back over to me and gave me a big smile.

'I remember doing this to my mum when I was a little girl. Don't worry, it happens all the time. Let's go and wait by the till.'

There was no point telling her I was Grace's carer, not her mother.

'Can you ask someone to watch the door?'

The assistant smiled. 'Of course, but kids never run outside. She'll be in here somewhere. They always are.'

147

11

'Count to ten, Angela!'

It was a full five minutes before I was reunited with Grace. It felt like five hours.

A customer who heard the announcement spotted her sitting on the floor in a corner, playing with one of those foot-measuring gauges, the ones with the tape measure and the sliding rule. Apparently, Grace was totally engrossed in sliding the ruler up and down, up and down, and she was staring at it as if mesmerised. She hadn't heard the announcement herself. The customer took her to the cash desk.

'Grace!' I exclaimed. 'There you are!' Relief flooded me.

'Sorry, Angela. I didn't realise you'd get worried. I was just hot.'

'Hot?'

'Yes. I needed some air.'

It seemed Grace had taken it upon herself to walk to the front of the store to get some fresh air. She didn't think to tell me what she was doing. She'd stepped outside before

148

wandering back in, and when she couldn't see me she'd entertained herself by playing with the foot gauge.

'I thought they'd call us both when our number came up,' she said, which wasn't an unreasonable expectation, I suppose. I stayed calm and told her she must stick with me in future, and it was up to her to look out for me as much as it was my responsibility to keep my eye on her.

'OK. Sorry. Shall we look at shoes now?'

I exhaled deeply, thanked the people who'd helped me and agreed. My heart rate had returned to normal but I had that horribly spiky feeling in my blood, the kind you get when adrenalin has coursed through you after a nasty shock.

'Do you like any of these styles?' I said when we finally stood together in front of the girls' school shoes.

Grace didn't reply. She had a vacant look in her eye and was twirling on the spot, gazing around the bustling shop. If I didn't know better I'd have thought she was being rude and ignoring me by not looking at the shoes as I'd asked her to do. However, I realised Grace had simply lost focus, as she often did.

'Grace, please have a look at the shoes.'

'What?'

'These styles are suitable for your size and age group. Have a look, see what you think.'

She gave a cursory glance at the row of shoes before spinning around on the spot again. She was fiddling with her hair now too, readjusting her hairband to push her curls as snugly as possible away from her hot little forehead. It felt incredibly airless in the shop, and when Grace's eyes fell on a water cooler on the back wall she headed towards it without saying a word to me. After what had happened, my eyes were glued on her. I immediately followed her, sidestepping lots of customers. 'Wait for me. I'll come with you, Grace.' She was completely oblivious to the fact I was behind her until she stopped in front of the machine and there I was, standing right beside her. Even so, she didn't really bat an eyelid.

'Grace, you can't just walk off like that. It's very busy. I don't want you to get lost again.'

'Oh. Sorry! Can I get a drink?'

'Yes, sweetheart. But did you hear what I said? You need to keep an eye on me as much as I need to keep an eye on you. Do you understand?'

'Erm, yes.'

She clearly had no idea what a fright she'd given me and how dangerous it was to wander off, and especially to step out of a shop as she had. I had another go at getting through to her as I watched her help herself to a drink of cold water. I don't think she heard a word I said. Her eyes were darting everywhere and she overfilled the plastic cup because she wasn't paying enough attention.

'Do we have to wait much longer? How long do we have to wait, Angela?' She spilt water on the carpet as she drank and talked. 'How long, Angela? It's boiling in here. Are you hot? Don't you want a drink? Look, you can get one, it's free! I can do it.'

I looked at our ticket. We were number 52 and they were only up to number 47.

'We're fifth. But hopefully it won't be too long.'

I let her get me a cup of water and she filled hers up to the top again.

'I need the toilet.'

'Are you desperate or can you wait?'

'I can wait.' She knocked back another large mouthful of water before I could suggest she didn't drink any more.

We went back over to the girls' section and, when I asked her again if she liked any of the styles, Grace pointed to what seemed to be the first shoe she set her eyes on.

'I like that one,' she said vaguely, looking bored and uninterested. Then she went to study a nearby stand of bags and umbrellas. She began fiddling with the display, spinning the stand around, taking things off and clipping and unclipping the fasteners on a rucksack. I asked her to stop and she groaned.

'How long now? Do you even *know*, Angela?'

I ignored the cheeky tone that had crept into her voice.

'We're fourth. Look, there's a seat now, let's sit down.'

Grace stayed seated for all of thirty seconds before getting to her feet and saying she needed another drink of water. I asked her not to drink any more for the time being, as she already needed the toilet. She groaned again.

'This is boring! How long now? Angela, are there any trees in the . . .?' She seemed to lose the thread of what she was saying.

'Where?'

'What?'

'Are there any trees in the . . . what?'

151

'The playground. I mean, like, what's it called? The school field.'

I pictured Grace's school. I knew it well. 'Let me think. There are, but not ones you can climb. But they do have a school garden where you can plant . . .'

'What's this?' Grace wasn't listening. She had picked up a small plastic ball a child must have left on the floor by accident. 'Can I have this? Can I, Angela? Do you want to play catch?'

She tossed the ball towards me. I wasn't expecting it and it hit me in the face. I felt a surge of anger.

'Oops, I didn't mean to do that. Sorry, I'm really sorry, Angela!'

She hadn't hurt me, luckily. I told myself to be calm and said to Grace that I was OK but she must put the ball down and not throw things like that again. Then I asked her to sit down and try to stay still.

'Sorry. How long now? Are we next? Are we, Angela?'

'Look at the number on the display, Grace. What does it say?'

There was a digital display, illuminated in red, showing which customer was next.

'What? Why are you asking me? I asked you! I can't work that out!'

'Of course you can. It says 50. See the number 50, lit up in red? We are number 52. Oh, look, it's gone up to 51 now. They'll call us when it's our turn. We're next.'

'What?'

I patiently explained how the very simple system worked,

but Grace wasn't concentrating. By the time our number was finally called, I felt completely frazzled. I was very grateful when the young assistant asked if Grace would stay very still while she had her feet measured. Grace did as she was asked; I really felt like asking the assistant to take her time, so I could enjoy even more of a breather!

'Have you seen anything you like?' the young woman asked.

Grace quickly scanned the shelves in front of her once more, as if for the first time.

'Erm, that one.'

She was pointing towards a different shoe to the one she'd picked out earlier. It had a crepe sole and thick, Velcro straps and to me it looked very plain and old-fashioned compared to the others. All of Grace's sandals and trainers were much more modern. She was interested in fashion and often talked about what her favourite pop stars wore, so I was quite surprised at her choice.

'That one?' the assistant said, arching one eyebrow. 'OK. I'm sure we'll have that in stock. We don't sell many of those. I won't be long.'

'Do you want to pick another to try too?' I found myself asking. I'd noticed that Grace's attention was really on the wane, and I was worried she'd pointed at any old shoe, just to get this over and done with.

'What? OK, that one.' This time she chose one that looked like it would suit her much better.

While we waited for the assistant to come back from the storeroom Grace sat in her socks, drumming her heels back into the wooden panel at the front of her cube seat. The beating noise this made got louder and louder, but she seemed oblivious to the racket she was making, even when people started looking over.

'Can you stop that please, Grace?'

'What?'

'Please stop kicking your heels into the seat.'

'Oh!' She stopped straight away; I don't think she realised what she was doing.

When the assistant returned she had disappointing news. Neither shoe was available in Grace's size.

'Can we just go?'

'No, Grace. Can you tell us which shoes you do have in this size?'

I felt like kicking myself at this point. I realised I'd gone through this rigmarole before, and more than once. You'd think I'd have learned by now that shoe shops are all but depleted of school stock at this time of year. There is no point in asking a child to choose a style; what you need to do is ask the assistant what they have left in stock in the child's size.

The young woman disappeared into the storeroom again.

'How long is this going to take? I need the toilet.'

'Can you hold on or do you need to go now?'

'I need to go. Now. I'm bursting. Is there one? Where's the toilet? I think I'm going to pee myself.'

We ended up leaving the shoe shop before the assistant returned. I took Grace across the road to our local department store, where we had to take the lift to the top floor. It stopped at the second floor and went back to the ground floor before finally taking us up again. The ladies' toilet was at the back, beside the cafe, which was rammed with parents and kids of all ages. There was a long queue for the toilet. Grace looked very on edge as we waited our turn. She started looking all around her, jerking her head around and jabbering on about whatever came to her mind.

'Have you been in here before? Angela? Angela? Do you need the toilet too? What's that thing over there?'

'It's a display stand, for a promotion, I think. No, sweetheart, I don't need the toilet.'

To be honest, I could have done with going, but I wasn't taking any chances. Grace appeared so distracted and agitated I didn't trust her not to go scampering off while I was in the cubicle. There was no way I was taking my eyes off her for a second.

'I'll wait here,' I said when it was finally her turn.

She looked more relaxed after going to the toilet.

'Better now?'

'Yes,' she smiled. 'Do we have to go back to the shoe shop?'

'Yes,' I smiled back. Grace's face fell and she started to sulk and whine.

Of course we had to take another ticket out of the machine in the shoe shop and wait our turn again, which made her huff and puff dramatically. This time we were seventh in the queue.

'Can we just go? Angela, can we come back another day?

Can't I wear my old shoes? Angela? Is there another shop? This is so boring. This isn't fair. Why do we have to wait? Why, Angela? Why? School is ages away. I've got loads of shoes.'

I gave up attempting to give her an explanation for each question; she didn't really want answers. She was just letting me know how fed up she was, and sharing her frustration.

'Grace, we're not leaving this shop again until you have a pair of school shoes.'

I was feeling extremely agitated. The shop was even more jam-packed than before and I was starting to worry they'd have nothing left in stock for Grace.

Count to ten, Angela, I thought. *One, two, three, four . . .*

'Number 72 please!'

Finally! Thank God for that.

I explained that we'd already been measured and just needed to see which styles were in stock in Grace's size. It was a different assistant, and the young man insisted on measuring Grace's feet all over again, as that was what he'd been told he must do on his shoe fitter training course.

Count to ten, Angela! One, two, three, four . . .

'Ow! That's pinching me. See, I told you already I wasn't that size. Where's it gone?'

'What?'

'That ball?'

'Grace, let's just focus on your feet, OK?'

The young man did an admirable job of keeping his cool with his tricky little customer. I was even more impressed when he emerged from the stockroom with a choice of three different shoes in Grace's size. None were the ones she'd picked out, but she didn't seem to notice, or care. She happily tried them all on and did a lap of honour in her favourite pair. The shop assistant was pleased with the fit and Grace said they felt comfortable.

'What d'you think, Angela? What do you think? Do you like them, do you?'

She'd chosen the least sturdy of all the shoes but I told her they looked great, and that I liked them. I wasn't going to rock the boat at this stage. They may not last long, but at least she had a new pair of school shoes.

'Really? Do you really think so? I'm not sure.' She was now standing in front of the mirror, examining her feet from every angle. 'No. Look at this bit.' She pointed to a tiny detail on the back of the shoe.

'What?'

'It's funny. Weird. No, I don't like them. What about these?'

She had picked up a shoe from a completely different range that wouldn't do for school; it wasn't even in one of the regulation colours. The assistant politely asked if she wanted to reconsider any of the other styles he'd brought from the stockroom, but she just talked over him.

'What are we doing after this? Angela, what's happening after—'

'Grace,' I said, slightly too sharply. I hated to admit this to myself, but she was really winding me up. When I thought about those words – *winding me up* – they gave me a start. This is what Grace had been accused of so many times, and

I told myself I could not be yet another person in her life who viewed her as a so-called 'wind-up merchant'. At that moment I wanted to be anywhere but in that shoe shop with Grace, but I gave myself a little talking-to and tried to be patient and kind.

'Listen, Grace,' I said, more softly this time. 'I'm as fed up as you. This has been much more long-winded than I hoped. I know it's boring, but this is the only shop that does school shoes in this town. Please pick a pair.'

'OK, I'll have . . .' She looked like she was mentally saying 'dip, dip dip' as she made up her mind. 'Those!' She chose ones with a buckle, which were quite pretty and not bad in terms of durability.

The dutiful shop assistant insisted Grace had to try both shoes on all over again, so she could take a walk around the shop floor and he could check the fit.

'Can you walk to the water cooler and back for me?'

Grace didn't walk, she ran, knocking into people as she did so. At the water cooler she dithered, didn't look back and started helping herself to a cup of water. I got to my feet; I was really getting annoyed now. I saw her give a sneaky glance in my direction before she filled her cup to the rim and took a long glug of water. Slowly, she wiped her lips with the back of her hand and then skipped back to the fitting area.

'I'm not sure they fit. I can feel my heels lifting.' The assistant checked the fit very carefully and assured us it was perfect, as there was the correct amount of room for growth. Grace looked slightly disappointed at this news. I couldn't work her out. One minute she was desperate to leave, the next she seemed to be spinning this out on purpose.

'Mmm,' she muttered finally. 'I suppose they're OK.'

'We'll take them,' I said. 'Thank you very much.'

'There's a shoe protector cream that's recommended for this shoe. Would you like me to get one for you?'

'No, thank you!' I snorted. My nerves were so frayed I could have screamed.

'Do I have to wear them?' Grace asked, just as I was presenting my bank card to the cashier.

'Are you joking?' I thought she was asking if she would have to wear them for school.

'What do you mean, Angela? What's the joke? No, I'm not messing. Let me carry the bag! Can I put them on again now, and put my trainers in the bag? Can I, Angela? Can I?'

I had absolutely no idea how her mind worked. All I knew was that mine was blown at this point!

'How was the shopping trip?' Jonathan asked later.

I didn't know where to start.

'I don't think Grace realises how frustrating she can be,' I stuttered. 'I'm sure it's not deliberate, but then again . . .'

I really was stumped. Grace had so many good qualities, but she could be incredibly irritating. I didn't fully understand why she behaved the way she did, but I was determined to get to know her better, and to keep my cool along the way.

12

'Reach for the stars, Grace!'

'We're going on a bike ride,' I explained to Grace. 'There's a country park not far away, and I'm going to pack a picnic.'

Her face lit up. 'Who's coming?'

I said it would just be the three of us, as the other girls who were living with us were out for the day. Grace had tried hard to be friends with the girls and I'd encouraged both of them to remember what it was like when they were settling in with us, and everything was still strange and new. However, despite them all being of a similar age, the two other girls hadn't really warmed to Grace. She would forget things they told her that were important to them, such as the name of their favourite band or which clubs they belonged to, and it seemed that whenever Grace struck up a conversation she managed to make some sort of blunder and annoy them. Given that the other girls could be moody and unpredictable themselves, even without any provocation, it didn't take much for Grace to rub them up the wrong way.

As I've said before, children who have suffered trauma in their childhood, and possibly from birth, have so much to cope with, because their neglected and traumatised brains don't always work in the way they should. Inevitably, there were things we would never know about what happened to Grace – and the other girls – before they moved in with us, but I knew enough to be aware I must make allowances for their behaviour. In each case, their family lives had fallen apart in one way or another, and they had all been deeply affected by this. All three needed extra help to cope with the aftermath of their disrupted childhood, and I had to remind myself of this all the time.

I never blamed any of the girls for being tetchy or difficult, but I tried to encourage all three of them to be generally nicer to one other. Routinely, I'd remind them to be kind and respectful and to treat others the way they would like to be treated. Unfortunately, despite me having numerous conversations with them along these lines, the other two girls seemed to struggle when it came to Grace. It was upsetting to witness, because from what I could see Grace didn't create trouble intentionally. More often, the opposite was true: problems seemed to escalate when she was actually trying very hard to please the girls.

'What are you doing? That looks good. Can I play? What about this? I can do that! I can show you. Look, this is how it goes . . .' Grace often bombarded them with chatter. She was full of energy and curiosity, and she would touch their belongings or poke her nose into their things without thinking or asking permission.

I'd recognised that she wasn't sharp at picking up signals, and she would continue even when it was obvious to anyone watching that her attention was unwelcome. For instance, if one of the girls moved themselves away because Grace was invading her personal space, she would take a step closer in. Inevitably, they lost their temper with her at times.

'She's doing my head in!' was the phrase they each used a lot. 'She's always in my face!' was another complaint I heard often. It was such a shame, as all Grace was trying to do was make friends and fit in.

Anyhow, whenever we had the chance to take Grace out on a day trip when the two girls were otherwise engaged, we took it. It's always good to try to give each child some one-to-one attention, and Jonathan and I were looking forward to our day out at the country park.

'What time are we going? What shall I wear? Which bike am I riding? Shall I use the purple one again? Is it still in the garage? Shall I, Angela? Do I need a helmet?'

I answered all her questions and told her that, yes, she could use the same bike she'd ridden last time, as luckily it was the perfect size for her. She excitedly helped me make the picnic.

'Am I allowed tuna in my sandwiches? I like tuna. What about those crisps, are we allowed crisps? Will we get ice cream? Is there a cafe or not? A van, an ice-cream van? Dogs. Are dogs allowed in the park? I hope we see some. I like dogs. Do I have to carry my own packed lunch?'

The questions went on and on. Though it was quite exhausting to be with Grace when she was in this mood, I loved her enthusiasm. It was far preferable to having a dispassionate, lethargic child who needed cajoling out of their bedroom. We'd known plenty like that, and lots of kids had pulled a face about being treated to trips to theme parks, beaches and caravan sites that we thought they would have relished. It was very disheartening when a child wasn't excited by anything; I always found it far harder to cope with than an eager and animated child like Grace. She may have been a handful, but at least she was childlike, as a ten-year-old should be. I found her exuberant moods pleasantly infectious and I couldn't wait to get going.

Jonathan drove us to the park. I can remember that we both remarked on the fact the windows steamed up in the car as soon as Grace got in. She'd been buzzing around so much getting herself ready, and she must have run up and down the stairs half a dozen times, fetching her hoodie, going back to do her teeth after forgetting the first time, hunting for a sun hat she wanted to wear, and so on. She still hadn't unpacked properly, which didn't help. She never seemed to know where anything was and often got agitated as she grappled with the zip of her large suitcase, trying to cram everything back in. All my suggestions about unpacking continued to fall on deaf ears; again and again she said she'd do it, but never did.

It was already a very warm day, and as Grace strapped herself in the car it felt like an extra radiator had been switched on in the back seat.

'Drink?' I asked.

'Yes please.'

I avoided handing out drinks in the car as a rule, to avoid spillages, but with Grace being as active and energetic as she was, she was always in need of a drink. I gave her a small plastic bottle of water and she drank the lot.

'Is there another one? Is there enough for the picnic? What time are we having the picnic? Angela? Are you wearing a bike helmet? How far will we go? Are you good at riding a bike? Jonathan, are you? Have you got your helmet? Are we there yet?'

'No we are not there yet! We've got plenty of drinks and we'll eat around one o'clock. Yes, I always wear a helmet, so does Jonathan, and we've been riding our bikes for years. We love cycling in the country park. We're not fast riders or anything like that. We just like to be out in the fresh air, for fun. How about you?'

'I like it,' she said vacantly. Though Grace had a habit of firing out lots of questions, she seemed to switch off when she got a string of answers back. She definitely paid more attention when you tackled one thing at a time, and I needed to be more sensitive to this. I resolved to take extra care not just when asking her questions, but also when answering them.

As soon as we got to the park Grace spotted a boisterous group of boys playing near a large fir tree. It had lots of strong, horizontal branches, and some of the boys began to climb on the branches closest to the ground. A couple of them sat on the widest branch, swinging their legs and rocking the tree for a joke, as if they were trying to shake their friends off. It looked like harmless fun, as they were only a few feet off the ground and the tree looked rock solid.

'Can I go on that tree?' Grace asked. 'Can I? I love trees.'

'I don't see why not. But let's have our bike ride first, and we'll come back. Hopefully the boys will have moved on by then. I'm sure Jonathan will have a go too.'

'Try stopping me!' Jonathan said.

Grace seemed satisfied with this, and we got the bikes off the rack on the back of the car and all put our helmets on. Jonathan and I had panniers on our bikes, into which we packed the picnic.

'Can I have a piece of cake?'

'Not yet, Grace. Let's save it for later.'

'Why? I'm hungry.' She pouted. 'I hate this helmet!'

Grace looked all hot and bothered. She unclipped the helmet and threw it on the ground. 'It's too small, I'm not wearing it!'

The helmet was the perfect size; it was just that Grace's hair was so thick. I realised it must have been quite uncomfortable having all those curls crammed under the helmet in this weather.

'Let's tie your hair back. That's the problem.'

'Haven't got a bobble. Why didn't you think of this before, Angela? You should have thought about that – you know my hair needs a bobble. Why didn't you pack one, you know I forget things! Can you hear me?'

I sighed and took a moment before answering her. This mustn't descend into an argument.

'Grace, sweetheart. I'm here to help you. Please don't

speak to me like that. And please don't throw the helmet on the ground.'

'But it's rubbish! I'm not wearing it!'

'OK,' Jonathan said. 'I'll put the bikes back on the rack. What a shame.'

He wheeled his bike back to the car and started to lift it onto the rack.

'What are you doing?' Grace looked startled, and very annoyed.

'Packing up. If you don't wear your helmet, we can't have a bike ride. That's why we came here. No point in staying if we can't ride our bikes.'

'What? But, what about the picnic?'

'Don't worry about that,' I said. 'I'll put it back in the cool box and we can eat it at home.'

'No! I want to ride my bike! I want to stay here!'

'Do you? That's good. So do I. Jonathan, I think you can take your bike off the rack. Grace wants to stay.'

'Really? That's great. Put your helmet on then Grace and we can get going.'

I helped her pull her hair into a little knot at the nape of her neck before putting the helmet back on. She didn't say a word and we set off, heading along a pretty path lined with trees. The sun was blinking through the treetops and I inhaled deeply. It was a glorious day. Butterflies were fluttering around and I was enjoying listening to birdsong as I glided across the dappled patches of sunshine on the pathway.

Jonathan was riding alongside Grace and, before long, I heard them chatting about the birds and butterflies. A little later, Grace started singing to herself as she cycled alongside me. She had such a beautiful voice and I complimented her on it, as I had done several times before.

'I wish I could be a pop star,' she said.

'Maybe you will be.'

'Right, yeah.'

'I bet you when the Spice Girls were your age they wouldn't have believed they would become such big pop stars, but look at them.' I paused before adding, 'If you want something, you should aim for it and try your best. Don't be put off before you begin, and don't let anyone else put you off either.' We turned a corner and I shouted out, 'Reach for the stars, Grace!'

She went very quiet. I realised, too late, that I'd probably bombarded her with too much information again. We waited for Jonathan to catch us up, as he'd stopped to adjust his panniers. I recapped slowly, so Grace could digest what I'd said, but she didn't reply. I glanced at her. She had narrowed her eyes and appeared to have gritted her teeth. She looked to be simmering about something, but I wasn't sure exactly what. Was it simply that I'd said too much, all in one go, and it had agitated her, or had I hit a nerve, touching on something that bothered her?

'You OK, Grace?'

'Can we have our picnic now?'

'Not long. We'll stop when we get to the next-but-one field. There's plenty of benches there.'

Grace ate the savoury food very quickly and asked for cake while Jonathan and I were still eating our sandwiches.

'Just a minute,' I said.

'Oh forget it!'

'Grace! What's wrong? I'm just finishing my sandwich. Then we will all have a piece of cake.'

'Grrr! Why do I have to wait all the time? Can I have another drink?'

I gave Grace some water, which she also pulled a face about. 'Is that all you've got?'

Something had definitely niggled Grace, and it was obvious that nothing I said or did was going to be right at this point in time.

'Please don't be rude. I've got a flask of tea. Would you like a cup?'

'What?'

She was now scanning the horizon and she started looking up at the sky.

'What's that bird?'

Jonathan got to his feet and followed Grace's gaze.

'Good spot, Grace,' he said, squinting into the sky. 'It's definitely a bird of prey. Let me see. Its wings are slightly rounded, see that? It's got a huge wingspan. I think it may be a buzzard. What do you think? Grace?'

He turned and looked down at Grace, only to see that she was now staring into space, in the opposite direction, and fidgeting with a button on her top. She was also kicking the ground. By now I'd worked out why the toes of all her shoes were scuffed. Grace had a habit of lifting one leg up behind her and repeatedly bashing her toes up and down into the ground, as she was doing now. She often did this when she was standing up, doing nothing else in particular, which meant she rarely stood completely still. When she tired of kicking one toe into the ground she swapped legs and had a go with the other shoe.

'Can I climb that tree?'

She pointed to a tree across the field that looked a similar shape to the one the boys had been climbing earlier, with plenty of low, horizontal branches.

'I tell you what, Grace. If you sit down while we finish the picnic, you and Jonathan can go over there while I pack up. Do you want some tea?'

She didn't reply but sat down cross-legged on the blanket next to me. While I got the cake out she flapped her knees up and down and hummed a tune to herself. Then she quickly ate the slice of cake I offered, said thank you and helped herself to some water. Though she'd ignored my question about the tea and hadn't responded to what I'd said about her and Jonathan going over to the tree together, the main thing was she was calm now. I'd seen that her mood could switch at any moment, and I was grateful she wasn't being belligerent.

'I'll tidy up here and I'll mind the bikes, if you like.'

Jonathan agreed. 'Come on, Grace. Let's go and check out that tree!'

She jumped up and started sprinting towards the tree. Jonathan chased after her.

'Wait for me!' he called. Grace was already on the lower branches when he reached her. I watched as he hopped up onto the lower branches too, and Grace immediately started to climb to the next branch, and the next. She didn't speak to him and didn't look back: all her energy and concentration was going into climbing the tree. Jonathan told me later that he suddenly had a horrible feeling in his stomach, the kind that grips you tight when you sense something is about to go wrong.

'Grace, don't go any higher.'

She continued to ignore him and started climbing the tree even faster. She was sure-footed, thank God, but she was quick too.

'Grace, can you hear me?'

Nothing. She didn't even flick her head around.

'Grace, I don't want you to go any higher. It's dangerous. I don't want you to fall.'

From where I was sitting I couldn't hear what Jonathan was saying, but I could see what was happening. I was already locking all the bikes together and stuffing the rug and the remains of the picnic into the panniers. I quickly headed to the tree. I didn't run or shout; I didn't want to do anything that might alarm Grace or provoke her to climb higher. If Grace's aim was to scare us – or wind us up, to use the phrase that seemed to follow her around – it was best not to fuel the fire in her belly.

I was nearly there. 'Grace, please stop there,' I heard Jonathan call. Outwardly he kept his cool, but I knew his stomach would be churning crazily, just as mine was. 'That's enough now. I can see you're a very good climber, but please stop now. That's enough. Let's carry on with our bike ride. Grace, I'm sure there will be lots of other trees to climb. We can go and try that one the boys were on. I don't want you to hurt yourself, or you won't be able to do any more climbing, will you? Can you hear me?'

Grace was now about six to eight foot in the air. She was facing away from us and, for once, she was standing incredibly still, rooted on a wide, sturdy branch. With one hand she was holding onto a bunch of several thin branches above her head.

Jonathan looked down at me. 'What shall we do?' he hissed.

'Let me try to talk to her.'

I remembered what I'd been telling myself, about keeping things simple and not bombarding Grace with questions or instructions.

'Grace, it's Angela.'

I waited.

'Can you hear me?'

No reply. No movement. Nothing at all.

'Grace, it's Angela.'

I waited again.

'Can you hear me?'

Finally, she started to slowly move herself around. I breathed out, not realising until that point that I'd been holding my breath.

'Are you OK?'

She nodded ever so slightly. She was still clutching the bunch of branches above her head as she carefully twirled her body around. It turned with her, snapping, stretching and straining as the thin branches formed one scraggy rope. It looked like it might give way at any minute.

'Can you hold on to that thick branch next to your left arm?'

'No.'

'Grace, you need to hold on to a thick branch.'

No reply.

'You are a good climber. Please take hold of that thick branch, so you are safer.'

I detected a slight nod of the head.

'Can you hear me? You can do this, Grace.'

She didn't look at me, but ever so slowly she started scanning the branches on all sides. Fraction by fraction, she clicked her head around in an almost mechanical, doll-like way. Then she suddenly let go of the thin bunch of branches above her head.

I gasped and instinctively threw my hands over my mouth. Her body dipped and her arms fell forwards as she crouched down and gripped the large branch she also had her feet on. Her bottom was in the air now and she held that position, panting and looking as agile as a jungle cat. This was not what I'd expected her to do, but at least she was stable. I was confident that from this position she could carefully climb back down.

'Well done. I think you can come down the way you went up now.'

She nodded and I felt a flood of relief, but then Grace went sideways instead of down the way I'd expected her to. She looked to be in a world of her own, and then she turned away from us and began to climb higher and higher, at quite a pace. I heard Jonathan audibly gasp.

'I'm going up,' he said assuredly.

I agreed. I knew he would climb slowly and quietly, without making a fuss. Grace might not even notice him until he was upon her; she was facing away from us and now seemed to be chuntering to herself as she concentrated on picking her way up and up. The tree was very old and I told myself hundreds and hundreds of people had climbed it before Grace. As long as nobody panicked, everything would be fine.

Grace's head shot around as soon as she heard Jonathan behind her.

'This is FUN!' she exclaimed, smiling. Her cheeky little face was scarlet and her hair looked wilder than ever, her curls glistening like so many shiny corkscrews in the sun. 'I'm reaching for the stars! Angela told me to! Angela said, "Reach for the stars, Grace!"'

Grace was now just about as high as she could go. I'd say she was at least ten feet in the air. The branches above her started to thin out and point skywards at this point; even someone as slight and lithe as Grace would not be able to climb them. She looked at Jonathan and laughed as she spoke to him again. I couldn't make out what she said, but Jonathan told me later she started to repeat, 'What goes up must come down! What goes up must come down. What goes up must come down.'

Grace continued chanting as she studiously, and expertly, started to pick her way back down the tree. It felt like I stood there with bated breath for an hour, though it could only have been minutes. My palms were sweaty and my heart felt so tight I had a pain in my chest. Jonathan had inflated the tyres on my bike that morning and a horrible image wouldn't leave my head of my heart being blown up not with air, but with shot after shot of adrenalin. It honestly felt fit to burst with stress.

Jonathan stayed as close as he could to Grace and had his eyes trained on her the whole time. At last, she was just a few feet from the ground. She jumped from the lowest branch dramatically, and Jonathan was just a step behind.

'Easy!' she said proudly. As he took his last step down, Jonathan caught his toe on a protruding lump of bark and landed clumsily on the grass beside Grace. I could tell he was really cross, but he kept his counsel, stood up straight and dusted himself down. The last thing we needed was to give Grace any excuse to take off again.

'I'm glad you're both back on safe ground. Both OK? Let's go and get the bikes.'

I wanted to get Grace away from the tree as quickly as possible; we'd talk to her about this properly later, probably in the car, when we'd be more likely to have her attention. She seemed oblivious to the fright she'd given us; it was as if she'd shut out the world for a few minutes and all her focus was on climbing the tree. There wasn't a flicker of acknowledgement that Jonathan had had to go after her, or that she'd ignored our pleas not to climb so high.

'Bikes? Oh yeah. Where are we going now? What are we doing, Angela?'

She was skipping towards her bike, looking like she didn't have a care in the world.

Jonathan widened his eyes at me behind Grace's back. Written all over his face were the words, 'What a nightmare!'

We set off on the bikes again.

'Please stay close,' I said, adding that if she didn't do as we asked we would have to go home. My nerves felt shot to ribbons.

Grace didn't argue, and thankfully she threw herself into the ride with gusto. Part of the track sloped downwards, and she held her legs out like oars and let herself freewheel. 'Yee-hah!' she called.

I knew the park well and I took the lead, taking us on a picturesque trail that eventually brought us to the top of the car park. Jonathan cycled behind Grace the whole way; neither of us wanted to take any chances.

There was a bin in the car park. Chip wrappers were scattered on the ground near it. I commented to a member of the park staff that I couldn't understand why people didn't put their rubbish in the bin, to which he replied, 'Those chip wrappers have been put in the bin a few times but that black bird keeps coming down and picking them out.' He pointed to a tree that overhung the car park.

I opened up the panniers on my bike, took out the rubbish from our picnic and stuffed it into the bin. I had a spare plastic bag, one I'd used to wrap our fruit and water bottles in, and I decided to use it to scoop up the greasy chip wrappers and put them in the bin too. Meanwhile, Jonathan said he'd start fixing the bikes onto the cycle rack on the car.

'You're a good citizen,' Grace said, when I explained what I was doing with the plastic bag. 'I learned about that in the

Green Club at school. Good citizens don't litter. Good citizens look after our planet.'

'I like the sound of the Green Club! I hate litter.'

'Can I still go to Green Club?' Grace asked. She looked very thoughtful and worried.

I'd already talked to Grace about which clubs she might want to join when the new school term started up, and she had told me she wanted to do singing and disco dancing. I'd told her I'd do my best to get her signed up either at school or in a local club, but this was the first I'd heard about Green Club.

Encouraging kids to join clubs is a high priority and we always let them pick what they want to do. Children benefit enormously from being able to have a go at what interests them. As well as trying new things and learning different skills, it's important for kids to socialise with other children, follow rules outside the home and school and simply have a change of scene or a fresh challenge. We've met plenty of kids who have never done any extra-curricular activities before they were taken into care. Some had never even been swimming or been taught to play a simple game of catch, and we've met several who have never even heard of board games most of us grew up with, like Cluedo or Operation.

'Green Club? It may not be called that in your new school, but we'll see what's on offer. And, do you remember, we talked about you doing singing and disco dancing clubs? All the clubs start up in September.'

She didn't reply and I wondered if she'd forgotten our earlier conversation.

'When you start school we can see what's available. If there's nothing at the school, we'll see what's on in the town.'

I was bending down and scooping up the chip papers as I said this. Again Grace didn't reply, so I turned my head to look up at her. I was startled by what I saw. Grace's eyes were on stalks, she was ghostly white and looked scared stiff.

'Grace? What is it, sweetheart?'

She was staring beyond me, at the ground beneath the bin. There was an empty whisky bottle lying there, which must have been hidden by the greasy papers. Instinctively, I scooped the bottle up and threw it straight in the bin, so Grace didn't have to look at it any longer. I'm a stickler for glass recycling normally, but Grace was my priority here and my gut told me I had to get that bottle out of sight as quickly as possible.

'Grace, sweetheart, it's OK. Don't worry. Everything's in the bin now.'

She was rooted to the spot, completely motionless, and the colour had drained from her usually rosy-red lips. She reminded me of Vicky, one of the girls we fostered when we started out back in the eighties, and who I wrote about in my first book, *Terrified*. Vicky used to freeze in terror when she was reminded of frightening and traumatic things that had happened in her childhood.

I figured it didn't take a genius to work out why Grace was so spooked by the whisky bottle. We knew her dad had been an alcoholic, and by her reaction it appeared whisky had been his poison.

'Grace? Can you hear me?'

She jolted her head from side to side, as if looking for the answer somewhere in the car park.

'What?'

'It's OK, Grace. Come on, let's help Jonathan.'

She continued to stare at me, and then she suddenly bolted. It took me completely by surprise; it was like she went from zero to a hundred miles an hour in the blink of an eye.

'What the . . .' I heard Jonathan shout as she charged past him. She headed to the fir tree she'd talked about climbing, the one the group of boys were playing on when we arrived. After what had happened, we'd avoided it and hoped Grace wouldn't remember that she wanted to climb on it. Jonathan was hot on her heels, but she was incredibly fast and nimble and had started scaling the tree before he could stop her.

'Don't go up high!' he called forcefully.

Even if he'd caught up with her on the ground, it wasn't guaranteed that Jonathan could have stopped Grace. Foster carers can't grab hold of a child in the way a parent might, to stop their own child running off, for example. This is drummed into us at training: the rule is that you can't restrain or even 'safe hold' a child in any way without permission, or without it being written into their care plan, even in an emergency situation. The only thing that is allowed is to hold a child's arm in a soft grip, but even then we have to err on the side of caution. Shockingly, one carer we knew grabbed tight hold of a child because he was going to fall in a stream and she tried to stop him. He was left with bruises, his parents reported the foster carer and, even though she was eventually cleared of any wrong-doing, she gave up fostering because of the stress and injustice of it all.

'Grace! Can you hear me?'

All we could do was reason; words were all we had.

'Can you hear me Grace?' Jonathan was calling up to her, who was a few feet up by now and resolutely ignoring him.

'Please don't go past the next branch. It's not safe. Stay on the lower branches.'

She scampered up several branches very adeptly, swinging herself up to a resting place, several more feet above the ground. There she sat panting and puffing for quite some time. She looked back but still didn't answer us.

I was at Jonathan's side now and we both stayed calm.

'What are we going to do now?' he said.

'She'll come down. Don't panic. She's actually a good little climber.'

'I heard that!' she called cheekily.

She started laughing, and to my surprise I laughed too. I think it was with relief. Thank God she was talking to us, I thought, and sounding more like her usual self.

It took a few more tense minutes before she decided to slowly make her way down.

'You don't need to worry about me,' she sang. 'I'm a good climber. Jonathan, do you think I'm a good climber? I was the best in my old school on the monkey bars, you know. Are you a good climber, Angela? Have you ever been proper climbing? Like rock climbing? Angela? Are you? Can you climb? Can you do monkey bars?'

We let her talk and talk, and finally she was on safe ground again.

By the time the car was packed up she went quiet again. We spent much of the journey back explaining to Grace that she had to do as we asked her. She couldn't run off like that, especially across a car park, and she must not climb trees without our permission.

'Do you, like, actually care?' she wrinkled her little nose.

'Yes, Grace. We care very much indeed. We want you to be safe and happy. We are here to help and support you, and you can talk to us about anything you like.'

'OK.'

She sat fidgeting and not saying very much at all for about ten minutes. Then, from nowhere, she piped up with, 'Lee and Lily, they don't care. They don't even like me. My mum cares about me. She would have me back at the drop of a hat, if she could.'

13

'She's a harum-scarum kid'

Around five weeks after Grace moved in with us we had another placement meeting. I had received a letter in the post a few weeks earlier, informing us of the date, time and venue of the meeting, which Social Services had decided to hold in our house. As it happened that was fine by us, though I must admit I did use to feel it would be nice to be asked if this was convenient, rather than being told when we were hosting the meeting in our own lounge!

This particular meeting had been arranged to fit in with Colette, who had agreed to come to our house to meet with the social workers, and then take Grace back to the family home for the weekend. This would be Grace's first visit home since moving in with us, and she said she was looking forward to staying with her mum, 'but not Lily and Lee'. There had been very little contact with home in the previous few weeks, as Colette had made no effort to call us and had often not been available when Grace tried to call her.

The school holidays were coming to an end and Grace

was starting school the following week, which she was excited about. We'd been on a visit to her new classroom and the head teacher had shown her around. Grace's eyes were everywhere, drinking it all in. Afterwards she talked non-stop about what her classmates would be like, whether the other girls were into disco dancing and Take That and the Spice Girls, and whether the school dinners would be as nice as the head teacher said they were.

When the two social workers arrived for the placement meeting, Barry had a word with Grace in private before she went up to her bedroom to wait for her mum's arrival. This was normal procedure, to give Grace the opportunity to discuss anything she felt uneasy about mentioning in front of Jonathan and me, or our support social worker Jess, or indeed her mum.

I prepared a tray of tea and biscuits and then Jonathan and I settled in the lounge with Barry and Jess. The four of us discussed all the various issues I'd flagged up in my notes in the preceding weeks, and I found myself feeling quite surprised by how much there was to talk about, considering Grace had only been living with us for a relatively short time.

I told the social workers Grace still hadn't unpacked and explained that she was still taking food to her room from time to time and trying to hide it. This hadn't happened very often, but I'd found more biscuit wrappers and the packaging from some cheese triangles just a couple of days before. I'd spoken calmly to Grace each time, reiterating there was no need to do this and that she could ask me for treats or food if and when she needed anything. Grace's response each time was to politely say sorry and that she wouldn't do it again, but she always did. Jess suggested I put a personalised tuck box in the kitchen for her, with Grace's favourite snacks and treats in it, and tell her she could choose what she wanted. She would not need to ask us, only let us know if it was empty. We both agreed this was a good idea. Barry recalled seeing something in Grace's notes about a shortage of food in the family home and wondered if this was what had led to Grace's habit. It was something that had crossed my mind too, having been told that when Grace and Lily were left home alone by their father as very young girls they were frightened and hungry.

I mentioned the tree-climbing episode and her disappearing act in the shoe shop and we recapped on Lena's accident. By now my friend Gail had confirmed to me that Lena was fine and, luckily, had got away with just two small stitches in her arm. Gail certainly did not want any money for the damage to the greenhouse and there had been no comeback from Lena's mum Shannon. I could only assume she saw it as an unfortunate accident, as we did.

Barry jotted down a few notes as I spoke.

'She's a harum-scarum kid,' he commented. 'I think that's obvious.'

'Yes, but she's got a good heart. She's not a bad kid, not at all.'

Barry nodded. 'Yes, that rings true to me, from what I've seen of her. I'd agree with that, one hundred per cent.'

We went on to talk about Grace's continued moodiness, the fact she was generally extremely lively and energetic and could be unpredictable, plus some of the worrying comments she'd made about her family, and Lee and Lily in particular. Barry said he'd also heard Grace complaining about how Lee and Lily treated her. Grace had told him that Lily not only told lies but was a bully. Barry had also heard the allegations about Lee smoking cannabis. He advised me that Social Services were aware.

'By the way, has Grace said anything to you about the clothes she claims go missing?' This was bothering me and I wanted to get to the bottom of it.

'Not specifically, but she did make a comment one time that she thought Lily was jealous of all her new clothes.'

This fitted. Grace did have a large amount of clothes, and most were of good quality and fashionable too. I guessed that previous foster carers had treated her to plenty of new things, just as we always did with the children who lived with us. Therefore, I could see how Lily might have become jealous, although, of course, I imagined that Grace would have swapped every last stitch of clothing she owned to be in Lily's position, still living in the family home.

I started to wonder if Lily took the clothes to be spiteful, given that it was unlikely any of Grace's things would fit her. Perhaps it was actually Lily and not Lee who was playing games with Grace's clothes? Or was it both of them?

The conversation moved on. I mentioned to Barry that Grace had got sunburned last time she went home, just before she moved in with us, and had suffered severe sunburn in the past, and I also told him about her frightened reaction to the empty whisky bottle.

'Well, Dad was an alcoholic,' Barry said. 'I don't suppose you'd need to be a rocket scientist to figure out she was traumatised by his drinking. It's the reason she first went into care, after all.' Barry went on to say that Grace was only five or six when her father died of the drug overdose, which he believed had been accidental. We all agreed it was terribly sad.

I made a point of mentioning the fact Colette had given Grace the impression she could move back home if she behaved better, and that I felt Grace looked up to her mum, was keen to please her and saw a return as a possibility rather than the empty promise it perhaps was. The social workers listened carefully and took notes. Neither seemed to disagree with my precis of the situation with Colette; this was a matter to keep a close eye on, Barry said.

We also talked through Grace's routine appointments. As well as the doctors, Jonathan and I had taken her to the dentist, who had advised that she needed to be extremely vigilant about brushing her teeth; she already had more fillings than average for her age. The optician gave her a clean bill of health and said she had excellent vision. I explained that the GP had not seemed unduly concerned about Grace on any level, but that Jonathan and I still had a feeling there was something going on that we didn't fully understand, or have a name for.

Jess assured us that we would all continue to talk about and monitor Grace's hyperactivity and the other issues we were worried about and said that, if necessary, they could look at arranging an appointment with a specialist. Barry commented that Grace might still be adjusting to her new home, and that might explain some of her behaviour. I wasn't convinced; I'd looked after countless children who'd arrived feeling unsettled and upset. Some had gone through unimaginable traumas, but in my experience that didn't make a child bounce off all the walls like Grace did at times, or have trouble following simple instructions despite appearing to be academically able. I told Jess that we would of course continue to help Grace as best we could, but that we would appreciate some expert advice if that could be arranged sooner rather than later. She suggested it might be best to do this through the school, and that perhaps we should wait and see what her new teachers said. I agreed to this, it seemed like a good idea and it wasn't long before Grace was starting school.

Barry reported that when he had spoken to Grace separately, she had told him she liked it in our house and that she had a friend called Briony and was looking forward to starting school. We'd learned she'd had problems settling into schools in the past and teachers had flagged up problems with 'too much chattering' and 'disrupting lessons', but I wasn't surprised. She'd been in nine schools to date; no wonder she wasn't exactly a model pupil.

Both Barry and Jess said they were satisfied with how things were going and they praised our efforts. The overall message was that we were doing very well, and that we should continue with more of the same. 'Well done to you both,' Jess said. 'I wish the rest of my caseload was working out as well as this!' She added that it would be interesting to hear what the new school would have to say about Grace's general behaviour in the classroom.

'You mean in terms of how she interacts with others?' Jonathan asked.

'Yes, exactly. Whether she is seen to be winding other kids up and so on. All those problems that have cropped up time and time again. I wonder if we'll hear the same complaints.'

Though nobody spelled it out in the meeting, I think we all shared a common thought, which was that, despite the fact she could certainly be a handful, Grace really didn't seem to deserve the extremely bad press she'd had from her family, former foster carers and previous teachers.

Colette was at least twenty minutes late for the meeting by now. While we waited for her to arrive, Jonathan and I took the opportunity to ask Barry if he had any other background information about Grace that he might be able to share.

He said he hadn't yet had time to read every page of the extremely large Social Services file on Grace, but he knew by now that each one of her eight previous placements had broken down amid complaints about her supposedly aggravating behaviour, and every one of the nine schools she'd attended had reported behavioural problems, typically describing her as 'disruptive'. Other words used were irritating, infuriating, provoking, grating, frustrating, annoying and exasperating. One foster carer had described her as a 'master wind-up merchant'. I knew Grace was no angel, but I just didn't see her as a child who was so disruptive she had to be moved from home to home and school to school. I would have liked to have been given some examples of Grace's behaviour to back up the criticisms, but Barry wasn't able to provide any, having not yet scrutinised all the paperwork in sufficient detail.

'If there's anything in the files worth passing on, rest assured that I will,' Barry said. Just at that moment the front doorbell rang out. 'Ah! Saved by the bell!' Barry chuckled, closing shut a large file he had open on his lap.

I stood up and went to answer the door. I met Grace on the stairs. 'Don't run!' I shouted, but Grace seemed to be in a frenzy of excitement about seeing her mum and sprinted down the stairs. Her eyes were shining and she was springing from stair to stair, full of beans.

Unfortunately, when Grace flung open the door her face immediately fell and she looked as if her batteries had suddenly run flat. Colette was not alone. There was a teenage girl standing by her side.

'Lily!' Grace gasped, 'I didn't . . .' her voice faded away and she seemed to physically shrink under the gaze of her sister. I watched in dismay as Grace's shoulders drooped and she folded her arms defensively in front of her before recoiling, taking several steps backwards. Meanwhile Lily stood strong and bold, her pointed chin jutted upwards and her broad shoulders held firmly back.

I was surprised at how physically different the sisters were. Like her mum, Lily was very tall, curvaceous and buxom. I thought she looked much older than thirteen; I'd have guessed at fifteen. Her long, poker-straight hair was dyed a shade of burgundy, she wore a lot of orange-tinted foundation on her face, and she was dressed in tight leggings and a low-cut T-shirt with a glittery motif on the front. Grace looked like a tiny little mop-haired fairy next to her big sister.

'How are you, *trouble*?' Colette asked Grace flatly, stepping into the hall without introducing me to Lily, who made no effort to even look at me. Lily strode in after her mum, one hand on her hip, inspecting our hallway and giving Grace an unnervingly hard stare as she did so.

'I'm OK, Mum,' Grace said in a tiny voice. I've heard lots of parents call their kids 'trouble' as a jokey term of endearment, but I didn't detect any affection or even a hint of playfulness in Colette's voice. Rather, she delivered the word sharply and almost accusingly. Not surprisingly, Grace looked awkward and uncomfortable. I wanted to scoop her into my arms and tell her everything was going to be OK, and that she had nothing to feel worried or self-conscious about.

'What's new then? Behaving, I hope?' Colette boomed this out; her voice was so loud it seemed to bounce off all the walls. 'Well then, Gracie? Cat got your tongue?' Colette rolled her eyes theatrically, which seemed to be for Lily's benefit. I felt very uncomfortable now too, because this seemed so wrong. It was as if Colette was throwing her weight around almost in order to show off to Lily, which I thought was a very odd thing for a mother to do.

Grace glanced at me anxiously while Lily gave a little

snort. She stared down at her sister, raising one of her thin, highly plucked eyebrows as she did so. An unmistakeable sneer appeared on Lily's lips, which she made absolutely no attempt to hide. I'm afraid it looked to me like Lily was enjoying seeing her sister squirm like this, and I had the feeling she was hoping Grace had misbehaved so she could enjoy the fireworks. Looking back, if I had to pick one word to describe Lily, it would have to be 'cocky'. I don't really like that word and don't use it very often, but that's exactly how she came across, even before she opened her mouth.

'Grace is doing really well,' I sang out with confidence, throwing a broad smile at both Colette and Lily. This was an instinctive reaction; subconsciously, I think this was my attempt to redress the balance and move things in a more positive direction. 'I'm Angela, by the way. It's nice to meet you, Lily.'

'Hi,' she said through curled lips.

I tried to prompt Grace to answer her mum's question about her news.

'So, your mum asked what news you have, Grace.' I gave her an encouraging smile and left a pause, hoping she'd fill the silence, but she didn't. Grace looked like a rabbit in the headlights and, though she opened her mouth, no words came out. 'We've been busy doing all kinds of things, haven't we?' I left another, shorter pause. 'It's been a busy few weeks and we've been out and about quite a lot.'

Grace nodded but still she looked too afraid to speak.

'Come on Gracie! Tell your mum what you've been up to, babe?'

Grace had plenty of news to choose from. We'd really made the most of the good weather and had packed in so many activities. Grace had been with me to visit my mum a few times and had been learning how to grow tomatoes and bake flapjacks. She'd thoroughly enjoyed herself at the town festival, where she bumped into her new friend Briony. The two girls played until they dropped on the bouncy castle, and Grace had found out that Briony went to the same school, which she was thrilled to bits about. Briony's mum Jill had suggested Grace might like to go for tea one night after school, and I'd said that that was a lovely idea, but maybe Briony would like to come to us first? Jill agreed to this without questioning why, and Grace was delighted. In fact, I think that made her day, and she really couldn't wait to have her new friend over and had talked about this several times. One weekend we'd had some of Jonathan's family round for a barbecue and we'd all played rounders on the field, which Grace had loved. We'd also been swimming and I'd signed Grace up for some lessons, as she wanted to learn how to do front crawl, having only ever mastered a very basic breaststroke.

Colette looked at her daughter expectantly and I hoped Grace might at least come up with a couple of things from the long list she had to pick from.

'Dunno, not a lot,' she said with a shrug. 'I got new school shoes.' She went bright red in the face as she spoke. I wondered if she was worried about telling her mum anything in case it sounded as if she was boasting, as I know some children feel anxious about that.

Colette looked at me and said somewhat suspiciously, 'Are you sure she's been OK?'

'Yes,' I said emphatically. 'I expect Grace will tell you all about what we've been doing, it's just a big day, that's all. She's been looking forward to seeing you.' I smiled brightly again. I wanted to make the atmosphere as light and optimistic as possible.

Afterwards, I told Jonathan that Grace's lacklustre 'dunno' reminded me of the time we'd taken two children on holiday to Disneyland Paris, or Euro Disney, as it was then. It had been a fabulous trip and the first time abroad for both of them, but when one girl was asked to write about what she did at half term she completely failed to mention the holiday. Instead, she filled a whole page in her school news book with a detailed description of a visit to McDonald's with her dad, then she wrote, 'Angela made me polish my shoes last night' and finished with a summary of the latest storyline on *Neighbours*. When Jonathan and I read it at parents' evening we didn't know whether to laugh or cry!

'Let's go up to the lounge,' I said, ushering Colette and Lily towards the stairs.

Lily muttered something under her breath when I asked her if she wouldn't mind removing her trainers. I wouldn't have asked Colette to remove her shoes – it was up to adults to offer – and in any case she told me she was keeping her sandals on, 'if you don't mind, Angela', saying they were clean and she never went anywhere without heels on. The strappy sandals were about four inches high; I don't know how she managed to walk in them, let alone drive!

Jonathan was pouring more tea and Jess and Barry were chatting and each finishing off a custard cream when I showed Colette and Lily into the lounge. Grace trailed behind them, looking cowed. How her mood had shifted, I thought. It was such a shame; Grace's expectations were so high and she had been so excited about seeing her mum, but all I saw now was a little girl who was anxious and nervous and desperately wanted to please. She needed nothing more than approval and love from her mother, but it seemed to me that she found herself squirming in her skin just for being herself.

The two social workers and Jonathan politely stopped eating and talking and got to their feet for the introductions.

'Hi guys!' Colette said to the room, giving a wave and a giggle, and flashing her large, white teeth in the process.

Colette and Lily sat in the two armchairs Jonathan and Barry had been occupying, leaving the men to squeeze onto the sofa next to Jess and me. Grace slunk to her knees and sat on the carpet.

'You don't mind me bringing our Lil, do you?'

The social workers asked Grace if she minded having her sister in the room and she said 'no'.

'OK, you can stay, Lily,' Jess said, 'but I might have to ask you to step outside if we want to talk privately about a few things, OK?'

'Whatever,' Lily said absent-mindedly. She was chewing gum noisily.

Jess displayed her usual professionalism and ran the rest of the meeting with impressive authority and charm. She was complimentary about Grace and told Colette she should be proud of her daughter for the way she had settled in so far.

'Angela and Jonathan are very experienced carers,' she said. 'I love working with them, because they have a way of making a real difference, often where others have found it very challenging.' She added that she believed the key to our success was that we followed all the advice we received from Social Services to the letter and were constantly sharpening our skills through our regular training and support groups. 'They are hardworking, diligent and consistent, and the children know the boundaries. That's very important,' Jess said. She gave a confident smile. Knowing Jess as well as I did, I realised this was her subtle way of trying to tell Colette not to rock the boat, either by clashing with us or by letting things slip when Grace went on home visits.

Colette yawned, quickly followed by Lily. 'Why does that always happen?' Colette hooted. 'One person yawns and it sets everyone off!' Lily laughed too while the rest of us shifted in our seats, wishing Colette would focus on the purpose of the meeting. We were here to discuss her young daughter's life, and it was awkward to see Colette behaving so insensitively.

'I *am* grateful to Angela and Jonathan,' Colette said, having suddenly seemed to remember where she was. In a blasé voice and rolling her eyes to the ceiling as she spoke, she added, 'God knows, I couldn't cope with her like they do.'

Grace looked mortified. Again, I wanted to hug her and

I wanted to protect her. The last thing she needed was to be upset by comments from her own mum.

Jess went on to say, very politely, that it would help everyone, and especially Grace, if Colette would try to follow the rules Grace was used to in our house during all her visits home. She clearly didn't trust that Colette had picked up on her subtle cues and decided to spell it out. 'This is very important,' Jess said. 'It will be helpful to everybody and most of all Grace.'

Jess now asked Lily to step outside. I took her to the kitchen, where she sat looking bored, while I made her a drink of squash.

'Are you OK there, Lily? We won't be long, I shouldn't think.'

'Suppose.'

'OK, see you shortly.' I switched Radio 1 on for her and gave her a magazine and she seemed quite happy.

When I went back in the living room Colette was saying, 'I do my best, you know, but sometimes it's hard. It's been totally nuts round our house!' Then she began making excuses for the fact she had hardly been in touch with Grace by phone since her move. I was reminded of what she'd said when I'd called her to try to make arrangements for a contact visit. 'Didn't I tell you, I'll call *you*,' she'd said. 'There's a lot of stuff going on at the moment, things you wouldn't believe! Nuts, it is. I'll be in touch, don't you worry. Gotta dash now.'

Colette was taking the opportunity to expand on why she had barely spoken to Grace over the past month or so and had been hard to pin down for a visit. She said she was only telling us this story because it had been playing out in the local paper, and she expected we'd all see it anyhow. I wondered if she was secretly proud of the fact part of her life was interesting enough to be worthy of a report in the local paper, as she seemed to be enjoying recounting the story.

'I still can't believe it,' she said, giving a little giggle. 'But this is what happened. I'll tell you the truth and the whole truth.' I thought, *Where have I heard that before?*

Colette looked very comfortable holding the floor as she told her story in painstaking detail. The essence of it was this: she had been involved in a spat with her husband Malcolm's ex-wife Linzi, who had accused Colette of stealing her jewellery. In fact, Colette said Malcolm had originally paid for all the jewellery and was adamant it was his property after he and Linzi divorced. He gave the jewellery to Colette but told her a 'white lie', saying he'd bought the heavy gold necklaces, rings and hooped earrings at a second-hand jewellers in town.

Linzi went to the papers with her story, providing old pictures of herself wearing the jewellery on holiday, dressed in a tight white leather dress. She also posed for new photographs at her home, wearing a miniskirt and low-cut top. 'Likes the spotlight, that one,' Colette said, before explaining that the pictures showed Linzi opening the empty drawers of a little wooden jewellery box and looking shocked that the jewellery was missing. Colette rolled her eyes dramatically as she relayed this detail. 'Can you imagine? Why would you be all dressed up like that at home? She's such a drama queen. I can't believe the paper was even interested.' She continued, barely pausing for breath. 'Anyway, I don't know how she had the nerve, with me and Malcolm raising her two boys. I told this to the reporter when I got my right to reply.'

It turned out Colette had also given a lengthy interview, and she posed for pictures too. I was perplexed by all this. I couldn't understand why either woman would want to air her dirty laundry in public like this. More to the point, how could you let something like this get in the way of you speaking to your daughter on the phone, or arranging to see her? Grace was in care, in a brand-new foster home yet again, but it seemed Colette had more time to talk to a local reporter, pose for photographs and have a public slanging match with Malcolm's ex-wife than make time for Grace. Also, why bring it up and talk in so much detail about it at this meeting? Grace's life was being discussed. Barry and Jess had far more important things to spend their time on; we all did.

On the back of this story, Barry adeptly mentioned the fact Grace had said her clothes went missing at home.

'Do you know anything about this?'

'No. All I know is that trouble follows Grace around. This is exactly why I can't have her living with me. She probably just loses stuff and blames other people. She's such a scatterbrain.'

Just as our elderly GP had done, Colette said this as if Grace was not in the room. I was furious. I was about to ask if it would be best if Grace also left us while we talked in private, but Jess was already on the case.

'Colette,' she said. 'Please can we focus on the issue at hand and remember that Grace is here with us.'

'Sorry,' she said. 'Is this true Grace? Are you really saying someone is taking your clothes? I suppose you're accusing Lily?'

'Er, I'm not sure,' Grace muttered. She blushed bright red again then spoke in a tiny whisper. 'It might be Lee.'

'Lee?' Colette looked incredulous and gave a hoot of laughter while Grace looked mortified.

'What would a teenage boy want with a little kid's clothes?'

'I dunno,' she said. 'I might have lost things at other foster carers' or something, I dunno.'

Barry wasn't going to let this go. 'Could it possibly be Lee is causing trouble?' he asked Colette. 'I'm not accusing him, just asking the question. Is it worth having a word with him, make sure he's not been going in Grace's room and taking things to wind her up?'

'Lee winding Grace up? Nah, it's the other way around. But OK, if it'll make you happy, I'll have a word. I'll make sure he doesn't nick anything this weekend.'

Grace had packed a very small bag for her weekend visit home, and I didn't blame her. I couldn't see why she would make up a story about her clothes being taken, given that she was at pains to prove to her family that she wasn't a so-called 'wind-up merchant'. Also, I'd seen her very upset about the items that went missing. I believed her concerns were real, and I could see she was genuinely worried about what might happen to her clothes this time.

When we waved Grace off with her mum and sister I felt terribly sorry for her, and fearful of what the weekend would bring. I'd originally thought it was good timing for her to have this visit home before she started school. I thought it would give her a lift to spend time with her mum, but now I really wasn't sure.

'See you on Sunday!' I shouted as she climbed into Colette's jeep. 'Enjoy yourself!' Jonathan called.

All the windows were wide open. Lily was in the front passenger seat, next to her mum. She was looking very pleased with herself for being up front while Grace had to sit in the back. *Poor Grace*, I thought. She seemed destined to be made to feel like the odd one out.

Grace turned her head and looked as if she was about to say something to Jonathan and me, but Lily must have pressed the button to close the electric windows.

'You don't have to be nice to her, you know,' I heard Lily say loudly as the windows slowly closed. 'She's not your mum.' Grace looked away as the jeep was sealed shut. Meanwhile, Lily looked back over her shoulder and gave me a smug look. Clearly, she had intended me to hear her barbed comment.

What a little madam, I thought. Colette must have heard what Lily said, but appeared to completely ignore her daughter's rude remarks.

14

'What's wrong with her?'

Barry brought Grace back to our house after her weekend visit home. She was in a terrible mood, ranting and raving about how Lee had been through her weekend bag and 'messed about' with her clothes as well as her collection of hairbands and even her underwear. She accused him of going in her room when no one else was there and stealing some specific items of clothing, even though she had deliberately taken very little home with her.

'He's a druggie and a weirdo,' she said, before she'd even taken her shoes off. 'He's taken my skirt this time. He's a creep!' She said she had found the Spice Girls top she'd previously accused him of taking: it was under his bed, apparently.

I had considered whether Lee may be stealing her things to sell, if it was true about him being on drugs, but that seemed unlikely. None of Grace's clothes were particularly expensive or had designer labels, but what was the alternative explanation? As Colette had pointed out, why would a teenage boy want a young girl's clothes? Grace's clothes were not unisex and wouldn't fit a teenage lad. Was he just a trouble-maker, intent on upsetting Grace? Colette had been very quick to defend Lee and say that Grace was the only one who did the winding up, but that was no surprise, given that she had been accusing Grace of being a disruptive influence for years. Worryingly, the spectre of there being some kind of abusive element to this was looming large in my thoughts.

I supposed that Lee's life had not been that easy, what with his mum Linzi divorcing his dad and Colette becoming his stepmother. Nobody had told me why Linzi didn't have custody of her two sons, but there must have been a reason, as back then it was much more unusual than it is today for a father to take on the kids when their mum was still alive and well and living in the vicinity, as Linzi was. Mind you, that was also what had happened with Grace and Lily, as they had stayed with their dad too. I had not been told why this had been the case.

'I'm sorry you're not in a good mood, Grace. What else happened over the weekend?'

She blushed bright red. 'I don't want to talk about it! Why would I want to tell *you* about it? You don't care, you're just looking after me for the money.'

'Grace, Jonathan and I are very fond of you indeed. We love having you here and we are looking after you because we care about you a great deal and want to give you a lovely home. We have our shop to make money, we don't foster children for it.'

'She said you'd say that.'

I wanted to ask if she meant Lily or her mother – or someone else – but I was wary of asking a leading question.

'I'm not sure I know who you are talking about.'

'Lily, I'm talking about. For God's sake! I might as well be talking to the fucking wall!'

'Grace. Please don't use bad language and don't be rude. I'm just trying to find out about your weekend and have a civilised conversation with you.'

'Well I've told you now. It was Lily who said it!'

I wanted to remind her that she'd said in the past that Lily was a bully and told lies, but I had to play safe.

'Lily?'

'Yes. Anyway, Lee does the same to her, you know. She said she's going to report him to the police if he does it again.'

'He does the same to her? So she's going to report him to the police?'

Grace went scarlet. 'Yes!' she shouted.

'You mean he takes her clothes too, is that what you mean?'

'No! Yes! What do you *think* I'm talking about? Grrr!'

She stomped up the stairs, leaving me feeling even more concerned and uneasy about the situation.

'I'll have to tell Social Services,' I said to Jonathan. 'I'm sorry to say my instincts are telling me there's more to this.'

He nodded sagely, looking crestfallen. 'Mine too.'

We were now both afraid that Lee might be sexually abusing Grace, and possibly Lily too. We had no evidence and hoped we were wrong; it was simply a gut feeling based on what she'd said and how she behaved when she talked about Lee. We had no option but to act on this, despite the lack of proof. I realised that once I'd mentioned this, Social Services might well want Grace to talk to a specialist of some kind, perhaps a child psychologist or a family therapist. It was like opening a can of worms, but it had to be done. I would not make accusations against Lee, of course, but I'd report what Grace had said, how she reacted and simply relay my concerns. The experts at Social Services would take it from there.

Grace didn't mention her mum at all and so when she came down for dinner, I asked after Colette.

'She's great,' Grace said, fixing a grin on her face. 'She is so lovely to me. She is doing her very best to get me home, you know, but it's not easy. There's a lot to sort out. She's up the wall with lots of stuff, and my stepdad is about as useful as a chocolate fireman.'

Not for the first time, Grace was full of phrases I assumed she'd heard at home or from other adults; some of the things she came out with didn't trip off her tongue very naturally and they weren't things you'd expect a ten-year-old to say.

'I see. She's doing her best?'

'Yes, but it's like this. I have to stay here for a while, until after I'm eleven. But Mum said that if I behave myself then she might be able to have me home when I'm in secondary school. Because then I'll be old enough to, like, get a job and pay some keep.'

My heart sank. I'd been involved in this sort of situation before, when a parent only wants their child home so they can take some money off them. I felt a flash of anger. Grace was only ten and it would be years before she earned enough money to pay any keep. Why had Colette even started this conversation, just when the rest of us were doing our level best to get Grace settled with us?

Grace was up at six o'clock on her first day of school. Her mood had steadily improved in the three days since her return from her visit home and she seemed to be in extremely good spirits.

'Why are you being so slow, Angela?' she asked on the walk to school. 'Hurry up! I don't want to be the last one there.'

I was walking slower than normal as I'd twisted my ankle slightly, tripping over the stray end of a sheet as I'd carried the washing in off the line. It wasn't serious, but I was taking things steady.

'I'm going as fast as I can, Grace! You're still going to be early, even at this pace. If we go any faster the gates might not even be open when we get there.'

Halfway to school, I heard the clatter of shoes on the pavement behind me and turned to see Briony dashing towards Grace.

'Wait for me!'

Grace turned around, yelped in delight and gave her

friend a high five. The two of them linked arms and started talking animatedly. I'd learned that Briony had left her old school at the end of Year 5 when her dad was relocated to our area with his job. Jill, her mum, had been in the shop one day, and she had confided in me that Briony had been very negative about starting a new school until she hit it off with Grace.

'I can't tell you how pleased I am that the girls get on so well,' she'd said.

'It's great for both of them,' I replied. It was a busy day and the shop was packed with customers. I wasn't sure if Jill knew that Grace would be new to the school too, but I didn't have time to chat and explain this. However, I was pleased I'd seen Jill again, and that she was so positive about Grace. I liked her a lot. She was clearly a devoted parent who was rooting for her daughter to be happy in her new environment.

Now, as we all walked to school together, Jill began to reiterate the fact she was so pleased Briony had made a new friend before starting school.

'I can't tell you how relieved I am,' she said. 'It was very, very tough for Briony, leaving all her old friends behind. Having Grace as a friend will help her settle in. We must fix up that play date.'

At that moment, Grace suddenly decided to run up the grass bank beside the path in front of us. It had rained the night before and the grass was wet and no doubt muddy in parts. I'd made sure she looked immaculate in her new uniform and shoes, and I wanted her to stay that way.

'Sorry,' I said to Jill, excusing myself as I called out to Grace and headed towards her as quickly as my sore ankle would allow.

'Grace! Come down please! You're going to get yourself dirty before you even get to school.'

'What? Oh, OK!' She raced back down as quickly as she'd run up the bank. She was panting and laughing as I picked some grass off her socks and straightened out her clothes and hairband. I'd spent ages taming her hair with tangle spray and it looked lovely. It was a joy to see Grace looking carefree and relaxed, exactly as a young girl should.

As we continued the walk to school, I gave myself a mental pat on the back for reaching this milestone. Grace was in such good spirits, and I hoped it would bode well for the start of her new school career. Another mum joined us, and I introduced her to Jill. 'You're so kind, Angela,' Jill said when we reached the gate. 'It's lucky I've met someone who's lived here for such a long time.'

I was really looking forward to seeing Grace when she came out of school at home time. I had a very good feeling about her first day and, sure enough, she came out in a really great mood, talking nineteen to the dozen about everything she had done.

'Guess what? We get "golden time" on a Friday if we've been good. Do you know what that is, Angela? And I'm allowed to try for my "pen licence" because my handwriting is good enough and, if I get it, then I can swap from a pencil to a pen. There's going to be a play. We don't know what it is yet, but I'm going to, like, audition. My mum does auditions. I'll be good at auditions. There's a club for the disco dancing. Briony wants to join too. Can I join, Angela, can I, can I?'

'Yes, Grace, I'm sure you can. Have they given you the details? I'll just need to check the time and day, but I'm sure it will be fine. Your mum does auditions?'

She ignored that last question and thrust a piece of paper into my hand.

'OK, great, that's ideal,' I said, looking at the day and time. 'We'll get this sorted out for you as soon as we can. I'm so pleased you've enjoyed your first day.'

'Oh yeah, and my teacher's lovely. She's called Mrs Platt. No, Mrs Pratt. Is it? What is it? I can't remember! It can't be Pratt, that's silly!' She burst out laughing before finally telling me she'd remembered. 'It's Mrs Lacey.'

'Oh,' I said, wondering how she'd got Platt and Lacey confused. 'Mrs Lacey? Right, I look forward to meeting her. I don't think I know her.' That exchange summed Grace up. She was full of enthusiasm and never failed to surprise me. I was sure starting at her new school was a really positive step and I felt a surge of optimism about Grace's future.

It was a short week at school – they'd started back on a Thursday – and before we knew it the weekend was here again. Grace was worn out by Friday night. She seemed to have put her heart and soul into her new start and I told her I was very proud of her, which I was.

The following week, every day brought more exciting news and waves of enthusiasm from Grace. There was a singing club at lunchtime, and Grace had signed herself up for it.

'The teacher said I've got a lovely, strong voice,' she reported. 'She wants me to be in the choir. And, guess what, Angela?'

'What?'

'At Harvest we're going to go round all the old folks' homes and sing to them.'

'Well isn't that lovely? I'm very pleased for you, Grace.'

The disco dance club was held at five o'clock in the hall one evening after school. Briony was there when I took Grace along, and I bumped into Jill in the corridor.

'We could share lifts,' Jill suggested. We'd both walked the girls home from school and then went back in the car for the club, as there wasn't much time.

I smiled and said we could think about that, once the girls had settled down. I think I said something along the lines of, 'I like to see what's going on in the clubs, don't you? They often let you watch at the end for a short while.'

Jill readily accepted this and said she agreed with me. In reality, I was stalling for time. It was still early days and I was in no rush to let Grace go in the car with Jill and Briony. If Grace were my own child I'd have been equally cautious, wanting to make sure I knew the other family well enough to trust them with the responsibility of driving my child. With Grace, there was an added element of course, in that I didn't want to start bothering Social Services with permission requests when it wasn't really necessary. I didn't need help with lifts, as I always had Jonathan to share the load of whatever we had on, either with the kids or in the shop. The school was only a matter of minutes away by car in any case. However, I wasn't going to rule out a lift share, because if Grace and Briony were good pals they would probably both enjoy going to the club together.

The two girls partnered up to start learning their first routine and afterwards Grace spent hours practising in her bedroom. She told me she wanted to be good enough to enter competitions one day, and to be picked for the school talent performance at Christmas.

'My mum will be *so* impressed,' she said, eyes widening at the thought, 'because she used to be a dancer!'

'She did? I didn't know that, Grace.'

'Yes. She worked in some, like, really fancy clubs and places. That's how she met my dad, you know?'

Grace hadn't mentioned her dad since she told me the Goldilocks story. Since then, of course, I'd learned from Barry that her father had passed away when she was five or six, and that he had died of a drug overdose.

'So your mum and dad met in a club?'

'Yes.'

She started looking around the kitchen and homed in on her tuck box.

'Can I have a snack?' She didn't always have to ask, but she did because it was so close to dinner time.

'Yes. Just a small one. Dinner won't be too long.'

She helped herself to a little box of raisins and sat at the kitchen table with a drink of fresh apple juice. The tuck box was working very well. Grace loved the fact it was especially for her, and since we'd had it she hadn't taken food up to her room once.

Unfortunately, encouraging her to unpack had not been so successful. Grace had started to leave a few things lying around her room, and she kept her school uniform in the wardrobe, as well as a few new items of clothing we'd bought for her, including a winter coat, but the big, grey suitcase still got regularly packed up with her toiletry bag, pyjamas, clean clothes and her cuddly swan. My heart tightened every time she did that, but at least Grace was progressing in the right direction and her bedroom was looking slightly more lived in. From time to time I gently reminded her that she was here to stay, and that it would be easier if she unpacked and put her things away.

'OK, I will,' she always said, but never followed this through.

'Jonathan and I met at a dance,' I told her, going back to what she'd been saying about how her mum and dad meeting in a club.

'Did you? Was it a disco?'

I laughed. 'Not really, no. I'm going back about twenty years, Grace. It was in the early seventies, when Jonathan and I were teenagers. It was just a village dance.'

'Can you dance, Angela?'

'Of course. I'm not the best, but I love to dance. That's the most important thing, isn't it?'

'Is it? My mum made loads of money dancing. She was really good at it. That's why me and Lily lived with Dad, because she, like, danced at night.'

'She danced at night?'

'Yes. She danced in special night clubs. She was a model too. Lily said Dad didn't like it. He was jealous.'

I made an innocuous comment about the fact lots of dancers had to work in the evenings. I hadn't forgotten Grace's reaction to the whisky and I was treading carefully, in case bad memories were being stirred up about her dad drinking when her mum wasn't there. At the same time, I wanted her to keep talking, if that was what she wanted, or needed, to do.

Grace sighed and took a glug of her apple juice. She had tipped the packet of raisins onto the kitchen table and was arranging them in the shape of a cross.

'Dad didn't like the club at all, but it was very famous. Mum's got a baseball cap with the name of it on. And a T-shirt, I think. She keeps the cap in her bedroom, on the end of the curtain pole. She was in newspapers too, because she was so famous and people liked to look at her pictures. She said she'll show me one day.'

Grace scrunched her face up, as if trying to remember something. Then she told me the name of the club where her parents met. I recognised it immediately. It was quite well known and I was pretty sure it used to be a strip club.

It was at this point that a thought struck me. I didn't know for sure, but I was beginning to wonder if the local paper had been interested in Colette, and possibly Linzi too, for reasons other than their spat about the jewellery. It had seemed quite an odd story for a paper to make such a fuss about, and I couldn't figure out why the women had gone to the papers instead of the police about the supposed jewellery theft. Now, perhaps, was it starting to make more sense? Jonathan speculated that when she was younger, Colette could have been something of a local celebrity because of her dancing and modelling. Maybe Linzi was too? It sounded feasible, from what Grace had said. We didn't have the Internet then, so we had no way of finding out more.

I noted down Grace's remarks for Social Services, just in case they needed to know. If all of this was in Colette's past it might not be relevant at all, but I felt it needed passing on. If Grace did start to have any kind of therapy, the more information we had about her family history, the better.

A couple of days later we bumped into Briony and Jill again on the walk to school. 'Which book did you bring?' I heard Briony say.

Grace looked nonplussed. 'Book? What, just my reading book.'

'No, silly! What book for that, you know, that thingie?'

'What thingie?'

'You know, we had to bring our favourite book from home, or a poem. I've got *Black Beauty*. My nana bought it for me.'

Grace had clearly forgotten all about this.

'Angela, have we got time to go home? Angela, have we? Angela, Angela?'

I explained that we didn't. Grace would be late, and she would just have to tell the teacher she had forgotten to bring a book from home. This may sound a bit harsh, but I'd learned from experience that chasing home to collect forgotten things was no help to the children in the long run. They only learn from their mistakes when there are natural consequences. My ankle was still a bit sore in any case, and it would have been impossible for us to make the dash back home and arrive at school before the end of registration.

Grace huffed and puffed a bit, but thankfully she didn't nag and accepted what I said. She also admitted she didn't know which book to choose anyhow and said she would get one from the school library.

'That's a very good idea, Grace.'

She skipped off in front with Briony.

I turned to talk to Jill and found her giving me a very strange look.

'Is everything OK?' I asked.

I wondered if she thought I'd been too hard on Grace; lots of parents I've known would have raced back to fetch the book, even at great inconvenience to themselves.

'Er, yes. She called you Angela. Grace. She called you Angela. I didn't realise you weren't her mum.'

Jill looked quite worried. I realised that even though we'd met on several occasions by now, Jill clearly hadn't heard Grace call me Angela before. I had assumed she knew I was a foster carer, though I hadn't really considered this either way, as why should I? It was no secret that Jonathan and I were carers. All the neighbours who came into the shop and congregated on the playing field at the back when their kids were playing out knew that different foster kids came and went. That said, because I only ever offered information if people asked direct questions, and I always take the lead from the child when it comes to what they want to tell people, it wasn't that big a surprise to me that Jill didn't realise Grace was fostered. It was clearly a surprise to her, though. Or should I say, it was a shock.

'Oh, didn't you?' I said. 'Yes, Jonathan and I have been fostering children for many years.' I felt my hackles rising, because Jill was now regarding me with a mixture of suspicion and anger.

'No, I didn't. Why didn't you tell me?'

She said this in an uncharacteristically rude way, a scowl forming on her face.

I politely told her that it wasn't the done thing to go around volunteering information about a foster child's private life.

'I don't think that's fair,' she blurted out. Her arms were folded in front of her chest now, and she was looking me straight in the eye.

'Oh,' I said calmly. 'I'm not sure I follow you.'

I carried on walking and looking ahead, my eyes on Grace. Jill followed my gaze; the girls had their heads together and were giggling about something. Jill gulped and girded herself to go on.

'What I mean is, I have the right to know. If she's going to be Briony's friend, I need to know.'

'Know what?'

'What's wrong with her.'

Jill delivered this statement emphatically. I could barely believe my ears.

'I beg your pardon?'

I'd come across attitudes like this before, but never from a mother at school like this, and never so blatantly. It took my breath away, and I almost felt embarrassed for Jill for being so ill-informed.

'Well?' Jill said. She softened slightly now; I think she could see how startled and unimpressed I was. 'I don't want to upset you or anything, but I just need to know. I have to look out for Briony. I'm sure you understand.'

I sighed and tried hard to keep my patience. I wanted to hide my annoyance and hoped my facial expression didn't give me away, but I'm not sure I succeeded as I still needed to work hard on this.

'Jill,' I said, 'there is nothing "wrong" with Grace. Children are placed in care because their parents cannot look after them, for any number of reasons.'

I could have said a lot more, but this seemed to be enough to get through to Jill.

'I'm sorry,' she spluttered. 'I just thought, well, you know?'

I didn't plug the gap in the conversation; I just looked at her questioningly.

'You hear all these stories in the papers about kids in care, don't you? Delinquents and tearaways and, I'm sorry to say it, but they've all been damaged, haven't they? Most of them, I mean.'

'That can be the case,' I said, 'which means they need as much love, care and understanding as every other child, if not more. They are all unique and you can't tar them all with the same brush. Don't worry Jill, I know it's hard for people with no experience of fostering to understand all this. Kids in care are often misunderstood. I'm glad we've cleared this up.'

I remained calm and was reasonable for Grace's benefit, though in that moment I could cheerfully have torn a strip off Jill.

'Of course,' she said, looking slightly abashed. 'But can I just ask one thing?' She didn't wait for me to answer before she ploughed on. 'What's the reason she's not with her parents? It would be helpful to know . . .'

'I'm sorry, Jill. I'd never talk about that.' I kept my tone pleasant and put a confident smile on my face; I always find that helps when delivering an answer someone doesn't want to hear.

'Oh,' she said, looking flummoxed. 'OK.' She rushed ahead without saying another word, and I watched as she led Briony away from Grace.

15

'You look so full of life'

'Mrs Hart, can I have a word please?'

It was Grace's teacher, Mrs Lacey.

'Yes, of course. Shall we both come in?'

I'd just collected Grace from outside her classroom door and the teacher had beckoned me over.

'Yes, please do.'

It was the night Grace went disco dancing and it was always a rush to get her home and changed and back to school for five. I hoped this wasn't going to take too long.

'Grace, would you mind taking these folders down to the office while we have a chat?'

Grace readily agreed. She was a very willing child, and she never really questioned it when she was asked to do chores. She started to run and Mrs Lacey reminded her to walk along the corridor.

'Is everything OK?'

'Yes and no. Grace is a clever girl. In many ways she is ahead of her peers. Her reading and writing skills are very good, she is enthusiastic and readily grasps new concepts, but she's let down by her lack of organisation. She's a chatterer, too, and is easily distracted by others. I feel we could get so much more out of Grace if she concentrated more and was more disciplined about doing homework on time, bringing in the right equipment and books, and generally having a tidier mind.'

I listened very carefully. I was impressed with Mrs Lacey. I felt she'd got to know Grace very well in a short space of time, and the description she gave resonated with me. I liked the fact she had talked about Grace's good points too, and her potential. I told her I'd picked up on similar issues at home, and that the problems she mentioned had been flagged up in the past.

'I wasn't aware she hadn't been doing homework on time or bringing in the right books and equipment,' I said, explaining that I always checked with Grace what she had to do.

'That fits,' Mrs Lacey said. 'I believe her when she says she forgot, or that she thought it was due in the next day. She is a very willing pupil and I don't think she's avoiding homework on purpose. I can see that she gets frustrated when she forgets things.'

'All of this sounds very familiar,' I said. I told Mrs Lacey Jonathan and I had discussed whether Grace should be assessed by an expert but she said we should hold fire and see how she responded to some extra help and support first. This seemed wise; it was not yet half term and Grace was still finding her feet.

I asked Mrs Lacey what more we could do at home to support Grace. Like all her fellow Year 6 pupils, Grace had a basic school planner that she was expected to fill in herself, noting down what work needed to be done and when. There was space for notes about important dates, when she needed to bring in her PE kit and so on. I regularly checked the planner but Grace had been writing things down on the wrong day, or forgetting to note them down at all. I discovered she had been given several slips and letters for me, including one about a school trip, but had failed to pass them on.

Mrs Lacey agreed to give Grace extra reminders and to provide me with a copy of her timetable, the basic homework timetable (even though this often changed according to what had been done in class) and the school events diary so I could help keep Grace on track. We both recognised that it would be wrong to intervene any more. The whole point of keeping a planner in Year 6 was to help prepare the child for secondary school and, ultimately, we needed to help Grace to help herself.

'How's she getting on with the other children?' I asked.

'Fantastically,' Mrs Lacey said. 'She's very popular. She seems to have formed a lot of friends already, and she has a smile for everybody, adults included.'

I'd witnessed how Grace not only interacted well with the other kids but said hello to mums in the playground who worked as dinner ladies and classroom assistants too. She was also the kid who always had a bit of banter with the lollipop lady up the road.

'Here she comes! How are you today young lady?' Beryl would grin.

'Good, thank you Beryl! How are you?'

'All the better for seeing you!'

Though I'd seen it for myself, it was great to hear from Mrs Lacey that Grace was such a sociable child. I thanked the teacher for her time and left the classroom feeling positive and well supported by the school.

Unfortunately, there was one fly in the ointment, on the social side of things. Jill now avoided me on the school run and, if we did happen to cross paths, she swooped in with some excuse or other, chivvying Briony along. It pained me on Grace's behalf to see this, but luckily she didn't seem to notice this was happening. There was so much going in those early weeks of school that I don't think she gave it a second thought. She was living in the moment, and she always seemed to find someone else to chat to on the walk to school.

For my part, I had never been 'in' with any school cliques. This was inevitable, I suppose, given that I looked after children who went to various different schools and often came and went within a school year, or after a very short time. I was friendly enough and was always polite to other parents in the playground, and I had a couple of foster carer friends who I knew from support groups and got on well with, but on the whole I didn't loiter for longer than I needed to at the school gate. I liked it this way. In the circumstances, losing Jill as an acquaintance was no great loss to me. Grace was the priority, and as long as she and Briony were allowed to continue their friendship at school and disco dancing without any interference from Jill, as presumably they would be able to, then that would have to do.

Happily, despite being in separate forms, I gathered that the girls did often play together on their breaks and they had a few friends in common. I gave Jill credit for this; even though the fact Grace was a foster child had clearly bothered her, at least she hadn't poisoned her daughter's mind against Grace.

'When's Briony coming for tea?' Grace asked one morning. 'We've been waiting *ages*!' The girls were still partners in the disco dance club, which I was pleased about, but even so I didn't imagine Jill was going to let her daughter come to our house, and I assumed she wouldn't be inviting Grace to theirs any time soon.

'I'm not sure, sweetheart. I'll talk to Jill.'

I said this before I'd thought about it, but what was the alternative? I couldn't ask Grace to talk to Briony herself; that wasn't fair. And I couldn't tell Grace it wasn't happening now, because I was still willing to have Briony over, if Jill was. Maybe she'd be OK now she'd got over the initial shock?

I took the bull by the horns when I saw Jill in the school car park after the dance club one evening. Grace was already strapped into the back seat of my car, and I asked her to give me a minute as I walked over to Jill's car, just a few metres away. I hadn't spoken to her since the conversation about Grace being in care.

'Jill,' I said, 'can I have a word?'

She was leaning into the boot and didn't turn around, even though I was sure she'd heard me. I'd seen her put Briony's bag in and it looked to me like she was now making a meal of rearranging the contents of the boot. I walked up behind her.

'Jill?'

She turned around and jumped in an overly dramatic way.

'Oh! Sorry, I didn't hear you!' she said, blushing and looking nervous. I didn't believe her for one moment.

'It's OK. You did have your head in the boot! Listen, Grace has asked me if it's still OK for Briony to come to tea.'

'Has she?'

'Yes.'

'Er, I'm not sure. We're very busy. We've got my in-laws staying and there's a lot going on. Can I get back to you?'

'Of course.'

I walked away with a heavy heart. I was so disappointed and upset with Jill. Not only was she prejudiced against a young girl who was in care, but she didn't have the guts to face me, or the truth.

I knew exactly how this was going to play out. Poor Grace would keep asking and I'd have to say I was waiting for Jill. We'd just have to sit this one out and see what happened.

For the harvest festival, Grace was joining a select group of children from the choir to visit the old folks' homes in the area, delivering hampers and singing two songs celebrating the harvest. That morning she tied her hair up in two high bunches that looked like pom-poms on top of her head and fixed each one with a pretty sunflower hair bobble. She looked fantastic.

'Grace!' I said. 'The old folk are going to be thrilled to bits to see you and hear you sing.'

'Do you think so? Do you, Angela?'

'Of course. You look so full of life. Just perfect!'

This was true. Since she moved in with us, Grace had gained some weight and was now a very healthy size. Her hair was shinier than ever, her skin was glowing and she appeared more self-confident.

'Thanks. You know what, when I lived with my dad I didn't have enough to eat. I'm so happy to give food to the poor! Harvest festival is cool.'

Grace was looking in the mirror in the hall when she said this.

'You didn't?'

'No. I wish someone would take hampers to children who don't have enough to eat. Why is it just for the old folk? I would do that, I would. I'd sing to them too, so they weren't frightened.'

'That's lovely, Grace. You're a very kind girl.'

Her face suddenly contorted into a frown.

'When am I going home?'

'For a visit?'

'Yes. Duh! I know I'm not moving home until I've finished primary school.'

I gently reminded her that this was not something that had been decided, and the chances were she would be staying with us for longer, which we hoped she would. Even though Colette had made remarks to Grace about her going home when she went to secondary school, that was not the plan, and I didn't believe it was what Colette really wanted in any case, not while Grace was still so young. Social Services wanted and expected her to stay on with us, and Jonathan and I were totally on board with this. Grace was making such good progress, and everybody wanted this to continue.

'We love having you here, Grace. I hope you'll stay. Anyhow, shall we call your mum tonight and see if we can fix up your next visit?'

'Yes, yes, yes!'

Colette had not been exactly forthcoming with dates for Grace's next home visit and it was time to put this right. They had spoken two or three times on the phone, but the conversations were generally short and Grace was unchar-acteristically quiet during the calls, and afterwards.

'How was that?' I'd ask.

'Great!' she'd say enthusiastically, but I was never sure this was her genuine reaction.

We decided that Grace would call her mum after dinner that night, and she could tell her all about the harvest festival.

Grace was full of beans as she burst out of the playground following her afternoon at the old folks' home. She couldn't wait to tell me all about her day. The local paper had been along and taken photos of the residents with their hampers. One old lady was also called Grace, she told me.

'They loved the harvest song. I want to do it all over again!'

Just as we were about to leave the school grounds, one of the part-time teaching assistants from Grace's class came rushing over to me.

'Mrs Hart, glad I've caught you! I've been trying to catch you all week.'

Mrs Blythe was a middle-aged woman who had worked at the school for many years. She was quite matronly and old-fashioned and I knew she had a reputation for sometimes talking out of turn. This stemmed from the fact that one time she'd discussed a statemented child's reading levels with another parent and was reported to the head. To be honest, it had sounded to me like the whole thing had been blown out of all proportion. I didn't know Mrs Blythe well, but in my experience she was always well-meaning and caring.

'Oh, hello. I've just been hearing all about the harvest festival. It sounds like it was a big success.'

'Yes, yes. It really was. Now then, I just need to ask you something about the school trip.'

After various shenanigans with Grace forgetting to bring home letters and permission slips, and then Social Services having to get involved to give the green light for her to go away with the school, everything was finally booked. Year 6 was going camping in their last term. This was a long way off, but Social Services agreed that we should go ahead and book it in the hope and expectation that Grace would still be with us. Colette had not raised any objections and Grace was now really looking forward to her first camping holiday.

We had a payment booklet and had made the first instalment, and Grace kept this in a safe place on her dressing table.

'No problem, what is it?' I asked Mrs Blythe.

'Can I ask you to fill in this form?'

She thrust a piece of paper at me and explained she needed health details from all the pupils, and that Grace had failed to bring hers back by the deadline.

'Oh, I'm sorry. I'll do it as quickly as possible. Grace, do you remember having one of these?'

'What? No, what is it?'

'A health form for the school trip.'

'Oh, no.'

Grace's attention had waned. She had a habit of dashing out of school full of energy, but her ability to focus or concentrate rapidly drained and she would hit the wall, becoming suddenly tired and uncommunicative. Once we got home and she'd recharged her batteries with a drink and a snack her energy levels would typically soar again, and she'd be off pogo-ing or running around the garden or the playing field.

'Sorry, Mrs Blythe. I'll have a look at it tonight, will that be OK?'

'Yes, thank you, Mrs Hart. I need it by tomorrow. I imagine she might be one of the ones we need to keep an eye on.' Mrs Blythe said this in a patronising voice and alarm bells started ringing in my head. I was grateful that Grace had wandered off to kick a stray ball at the wall.

'Why do you say that, Mrs Blythe?'

'Grace is in care, isn't she? I imagine there are a few things we need to know about.' Mrs Blythe gave me a sanctimonious look. 'Night terrors? Nits and worms, that sort of thing? We'll need every child to be free of nasties. Does she wet the bed?'

'No!' I cut in sharply, desperate to silence Mrs Blythe in front of other kids and parents who were milling around. Anyone could be listening. This was such an inappropriate place to have this conversation, and so uncalled for. I was outraged and could feel my blood rising. I was still trying to come to terms with the way Jill had behaved once she discovered Grace was in care. But surely Mrs Blythe knew better, after all her years in this job?

'I don't believe there are things you need to know about,' I said forcefully. 'Grace is in excellent health.' I folded the form up and put it in my bag. 'But like I said, I'll fill it in tonight. Thank you. Goodbye.'

Grace hadn't heard a thing, thank goodness. I was going to report this to the head by phone first thing the next day. I didn't want Mrs Blythe to make the same crass error of judgement with any other foster child, or to treat any child differently because they were in care.

After dinner that evening, Grace phoned home. Jonathan was passing through the hallway when she was speaking to her mum and he heard her talking excitedly about the choir and the harvest festival.

'When can I come home?'

There was a pause and Grace called out to Jonathan, who was just about to walk into the kitchen.

'Is Angela there? My mum wants to talk to her.'

'Sorry Grace, she's nipped upstairs. Shall I talk to your mum?'

'OK!'

Colette seemed taken aback that Jonathan, rather than me, was the one making the arrangements for the weekend visit. She said she'd call back when I was around but he insisted he could deal with it.

'I couldn't rely on my fella to make any arrangements!' she hooted. 'Not unless he was fixing up a night with the boys down the local!'

They agreed on a date and then Jonathan tried to make some small talk, as he thought Colette might like to hear a bit more about how Grace was getting on.

'Grace loved the harvest festival,' he said. 'And she's got such a lovely singing voice.'

'Is she behaving though?'

'Yes. She's doing really well.'

'Well, miracles do happen! Let's see how long that lasts. My neighbour fosters kids. Honeymoon period and all that? I hope it lasts, and I take my hat off to you.'

'We are enjoying having Grace living with us.'

'Yeah? Well that's good to hear. Look, I've gotta go now, sorry.'

'Shall I put Grace on to say goodbye?'

'No, no need. There's my doorbell. Lee? Cameron? Can you get that? Bleedin' hell! Sorry, I'll pick her up on the Saturday morning, ten for half ten. See you in a couple of weeks.'

The line went dead.

'Is Mum still there?' Grace asked.

Jonathan had to tell her that her mum had had to dash as there was somebody at the door.

'Who?'

'I don't know.'

'Didn't she say?'

'No, she didn't know.'

Graced sighed and ran upstairs.

'That just about sums it up,' Jonathan commented later. 'Poor Grace. Rarely gets to speak to her mum, and when she does, what does Colette do? Rushes off the phone.'

'It's such a shame,' I said. 'But I've been thinking. Grace has come on leaps and bounds since she's been here. Hopefully Colette will be pleasantly surprised when she sees her again. Things may start to improve between them, at long last.'

16

'It's not my fault!'

Grace was subdued when she returned from her weekend visit home, and very tired too. She told us she didn't go to bed until two in the morning and her mum and stepdad had gone out and left her stepbrothers in charge. Grace didn't want to talk about what the family did all weekend, and it took several weeks before she mentioned the visit again.

'Lily thinks she's my mum,' she said out of the blue one day. 'She bosses me about and tells me what to wear. She treats me like a baby.'

Grace went on to say that Lily had not only told her what to wear but she'd forced her to change into certain outfits. 'And, she put on a stupid voice, like she was pretending to be Mum.'

Grace put a hand on her hip, stuck out her chest and wagged her finger as she demonstrated how Lily behaved.

'Grace, you're a wind-up merchant! Grace, do you hear me? Grace, put this dress on, now! Or I'll get Lee to beat you up!'

It made me feel very uncomfortable to hear all this. I know a lot of big sisters like to mother their younger siblings, but it sounded like Lily was using her power over Grace to bully and belittle her. On top of that, she was using Lee as a threat to Grace, when she was clearly already very wary of him.

'You know why we can't have you living with us, don't you, little Gracie? Look at Mummy while I'm talking to you. It's because you're a naughty girl. Now do as I say, bad girl! Put this on! Put that on!'

In addition, Grace said that Lee had stolen her entire weekend bag almost as soon as she'd arrived. She had to hunt all over the house for it until she finally found it in his bedroom, thrown in the bottom of a cupboard.

'I used to think he was weird for taking my clothes. I mean, what does he want with them? Now I know he's just a bastard! He's just a wind-up. He doesn't even want them – he just wants to take them! I hate him!'

I thought about this long and hard as I wrote my notes for Social Services, and I discussed it with Jonathan at length. From what Grace said, it seemed Lee hadn't actually helped himself to any clothes this time; he'd just hidden the whole bag. I was questioning his motivation, while Grace thought she had all the answers.

'He just does it to torture me! He's a creep! He didn't even want my clothes! He just hid my bag to be a total bastard and to wind me up! And they say *I'm* the wind-up! It's a big, fat lie!'

Grace's language and her whole way of talking changed

whenever she went home, and I had to keep reminding her not to swear. Jonathan commented on how demoralising this was.

'It's like she takes one step forward when she's with us, and two steps backwards when she goes home.'

My mother noticed the change too. She came over for a Sunday lunch and was shocked to hear Grace displaying bad table manners and being impolite.

'Shall we play a board game?' Mum offered after lunch.

The other two girls were enthusiastic and pulled out our old Cluedo game.

'No, that game sucks. It's boring and I'm not in the mood,' Grace said, curling her lip rudely.

'She's like a different little girl,' my mum said to me quietly, looking puzzled. 'She's not herself at all. Has she fallen out with a friend, dear?'

We never gave Mum any personal information about the kids and she always seemed to be blissfully ignorant about the myriad of problems a child in care might be facing.

'I don't think so. She's just not in the mood. Sorry, Mum.'

Grace had a hula hoop and she went in the garden and played with it for ages, counting the number of times she could twirl it around her slim waist. I watched her from the kitchen window as I was washing up. She was spinning the hoop so furiously it was exhausting to watch. When she did pause, she stood in a trance-like state for about twenty seconds each time, staring into space.

'She's not right,' I said to Jonathan. 'She needs to talk to someone, sooner rather than later.'

By now Grace was on a waiting list to see a child psychologist. This had been arranged with the agreement of Social Services in response to various issues that had cropped up since Grace had moved in with us, and particularly the concerns we had raised about Lee.

'You're right. Let's chase up that appointment.'

I did this the very next day but was told there was an extremely long waiting list and Grace would simply have to wait for a letter to arrive in the post. It could be several months before an appointment was available.

In the meantime, Grace's teacher called me in again to discuss her forgetfulness and lack of concentration. Grace's problems seemed to have escalated after her visit home. In the space of about ten days she lost her pencil case and her PE kit, including a brand-new pair of trainers; she turned up for disco dancing without the correct leggings and leotard; she was in trouble for knocking a reception child off a chair when she was running in the lunch hall, and she completely forgot to do two important pieces of homework. In addition to this, she was lagging behind in maths. I volunteered to buy some extra books and work with Grace at home, as she was in the bottom group and the teacher thought she could do better.

Frustratingly, it was difficult to be sure whether Grace was underperforming because of her academic ability or because she had missed so much school due to her frequent moves between foster homes.

I continued to make a concerted effort to cut out as much sugary junk and processed food from Grace's diet as I could. She didn't seem to be allergic to any particular foods, it was more a case of noticing she became hyperactive and less focused when she had sugary snacks and drinks and highly processed foods. Conversely, she was calmer when she stuck to wholesome, home-cooked food. The food diary I'd kept helped me see this and, on the whole, I felt her diet was helping her moods. When she went home for the weekend, I'd mentioned to Colette that it would be helpful if she could stick to the same rules I followed, but Grace told me she had frozen pizza, microwave chips, cans of Coke and a stick of rock that weekend. She developed toothache soon afterwards and I took her to the dentist, where we discovered she'd pulled out a piece of a filling and had to have it replaced. The dentist asked her if she was cleaning her teeth twice a day, to which she replied, 'Yes, when I'm at Angela's.'

After the success I'd had at home, using wholesome foods and home-cooked recipes to help curb Grace's hyperactive behaviour, I started to read as much as I could about the other issues she had, namely the disorganisation, the lack of concentration and her forgetfulness. One day, in the fostering magazine I subscribed to, another carer had written a piece about a child who sounded quite similar to Grace. The carer described an exercise she'd asked this little boy to perform and how he had fared. I decided to ask Grace to do the same thing.

'Can you place the blue book on top of the red book and then place both books to the left of the green book?'

She tried three times before giving up, totally defeated, despite me repeating the instruction every time, as she asked me to.

'That's stupid!' she said, though I could tell she was more frustrated than annoyed. Try as she might, she simply couldn't get her head around this simple task.

I mentioned the exercise to Grace's teacher. 'Do you think the time has come for her to be assessed by an expert? Perhaps an educational psychologist? She's a clever girl but I'm convinced something is holding her back. I think it's something we need to get to the bottom of.'

As I'd done previously with the GP, and with the social workers, I recapped on all of Grace's symptoms and voiced my concerns that we might be missing something and she might need extra help.

Mrs Lacey listened carefully and agreed, and Grace's name went on another long waiting list.

In November, Grace spent another weekend at home. Jonathan and I were not looking forward to it, or at least to her return. True to form, she came back overtired, moody and angry with her siblings. This time, she was also critical of her mum, and of her stepdad Malcolm.

'They were drinking all the time,' she said. 'Dad . . .' her voice trailed off. 'Malcolm drinks whisky. I really hate whisky. It fuckin' well stinks! Do I have to go home for Christmas?'

'No, Grace, you don't have to go home for Christmas. It's up to you. Please try not to swear.'

'Grrr! Well, I want to stay here. It's nicer here.'

I was quite nervous about how this would go down with Colette, but when I mentioned it she didn't turn a hair. In fact, I got the distinct impression it was convenient to her not to have to make arrangements or put Grace up. She didn't make any mention of presents, and the whole of December came and went without Grace seeing her family. There was a brief phone call on Christmas Day, which Grace seemed grateful to get out of the way, and she didn't question the fact she had no gifts from her family.

By New Year, Grace was in a really good place. I'd go as far as to say she was better than she had been since she moved in. She was really looking forward to going back to school and her eleventh birthday was coming up. She'd asked for an ice-skating party, and we'd allowed her to invite several friends for a skate and a birthday tea at the ice rink in the next town. All the girls accepted straight away, and Grace was counting down the days. Happily, Grace limited the invitations to the girls in her form, which seemed to be the done thing at the school, and so there was no awkwardness about Briony. Inevitably, their promised play date had never happened. Grace had mentioned it a few times but she'd either forgotten or given up asking by this time. Both girls had made lots of other friends, but they still went dancing together and their friendship had become very casual and easy-going.

The same could not be said of Jill and me. She made a beeline in the opposite direction whenever she saw me, and I had not spoken to her since the day I saw her in the school car park and attempted to invite Briony for tea. I think her prejudice may well have been compounded by the fact she joined the Parent-Teacher Association and got in with a group of mums who organised all the school fetes, coffee mornings, fundraisers and so on. At the Christmas fair I'd spotted Jill manning the cake stall. Next to her was none other than Lena's mother, Shannon. I could only imagine the conversation the two of them had had. When I walked past they exchanged glances, tried to pretend they hadn't seen me and made a show of being suddenly locked in conversation.

I hadn't seen Shannon since the barbecue and had no idea Lena was a pupil at the same school, a couple of years below Grace. In normal circumstances, I'd have made a point of talking to her. Shannon had never phoned me after I asked my neighbour, Gail, to pass on my phone number, and I would have taken this opportunity to have a chat and draw a line under the whole unfortunate incident. I knew from Gail that Lena needed stitches but was fine. Nevertheless, I would have made the effort to speak to her mother, but instead I carried on walking, straight past the cake stall. Willing Christmas fair volunteers Jill and Shannon may have been, but it was very clear to see that the season of goodwill was not going to extend to me, or Grace.

During Grace's ice-skating party I managed to snatch a few minutes of peace and quiet to myself. Jonathan was on the ice, helping to supervise the girls, while I was in the cafe overlooking the rink, organising the cake and party bags. As I folded napkins and stuffed the bags I looked at Grace giggling with her friends. The other two girls we were fostering were with family members that day, which was a shame as all three girls had been getting on well lately. They were never going to be best buddies but the other girls had become more accepting of Grace and had wanted to spend time with her. I'd heard them having a few laughs together and it would have been nice for them to join in with the party. Grace and her friends were having lots of fun, skating to the beat of the disco music that was being played from giant speakers, and as I watched them I found myself smiling and thinking back over recent events.

Grace had settled into school very well after the Christmas holiday. We hadn't heard from Colette for weeks and Grace hadn't mentioned her mum or indeed any members of her family. I wasn't concerned about the lack of communication because, for the time being at least, this appeared to suit Grace. We'd had very few outbursts or episodes of sulking recently, and she seemed to be on a fairly even keel in terms of her moods and emotions.

I watched Grace pulling silly faces and making her friends laugh. It was obvious to me that her confidence and self-esteem had been steadily rising, and it was impossible not to notice this improvement had happened when she stopped visiting home.

Colette hadn't attended the last placement meeting we'd had, and it was left to Jonathan and me to share information with Barry and Jess and discuss plans going forward. I was in no rush to talk about arranging the next weekend contact visit when Grace appeared to be doing so well, and had not brought the subject up.

When Barry had asked Grace if she was happy living with us, she told him she 'definitely' was. My heart swelled when I heard that. I was so pleased that Grace was happy in our home. She had a questionnaire to fill in this time, which Barry had brought to the meeting at our house. It was a standard form, asking her various things about how she felt the placement was going, how happy she was at school and so on. Grace had boxes to tick and was positive about everything.

I felt proud of her as I thought about all the good news I'd shared with the social workers during that meeting. She had been working very hard on her maths at home and at school and had been moved into a higher set. All her predicted grades for the end of Year 6 had risen, which was excellent news, as these would be shared with whichever secondary school she went to in September. Grace had also joined the netball team and loved it. The only problem with her playing netball was that her trainers didn't last five minutes, as the soles seemed to come detached every time she wore them. I took two pairs back and complained before I realised that she would stand on one foot and twist it around continuously, causing the sole to detach! Anyhow, she enjoyed netball so much that she had even started talking about going to one particular secondary school in our area when she moved up next year, saying she liked the fact it had a very sporty reputation.

Watching her whizzing along on the ice, throwing herself into the skating so energetically as she did with all physical activities, I thought that Grace would be well suited to a school where sports were prioritised. In fact, being active and enjoying sports was incredibly important to Grace's overall wellbeing. She needed to be busy, and to have an outlet for all her energy.

I remembered how Barry had commented that it was a very good sign that Grace was talking about attending a secondary school in our catchment area, as it showed that she had accepted she was staying with us now and not moving back home any time soon, as that would not be happening for another eight or nine months.

I felt a little pang in my heart when I remembered the next thing Barry had said: 'By the way, I trust she's finally unpacked?'

He had said this with a big smile on his face, giving one of his friendly winks. Clearly, Barry didn't think for one minute that Grace would still be living out of her suitcase several months after moving in with us, but we had to tell him that unfortunately this was one mountain we still had to conquer. Grace continued to cling on to her old grey suitcase. I'd hear her zipping and unzipping it at night as she got ready for bed and my heart would ache. From time to time I'd nudge her to unpack it but despite always promising she would, she never did. As ever, I didn't push her. I hoped to goodness that she didn't think she was going to be uprooted again at a moment's notice and I reminded her frequently how much we loved having her living with us. Jonathan wondered if the suitcase had become something of a comfort blanket: after all, it had been her constant companion on her journey through care. We both hoped that was the truth, and that she wasn't living in an anxious state, constantly on alert and thinking she would be moved on to another foster home.

'Angela!' Grace called. She'd spotted me watching from the cafe and gave me a big wave as she skated by.

I waved back. She was flourishing, I thought, and she'd settled in so well. That suitcase would be unpacked soon, I was sure of it.

When Grace and her pals came off the ice to have the party tea, her clothes were soaked through.

'What happened?'

'I fell over a lot!'

It turned out that not only had she got herself wet, but both her knees were black and blue because she had clattered so hard into the walls of the rink whenever she wanted to stop.

'I think we need to teach you how to stop yourself without using your knees as brakes,' Jonathan teased.

'You can talk!' she retorted. 'You used your whole body as a brake!' This got a huge laugh, as it was true that Jonathan had taken several tumbles on the ice, much to the girls' amusement.

The party was a great success and Grace said she absolutely loved it and asked when we could go skating again. She went to bed earlier than normal that night and fell asleep almost immediately.

'I had the best party ever,' she told me when I went up to say goodnight.

'That's good, Grace. I'm so pleased. It was lovely to see you having such a great time.'

She screwed up her face and seemed to be trying to remember something. 'I've never had a birthday party like this before. Thank you, it was very kind of you.'

'You're very welcome, Grace. I had a great time too. It's wonderful to see you enjoying yourself.'

I felt very emotional when I left her that evening. This was the real Grace, I thought. She was a lovely person with a good heart. Sometimes those fundamental truths about her were obscured by so many other factors, such as her moodiness and hyperactivity. More than anything else, I wanted to keep bringing out the best in Grace, and to give her every chance to be the best she could be.

The following week, when Grace came to write her thank you cards, she had a complete brain fade and couldn't remember who had been at the party. She got about six names and had to look at the photographs to help her remember the other three girls. This was quite typical; I'd learned that visual aids and lists really helped Grace, as did piecing information into small, bite-sized chunks. It was so obvious that her brain worked in a different way to most people's. This knowledge, garnered simply from spending time with Grace, observing her and tuning in to her, was incredibly helpful. It meant I always stopped and thought about how she might see things, and how I could help her deal with situations in the best way. That said, having a diagnosis or a name for whatever it was that caused her brain to work differently was still something I felt was very important to pursue. We couldn't have too much information, that's how I saw it.

Incidentally, there was no card or present from any

member of Grace's family, and Colette didn't even call her on her birthday. Grace made no comment about this at all. When her mum phoned her a few days later Grace didn't mention the party, which I could understand. It was sad, but I felt she had no expectations and was therefore able to accept things the way she did.

Grace went home a few weeks later, in early February, having not seen her family since before Christmas. She didn't seem keen to go but didn't make a fuss, and afterwards she said very little about the visit, though she was moody and seemed irritated. I had the feeling that Grace had come to accept that visiting her family was something she had to get on with, rather like she'd had to accept the way her mum had ignored her birthday.

In late February, the first of Grace's appointments finally came through. She had three sessions with a child psychologist that seemed to go well. Jonathan and I dropped her off and collected her each time, and though she didn't discuss anything with us, she appeared to take the sessions in her stride. She was always calm afterwards and never seemed agitated. In fact, she didn't seem to dwell on what happened during the sessions at all.

'How was it?' we'd always ask.

'Fine. What's for tea? Is there netball practice tonight?'

'If there's something you'd like to talk to us about, you know you can ask us anything at all. Or you can talk to me, or to Jonathan, on your own.'

'I know. But it's fine. I'm fine! Can we go swimming at the weekend?'

We were never given any information about what was discussed or even what was concluded, though the fact the psychologist was happy to sign Grace off after three sessions gave us a good indication that there was nothing too serious to worry about; at least, that's what we hoped.

After her sessions with the child psychologist Grace seemed more relaxed and had a new sort of lightness about her that was very satisfying to see. For the most part it was really good to be around her. She still had mood swings and bad days – we had a particularly terrible trip to the park when she refused to walk with us and nearly ran in front of a car – but the negatives were outweighed by sunny moods and good days. Though I certainly didn't want her to lose touch with her family, it was still apparent to me that the more distance she had from them, and the longer the gap between visits, the better Grace behaved and the happier she seemed in herself.

When her second set of appointments came through and Grace saw the educational psychologist, things improved even more. After attending several appointments on her own, Jonathan and I were summoned from the small waiting room to the consulting room upstairs. I'll never forget that day. Grace was sitting on a wooden chair in a very small, old-fashioned room. There was a tiny, metal-framed window looking over rooftops at the far side of the town. The room was slightly chilly and dimly lit, and there was a musty smell in the air.

In the midst of this rather uninviting scene, there was

Grace, positively beaming. She had the biggest grin on her face I'd ever seen and her eyes were shining.

'I believe Grace has ADHD,' the young female psychologist told us.

'I see. I've never heard of it.'

It seems unbelievable that there was ever a time when I hadn't heard of ADHD – we've since looked after many children with attention deficit hyperactivity disorder. But as I said earlier, this was more than twenty years ago and most people had never heard of it. The psychologist patiently explained that ADHD was a behavioural disorder that included symptoms such as hyperactivity and inattentiveness. She talked about fidgeting, difficulty sitting still, running everywhere, climbing, talking too much and being moody or temperamental. Forgetfulness and clumsiness were also common symptoms, she said. We recognised all the symptoms she talked about and it came as a very welcome relief to know this disorder had a name, and that we were no longer in the dark, muddling through it alone as we had been doing for many months.

Jonathan and I looked at Grace and instinctively found ourselves smiling too.

'So I'm not a wind-up merchant. See! I have a thing. I have this . . . thing! What's it called?'

'ADHD,' the psychologist reiterated.

Grace looked liberated; I can't think of a better way to describe it. She looked like she'd just walked out of jail or cast off shackles. She had a 'thing'. It had a name. She was not the deliberately disruptive, aggravating child she had been accused of being so many times. She had ADHD, and it affected the way she behaved.

'What can we do to help her?' I asked. Not knowing anything about ADHD, I had no idea what to expect in terms of medication, therapy or anything else.

The psychologist talked about how Grace could use lists and create visual reminders to help with forgetfulness, as we'd already started to do. She also talked about maintaining a healthy, natural diet and using exercise to burn off her energy. Regular sleep was also important, to help boost concentration and to generally improve Grace's mood. No medication was offered; I'm not sure anything was available back then and, in any case, the psychologist was confident Grace could manage her symptoms naturally.

'It sounds like you're already on the case,' she said. 'It really is a question of more of the same.'

I wanted to ask about the background to ADHD. Was it something you were born with, or did environmental factors play a part in how it developed? We'd seen for ourselves how Grace's symptoms worsened when she went home for the weekend. The change in diet, lack of exercise – she had often reported that the family 'just stayed in and watched telly' – plus the late nights and sleep deprivation clearly had an adverse effect on her mood.

The session was nearly over though, and the psychologist seemed keen to call in her next patient. She got to her feet and held out her hand to shake.

'Goodbye Grace, and good luck. It's been lovely meeting

you.' The psychologist said something about writing up her final report and sending a copy to Social Services.

'So that's it?' I asked. I was surprised at how swiftly the session had ended, and that the psychologist wasn't going to see Grace again.

'Grace really doesn't need to see you again?' Jonathan said.

'No, not at all,' the psychologist replied kindly. 'As I said, this can all be managed at home and you are already doing well. I wish you all the best of luck. Are you happy, Grace?'

'Yes!' she said. 'Very happy!'

In many respects, nothing had changed. We simply needed to continue doing more of what we'd already started. Having a professional give us this diagnosis meant we felt more confident about what we were doing, but there were no dramatic changes to be made in the day-to-day way we managed Grace, and she would not be prescribed medication, or be statemented. Despite this, it felt like *everything* had changed.

When we walked outside the sun was shining and Grace punched the air. I thought to myself that it looked like she had grown that day. Her head was held high and she looked like she was walking on air.

'I can't wait to tell everyone!' I'm not sure exactly who she was talking about, but I imagine she wanted to let her mum and the rest of the family know that she had a 'thing' called ADHD and that she was therefore not the deliberate troublemaker she had been made out to be.

I had so many questions and wished I had more

answers. In my mind the journey was far from over, it had simply taken a new turn. I wanted to start researching ADHD in order to help Grace in every way possible, but right now it was time to focus on Grace's overwhelmingly positive reaction to this news. She was no longer the misunderstood little girl she had been for so many years. I realised she must have carried around so much confusion before this diagnosis, knowing that she wasn't aggravating people or being scatty on purpose yet not recognising her symptoms or understanding how to deal with them.

After the appointment we went for a bite to eat in town, choosing a small cafe that specialised in homemade sandwiches, scones and fresh juices. We all had a very simple meal, but I remember it as if it were a slap-up celebration in a fancy restaurant. The atmosphere was fantastic because Grace was on cloud nine, and Jonathan and I were buoyed by her joy and optimism.

Later that day, I asked Grace to bring the washing in while I put the shopping away, as showers were forecast. She ran to put her trainers on and then I watched as she got to the back door and stopped dead. She stared into space and then turned to look at me.

'What is it?'

I'd seen her do things like this before, but normally she gave no explanation or looked embarrassed.

'Oh,' she said, scrunching up her little face. 'I can't remember what you asked me to do!'

'I asked you to bring in the washing, because it might rain.'

'Oh yeah! OK!' She shot out, then ran back for the peg basket she'd forgotten to take with her. 'Washing. Yes. I'll bring it in!'

Grace's life improved in leaps and bounds. She hadn't been given a magic cure, of course, but by understanding that she had something called ADHD she might just as well have been.

'I'm different,' she'd say when she got muddled. 'It's not my fault!'

Colette was informed about the diagnosis and I really hoped it would be an eye-opener to her, and that she would be more understanding of Grace's behaviour. Only time would tell.

I started to read anything and everything I could get my hands on, which wasn't a great deal in those days. I relied on library books and borrowing the odd article or cutting from other carers at our support group. Gradually, I started to pick up useful tips and helped to put as many aides-memoires in place as I could. For example, we had Grace's timetable printed out in triplicate and pinned it on the kitchen noticeboard and a corkboard in her bedroom, and also made sure she kept a copy in her book bag.

We had a list inside every bag she used for sports so she could check she had the correct kit. There was a chart on her wall for homework, a chalkboard and a new calendar she could use to jot down notes, important dates and reminders. Of course, I made sure the school was informed of the diagnosis, and while this would not mean she would get any extra help in the classroom or be statemented, at least the teachers might understand her better. Having said that, at the time ADHD was new to the teachers as well.

We encouraged Grace to keep up her dancing and netball and made sure we got out for long walks and bike rides whenever we could. She also joined the swimming club at the same pool where she had her lessons. Grace was a very good swimmer and had mastered the front crawl like a natural, and very quickly too. Of course, I carried on making sure she ate as healthily and naturally as possible, and it became second nature to me to read food packaging and avoid artificial additives when I did the shopping.

On Mother's Day I woke up to a wonderful surprise. Grace had made me a beautiful card with a picture of a vase of tulips on the front. In it she wrote, 'To my foster mum Angela. You're the best! Lots and lots of love from Grace. XX' She brought me a cup of tea and told me she had a present for me too, but that she hadn't wrapped it up yet.

'How exciting,' I said. 'I can't wait.'

After breakfast I went up to the children's bathroom to make sure it was clean and tidy. Grace shot out of her bedroom when she heard me on the landing. 'It's ready!' she said before dashing back into her room and slamming the door shut behind her. *Typical Grace*, I thought. *She's such a ball of energy.*

'Here it is!' she said finally, emerging from her bedroom once more. She was fizzing with anticipation as she handed me a small, neatly wrapped box with a pink bow on top. I untied the bow – it was one I recognised from our shop! – and peeled back the paper. She'd used a lot of Sellotape and the paper ended up in tiny pieces.

'Turkish delight! My favourite. Thank you Grace, that's so kind and thoughtful.'

I was very touched. I hadn't expected to receive anything for Mother's Day. I put the box on the windowsill for safe keeping, as I still had jobs to do upstairs, and I scrunched the torn paper into a ball.

'Can I pop this in your wastepaper basket? I'll be emptying all the bins shortly.'

Normally Grace had no problem about me going into her room, but a worried look flashed over her face as I took a step towards the door. I wondered if I'd offended her by making such a mess of the wrapping paper, or if there had been a gift tag I'd missed.

'No!' she blurted out. She seemed to have suddenly lost her composure and her voice was strained and unnatural. 'I mean, yes. I can take it. Give it to me. Give it to me, Angela!'

Grace had flushed bright red and I noticed her eyes were flitting everywhere. This was a habit she had when she was feeling hyper or stressed and probably needed to burn off some energy. She thrust her hand out.

'Give it to me!' she repeated. 'I'll take it.'

'It's OK, I can do it. I need to empty the bin in any case.'

'I'll get it,' she insisted. 'Stay there.' She said this quite desperately.

'Is something wrong, Grace?'

'No. Why should there be?'

My instincts were telling me I needed to go into Grace's bedroom. She was uncharacteristically uneasy and embarrassed; something wasn't right. I do try to respect each child's privacy as much as possible, but Grace had shifted herself backwards in an attempt to physically block the doorway now, which made me even more suspicious.

'No, Grace, I don't see what the problem is. Let me in, please.'

'No. I'm, er, in the middle of something,' she panicked. 'You can't go in. Angela, no, you can't go in.'

'Grace?' I fixed her with a look that told her I knew she was up to something, and she moved out of my way, very reluctantly. She was breathing heavily now, and there was a sheen of sweat on her brow. I pushed open her bedroom door and took a sharp intake of breath.

'Grace!' I gasped. 'I, I can't believe it! What's *happened*?'

Grace stood wide-eyed and speechless. I tried very hard not to cry.

17

'She doesn't care!'

'I'm sorry, Angela. I'm really sorry. You weren't meant to see this.'

I really couldn't believe my eyes and my heart rate went through the roof. Grace's bedroom looked like it had been ransacked by an extremely messy band of burglars. The dressing table was piled high with knick-knacks, books, jewellery, hairbrushes, flannels, hairbands and various items of stationery. The clutter was covering every inch of the shiny glass top. Clothes were strewn across the carpet. T-shirts, jumpers, leggings and jeans were jumbled up together in untidy piles. Drawers hung open, stuffed with underwear. Dresses, skirts and flip-flops were in a heap on the rug. The wardrobe doors were bulging, clothes and toys hanging out of them. The bed was stacked with magazines, a skipping rope, CDs, puzzle books, more books, a collection of toiletry bags, pencil cases, cuddly toys and a portable radio and CD player.

Dumbstruck, I tried to step further into the room but

there was nowhere to put my feet. The entire room looked like a scene from a car boot sale.

'What on earth . . .' I felt panicked, not understanding what had gone on. Grace's room was always so neat and tidy because of the way she packed her things away in her suitcase every day. Even when she accumulated more belongings she would stuff them in bags and boxes and somehow managed to keep the room looking more like a hotel room than a young girl's bedroom.

'It was meant to be done first, before you saw it. I'll tidy it all up, I promise. I'm sorry.'

'It's OK, Grace,' I said, the penny slowly dropping.

My eyes darted to the top of the wardrobe, and then to the back of the room. There was Grace's big suitcase, standing by the wall. When I saw it I felt as if stress streamed out of my body. The zip of Grace's old, grey suitcase was unfastened and one side was flapping open, revealing nothing but the faded satin lining of the case. The rest of her large assortment of bags, holdalls and boxes were also strewn at the back of the room, and they were empty too.

I feasted my eyes on the hollow shell of the suitcase for a moment before looking at Grace's pillow. There was her cuddly swan, sitting on top of a dressing gown and a mish-mash of pyjamas, as if presiding over this grand event.

'I'll tidy up, I'm sorry. I was going to do it and then I started wrapping up your present and . . . please don't cry. I'm sorry.'

'Grace,' I said, hastily trying to compose myself as I helped myself to a tissue from a crumpled box on the floor. 'I'm not angry or upset.' I took a deep breath and dabbed my eyes; I hadn't been able to stop a few tears from escaping.

'What?' She looked totally confused.

'Grace. I'm just so pleased that you've finally unpacked.'

'What? You're crazy, Angela!' she laughed. 'It's no big deal. I thought you were mad at me for all this mess.'

'No, Grace. You've finally unpacked! I'm so pleased. After all this time, I'm so pleased.'

It had been eight months. I'd wished every day that Grace would stop her heartbreaking routine of repacking her suitcase and all her belongings, as if she were afraid she'd have to move out any moment. Finally, she'd done it. I had a smile stretching from ear to ear.

'What shall I do with it?' she said.

I followed her gaze. 'Oh, your suitcase. It can go on top of the wardrobe, up there, if you like? If you still want to keep it in your room, that is.' I said this instinctively, as it occurred to me that it might be better for Grace if she didn't have the case on show. After all, it was a visible reminder of the many moves she'd made between foster homes.

'Yeah, it can go up there.'

'OK, I'll put it up for you. But first, you're going to have to find a home for everything. As it is, I can't get to the back of the room with all this stuff on the floor!'

'I know. I didn't want you to see it like this, especially not on Mother's Day! I thought you'd be really annoyed with me. I'll tidy up, honest. I had no idea I had so much stuff.'

She beamed at me and I told her again how pleased I was that she was finally making the bedroom her own.

'Do you need some help?'

'I might do, but I'll have a go myself. Thanks, Angela. You're the best!'

When I walked out of Grace's room I felt like I was floating on air. This was such a momentous day and I felt buoyed with optimism. The sun was shining, spring flowers were starting to bloom and I felt all was well in the world. I truly had a sense that Grace was going to keep soaring and leave the troubles of her past behind.

I'm happy to say she seemed even more settled and content from that day on. The fact her ADHD had been officially identified undoubtedly helped. Grace was never afraid to ask for extra support or discuss the fact she had forgotten something or was having difficulty focusing, as she had done in the past. The result was that her confidence grew even more, and she was thriving.

At Easter Grace joined a musical theatre company and thoroughly enjoyed combining her talents for singing and dancing. Before her first show had finished its short run she was already talking about auditioning for the next. Her weekly schedule would have been exhausting for many young girls, but she thrived on it and loved being busy every night of the week. The noticeboard in her bedroom was a maze of ever-changing reminders:

Red tights! Don't forget script 4 Friday. **New goggles??** ~~Paula – lift after school~~. Bicarb of soda – cookery **Tue**. **MEET MRS RIVERS 3.15 THURS!!!**

'Can you help me, Angela? Can you watch me? Can you sew this on to here? Can you teach me how to do that?'

Grace never stopped, but she was happy that way. I loved watching her perform and she made even more friends through the theatre group. There was never one best friend; everybody liked Grace and she got invited to all the parties, as well as to treats and events when a child was only allowed to invite one or two friends.

At the end of the netball season she won the players' player of the year award, which she was genuinely surprised about and proud of. I can remember Jonathan commenting that her exuberance and enthusiasm seemed to rub off on other people. My mum often made similar observations. 'She lights up a room,' she said more than once. 'What a lovely gift to have.'

Grace volunteered to wear a cuddly bear costume around the streets to promote her latest show, which the theatre group was putting on at the main playhouse.

'You're brave in this warm weather,' I smiled. It was May, and the weather was great.

'It's all for a good cause, Angela!'

The theatre was donating part of its profits to charity and Grace was keen to sell as many tickets as possible. Several adults supervised Grace and her friends and I offered to carry one of the collecting tins. I must admit, after a couple of hours of tramping around the town my feet were killing me and I was longing for a sit down and a cold drink! Most of the others in the group had had enough too, but Grace's enthusiasm and energy never waned. She was relentless, approaching everybody she possibly could, engaging members of the public of all ages in chatter, making them laugh and effortlessly charming money from their purses in exchange for tickets.

'Aren't you tired? Aren't you hot? Don't you need a break?' The adults, and some of the other youngsters, took it in turns to ask her these questions.

'No! Why stop now? We're on a roll! Onwards and upwards!' She marched on while the rest of us smiled at her pluck and joie de vivre and continued to support her until the shops closed and the town emptied out.

Colette had stopped attending the regular placement meetings we had with social workers and she no longer shared lifts with Barry when Grace made her visits home. This meant I had not seen her for a long time. There were some occasions when I felt it would have really pleased Grace if her mum had put in an appearance, such as when she was in a show or a swimming competition, but Colette never came to anything, even when I knew Grace had mentioned a particular event and invited her along. 'You can come if you want,' I'd hear her saying on the phone. It seemed a shame her mum never took her up on any of these offers, but that was the way it was. Grace never complained about this, though slowly but surely I noticed that she stopped mentioning such things on the phone.

It felt to me like Colette had drawn a line in the sand. She saw Grace on her contact visits to the family home – there had been two more, about six weeks apart, since her visit in

February – and that was it. There had been no further mention of Grace moving back in; that topic seemed to have been long forgotten. As for whether Grace's ADHD diagnosis had a positive impact on how her mother treated her, unfortunately I didn't see or hear any evidence of this. Barry had been the one to share the news with Colette, and her reaction had been to say, 'See! I knew she wasn't right!' This upset me. I'd hoped the diagnosis would soften Colette's attitude to Grace but it seemed the opposite had happened, and she had used Grace's ADHD as ammunition, to prove she had been right all along about her daughter's difficult behaviour.

At the end of May, Barry mentioned to Grace that they needed to arrange her next home visit for early June, but she complained bitterly. She knew that the aim was for her to have a contact visit with her family approximately every six weeks and we'd achieved this over the past few months, but Grace was having none of it this time. Barry had to really coax Grace in order to get a date in the diary.

'But it's Paula's party. Do I have to go? There's a swimming gala that weekend too. It's not fair! Can't I go the week after, or the week after that?'

Barry eventually managed to get Grace to make a visit home about nine weeks after her previous visit. She told me over and over again she wasn't looking forward to it.

'I'm sure you'll enjoy it once you're there, sweetheart. It's a while since you've seen your family.'

Grace complained that she was fed up with the long journey and the inconvenience of packing bags and missing all the stuff that was going on with her friends.

'What's the point?' she moaned, as she threw her pyjamas and toothbrush into a bag.

She was stony-faced when she set off in Barry's car, and angry and exhausted when she came back.

'Mum's so annoying!' Grace snapped. She told me that on both the Friday and Saturday nights her mum had played loud music when she was trying to sleep.

'Oh dear, I'm sorry to hear that.'

'Yeah. I was trying to get some sleep and I couldn't. It went on for hours.'

'I'm sorry to hear that, sweetheart.'

'Well, she wasn't sorry! She doesn't care!'

Grace looked slightly shocked by what she'd said and I noticed she tried to backtrack.

'But she's, like, got a lot on her plate. And everyone's got to let their hair down, haven't they?'

Almost as an afterthought, Grace told me that Colette had split up with Malcolm. I wasn't sure if this was a permanent split or not, as his two boys were still living in the house. Grace also told me she heard that Cameron was also a 'druggie like Lee', which I had to report to Social Services. I made sure I explained this was potentially hearsay from Grace as I had no proof it was true, but I had to let the authorities know.

That night, as she was getting into bed, Grace blurted out, 'Mum's worse than Dad!'

She rarely spoke about her dad, but on the odd occasion when she had I'd noticed she spoke generously about his past behaviour. The general impression I had built up was that she viewed her dad as a kind of lovable rogue whose heart was in the right place, but who just couldn't control his addiction to alcohol. I'm not sure how accurate this was, or if Grace was looking back through rose-tinted glasses. I suspect the latter.

Grace yawned and began to tell me that her father once locked her in the car outside the pub, telling her, 'Don't move, or I'll belt you.' She said he left her alone for what felt like hours, in blazing heat, and she was scared. Grace said she was crying when he returned, and when they got home he smacked her legs, even though they were sunburned.

She had never once mentioned drugs or the fact he died from a drug overdose. In fact, I don't recall her ever saying anything at all about his death, or openly referring to the fact he had passed away.

I listened and let her talk for as long as she wanted without interrupting. She didn't expand on why she had suddenly said her mum was worse than her dad.

'I'm tired. I'm going to sleep now.'

I wished her goodnight and her eyes were closed before I'd left the room. I think she was probably asleep before I got downstairs.

'I don't want to go home again for a while,' she said the morning after, when we had breakfast together.

'Don't worry. We don't have to fix anything up again just yet.'

'No, but I'll still have to go! I can't put it off forever, you know, Angela!'

Grace then proceeded to pick an argument with the other girls in the house, bickering about which 'greedy guts' had eaten the last of her favourite cereal and, audaciously, accusing the others of causing trouble on purpose. It was such a shame to see this as, on the whole, all three girls had been getting along fine for a long time.

'Grace,' Jonathan said. 'Please don't be rude. That was not a kind thing to say. Can you please say sorry?'

'What? Me? You mean me say sorry? What about *her*?

Grace ran out of the kitchen, slamming the door behind her. She stormed upstairs and remained in a sulky mood for the rest of the day.

When she reappeared she demanded sweets and crisps and fizzy drinks, telling me I was mean for not giving her everything she wanted because 'my mum lets me'. I was upset by Grace's behaviour, and by what she reported from home.

When Grace was rude or badly behaved we didn't ever ground her. Experience with other kids had shown us that this didn't help and only served to make the child feel even more upset, alienated or angry. Instead, we tried to talk to Grace calmly, and we always encouraged her to keep up with all of her activities, whatever mood she was in, because if she wasn't busy she was invariably much more difficult to handle.

'I think secondary school will be great for Grace,' Jonathan said, trying to look for a positive.

I hoped he was right. She had started to talk excitedly about her new school – she had got into her first choice, the one with the sporty reputation – and I hoped she'd respond well to all the new challenges it would bring.

'Let's hope it's the making of her. She's such a hard little worker and deserves every success.'

Around this time I had a chance conversation with a friend I'd known for years. She used to live in Colette's area and went to school with her. She told me several things about Colette's upbringing that I found distressing, but eye-opening. I learned that Colette had not had an easy life at all, having been shockingly abused in her childhood. Though this did not excuse how she treated Grace, I was left feeling a lot more sympathetic and understanding towards Colette than I had been at the start.

Nowadays, with many more years of fostering and life experience under my belt, I often think of Colette when I meet the parents of other children we foster. It's easy to feel angry or bitter towards a parent, especially when you have a damaged child on your hands whose pain has been caused or exacerbated by their mum or dad's behaviour, or both, but I try never to judge. Everybody has a story, and you never know all the details of their journey through life. I felt very sorry for the way Colette's life had turned out; it seemed to me that she had never managed to break out of the dysfunctional world she herself had grown up in, which was a great shame. It reminded me of a child who had been in a placement with a friend and carer from my support group – her mother had been in care and it turned out her grandmother had also been brought up in care. I struggled to understand why this would happen when I was new to fostering. I'd thought, wouldn't they fight tooth and nail for their child not to go into care? Thankfully, with the help of my friend, when this child grew up she was able to bring up her own children without even a hint of them needing to go into care.

18

'It wasn't comfy sleeping on the sofa'

One day, Colette phoned out of the blue. Grace had started at secondary school and had thrown herself into it with great enthusiasm, which was wonderful to see.

'I like it, Mum,' Grace said in a reassuring voice. 'Yes, everything is good. Yes, OK. Yes, that would be good.'

'Everything all right?' I asked afterwards.

Grace was frowning and seemed a little puzzled.

'Yes, Mum just wanted to find out how school was.'

'That's good. You sure you're OK?'

'Yes. She was nice to me. *Very* nice.'

'That's great!'

'Yes, it is,' Grace said, looking as if she couldn't quite understand why her mother had been so nice on the phone. Prior to this, Colette had gone through one of her phases of keeping a very low profile. She had not even phoned to wish Grace good luck at the start of her new term, even though she must have known what a big step it was for her daughter to start secondary school. I figured there must have been a reason; Colette must have had other things to deal with. Thankfully, Grace didn't seem to expect a call or anything else from her mum in that period of time, so she had not been disappointed, at least as far as I could tell.

'Mum wants to see me soon. She said she was sorry she hadn't phoned for a while. She said she *missed* me.' Grace emphasised the word 'missed' and narrowed her eyes. She looked deep in thought and unsure how to react. My heart went out to her in that moment. She obviously didn't expect her mum to be interested in her new school, and she hadn't anticipated that her mum would be the one to orchestrate a visit home and say she missed her, as this was not normally how things worked. Usually, Barry organised the visits, and sometimes we had trouble getting hold of Colette when Grace tried to call her to finalise arrangements. I thought what a pity it was that Grace had such low expectations of her mum, but I also felt a surge of optimism. I'd never known Colette to be so proactive; hopefully this would be good news for Grace going forward.

As the weekend of the next contact visit approached, Grace started to complain about the amount of homework she had to get through, the length of the journey to and from her mum's house and the fact she was going to miss a rehearsal with her theatre group, which was putting on a panto.

'I'm not sure I can go,' she said.

Here we go again, I thought. *This is just what happened last time.*

I tried to come up with positive things to say, but the

more we talked about the visit the more Grace scowled and grumbled and sulked.

'It's been a while since you saw everyone. I'm sure you'll enjoy it once you get there.'

'That's what Barry said. And Jonathan! Have you all been talking about me behind my back?'

'No, sweetheart. The fact is, we all care about you and have your best interests at heart. We all hope you'll enjoy seeing your family.'

She groaned and sighed dramatically. 'I don't have any choice, do I?' She didn't wait for an answer. Though Grace liked to say her piece when she was resentful about something, at the end of the day she was a pretty compliant kid. I don't think it entered her head that she could point blank refuse to go, as some children would have tried to get away with.

Grace looked frazzled when she got into Barry's car. She waved forlornly from the car window and I felt very sorry that her life had to be organised this way. It would have been easier if her family home was closer to ours, but unfortunately this was the way things had panned out, and we just had to get on with it.

I missed Grace when she was gone and found myself wondering what she was doing at various times of the day. I hoped she was managing to relax and enjoy herself with her family. I'd got very used to Grace's ways by now, and it was odd not to have her around, chattering nineteen to the dozen, helping with the chores while simultaneously getting under my feet and needing lifts here, there and everywhere.

It moved me to tears when Barry dropped her back at our house, because Grace ran up to me and gave me a big hug. She didn't do this often, and this time she clung on to me.

'Are you OK, Grace? How did it go?'

'Can I go to my room?'

'Of course you can. I've got the dinner on and I'll give you a shout when it's ready.'

Grace didn't reply when I called her later, so I went up to her room and tapped on the door.

'Grace? Dinner's ready.'

'Oh, er, yeah.'

'Are you coming down? I'm about to serve up.'

She came to the door and when I looked at her I could tell she was feeling miserable. Her chin was down, there was no spark in her eyes and she was hunched over. Even her voice gave away her emotions; it sounded deeper than normal, as if she was choked up. I was afraid that Lee or Lily had been mean to her, or perhaps even Colette, despite the fact she had been so pleasant to Grace on the phone and had been proactive in fixing up the visit.

'What is it, sweetheart?'

'I'm tired. It wasn't comfy sleeping on the sofa. And Lee woke me up in the morning. And . . .'

'And?'

'I don't like Lily's boyfriend.'

'Lily has a boyfriend?'

'Yes.' Grace yawned and rubbed her eyes. They looked red and I wasn't sure if this was from tiredness or because Grace had been crying, though she rarely shed a tear.

'You slept on the sofa?'

'Yes! Didn't you hear me? That's what I just said!'

'I thought it was. Would you like to tell me anything else about the weekend, because I'd like to hear more about it? And I'm sorry you weren't comfy on the sofa.'

She pushed past me and ran down the stairs, then sat at the dinner table with a face like thunder.

'What's the matter, Grace?' one of the other children asked.

'Nothing.'

'Are you sure? Are you OK? You look a bit, like, cross.'

Grace banged her fist on the table. 'Grrr! Just all leave me alone, will you?'

Jonathan intervened and reminded Grace to be polite, pointing out that the other child was only being kind and showing concern. Grace didn't reply and ate her food silently, then went back to her bedroom. She didn't speak to anyone that night, and the next day she was moody and monosyllabic.

Unfortunately, this was a pattern that repeated every couple of months, whenever Grace went to the family home. She also had plenty of angry and sulky episodes when she was at home with us, and at school, but the deterioration in her moods was always far more noticeable and extreme whenever she had stayed at her mum's house.

After one particularly tetchy visit, Grace told me that the reason she had to sleep on the sofa was because Lily was allowed to have her boyfriend staying overnight in her room. Prior to this, Grace had always shared her sister's bedroom. By this time, Lily was nearly sixteen and Grace was twelve.

'Mum said I was ungrateful,' Grace said. 'But I only said the sofa wasn't comfy. All she cares about is Lily! It's a joke! Lily gets away with murder and I only have to make one tiny mistake or say the wrong thing and I'm carpeted!'

From what I heard, it did sound like Grace was shouted at by Colette for the simplest things, like buying the wrong loaf of bread in the corner shop or accidentally chipping a mug when she did the washing up. Meanwhile, it appeared that Lily was treated like a little princess even when she behaved appallingly. At least, that's the picture Grace painted, and I have to say I didn't disbelieve her.

Despite the fact Colette's split from Malcolm did turn out to be permanent, Lee and Cameron were still living in the house. Nowadays, Grace very rarely spoke about them. I had never met either stepbrother or even seen a photograph of them, or the family home. Grace told me that neither boy had a job, though they were now both over the age of eighteen. I knew precious little beyond those few facts.

On several occasions I'd suggested to Grace that she might like to put some photographs of her family in her life story book – or set of books as they'd become – but she never brought any pictures or souvenirs back from her contact visits, not ever. It meant that even after all this time I struggled to picture Grace when she was with her family, and I felt I knew next to nothing about them. This contributed to the pangs I experienced every time Grace disappeared in Barry's car. My heart would sink like a stone whenever she returned in a bad mood, complaining about the weekend.

Life wasn't perfect at home with us, of course. Grace could still be extremely over-exuberant, which led to arguments with the other girls and a few discipline issues in the class-room, and she had difficulty knowing when to stop, which irritated her friends sometimes. Nevertheless, she was as popular as ever and had a large social circle. She was also blossoming into a beautiful teenager. In fact, she was so striking she was scouted by a local model agency and featured in an advertising campaign, which was a great boost to her self-esteem. I set up a children's bank account for her and we talked to her about the importance of saving money.

Inevitably, the ADHD pervaded all areas of her life, but I felt we all managed it as well as we possibly could. There were frequent episodes of extreme hyperactivity and Grace suffered some dreadful mood swings, particularly during the onset of puberty. On the advice of one doctor she took Evening Primrose Oil as a natural remedy for some of her symptoms, which she was convinced made her calmer. I'm not sure if this was just a placebo effect but, whatever the truth, she swore by it and relied on it for years.

When Lily was still only sixteen, she fell pregnant. Grace broke the news to me by saying, 'Good and bad news. Lily has split up from her boyfriend but I still can't go back in her bedroom because now she's having a baby!'

By now Grace was thirteen. I'd mentioned to Barry that Grace had no bed in the family home, but he said that unfortunately sleeping on a sofa for a couple of nights here and there wasn't a crime and that there was not much anyone could do about it. The family remained on Social Services' radar because of previous fears about drugs in the home, and Barry told me that if there were any genuine concerns about the living conditions, they would be picked up on and dealt with accordingly.

'Grace is safe in the home or we wouldn't let her stay,' he reassured me, but I didn't feel great about her situation. She needed to feel more than safe. I wanted her to feel welcome, and that she was on an equal footing with her siblings when she was staying in the family home. Being relegated to the sofa just didn't seem fair.

When Lily's baby was born – a boy called Harley – the family dynamic naturally shifted. Grace told me that Colette was delighted at becoming a grandmother and was determined to perform the role well.

I spoke to Colette on the phone not long after Harley's birth, and almost didn't recognise her.

'Angela, how are you?' she asked, sounding excited and full of the joys of spring.

'Who's calling?' I asked, before looking at the incoming number displayed on the handset of our landline phone and realising it was Colette. 'Oh, sorry Colette. It's you! I didn't recognise your voice at first. I'm fine. Congratulations on becoming a grandmother!'

'Thanks very much. It's the best thing in the world. He's

adorable, our little Harley. And Lily's such a lovely mum. We couldn't be happier!'

Afterwards, I commented to Grace that her mum sounded very excited about the baby. She told me, 'Mum said, "I want to be the best nana ever!"'

When I thought about this, I had mixed feelings. Of course I was pleased that Colette felt this way and I really hoped she'd live up to her pledge, but I couldn't help thinking about how this statement might impact on Grace. I know that, if I'd been in her shoes, I'd have been wondering how her mother could welcome another child into her life when she herself had been shunned and placed in care.

Thankfully, Grace didn't seem bothered about what her mum had said, or at least she didn't seem to analyse it the way I did. She sounded pleased by her mum's positive reaction to having a new baby in the house, which I think says a lot about Grace's character. She was a very kind soul and, though she could lash out when people were mean to her or she was in a bad mood, it was not in her nature to be bitter or go looking for trouble. If anything, she looked for the good in people, even when she had reasons not to.

According to Grace, from the moment Lily had found out she was pregnant Colette banned Cameron from bringing his 'druggie' mates into the house, saying that if anyone wanted to do any smoking 'of any kind' they had to go in the back yard before they lit up. Lee apparently became quite reclusive, which I thought was very sad for him, though it made life easier for Grace. He now had virtually nothing to do with her, and thankfully this meant the accusations about him winding her up by taking her clothes had stopped. Grace told me Lee would walk straight past her without speaking if she ever saw him around the house. 'I'm happy with that,' she said pointedly.

'I'm amazed Colette still has those two lads living with her,' I commented to Jonathan. 'You'd have thought they'd have moved out after she split up from Malcolm, and certainly now there's a baby in the house.'

'Money?' he said. 'I don't like to be an old sceptic, but don't you think that's why?'

Unfortunately, Jonathan was right. Grace eventually told me that Colette only agreed that Cameron and Lee could stay living with her after Malcolm left because they paid her keep. She'd told each of them they'd be out on their ear, 'quicker than you can wink' if they ever didn't pay up. With neither of them having a job, I figured the money they gave Colette could only have come from their benefits, or possibly drug dealing. Mind you, I was very unsure about the drug-dealing allegations that had filtered through to us. I imagined Social Services, if not the police, would have taken action about this by now if it were true.

Grace was clearly very taken with little Harley, and from the moment she became 'Aunty Gracie' she started to go home much more willingly, and more frequently. Lily took to motherhood well, it seemed, and from what Grace said it appeared to have knocked off the edges of her bossiness and sharp tongue. 'Lily's changed, a lot,' Grace commented.

'She's tired all the time but she's nice to me now. I think it suits her, being a mum.'

Grace helped her sister to feed and change Harley and seemed to be enjoying the visits home a great deal more than she ever had. Instead of just sitting in front of the TV, Grace went out for walks to the park with her mum and sister, taking turns pushing Harley in his pram.

'Mum asked me when I was moving back,' she said after a particularly successful visit, when Lily had said she was considering making Grace Harley's godmother. Her words took me by surprise, and not in a pleasant way. I gulped. 'Did she?'

'Yes. Mum said she'd have me back any time! Lily wants me back too.'

Grace was smiling and was clearly delighted that her sister and mum felt this way. It was perfectly understandable. We all seek approval from our parents and siblings, and to Grace it was clearly a huge vote of confidence to have been invited back home, and to be considered for the role of godmother. I think she must have viewed it as a massive endorsement for how she had progressed, and how well she was doing generally in her life.

To my knowledge, apart from what she'd said in the very early days of the placement, Colette had not talked about Grace moving back in with her for a long time. I'm not going to lie; it came as a bombshell to me that this possibility might be back on the agenda. Despite the positive changes since Harley's birth, my head spun at the thought of Grace returning to live with her family.

At this point in time, she was doing very well at school, having started her GCSE courses, and she continued to do well in every avenue of her life, keeping up all her activities and getting on well with all her various friends. Though she never chased it, Grace's modelling work had continued to trickle in. She didn't take on many jobs as she had so many other commitments to prioritise, but the work she did agree to paid well and she enjoyed it. She appeared in several magazines and did some semi-regular work for a catalogue and a regional hair salon. The savings account I'd started for Grace now had a healthy balance. Through speaking to a contact she made at the modelling agency, Grace developed an interest in advertising and marketing and said she might like to work in one of those fields when she left school.

I went over all of the above when I told Jonathan what Grace had said about potentially moving back in with the family.

'She can't give all this up, can she?' I said desperately.

'Don't panic. It's understandable she's happy it's being discussed, but I can't see it happening in reality, can you?'

I had to admit I couldn't, not really. 'She's got too much to lose here, hasn't she?'

As I spoke I found myself thinking how naive that hopeful statement of mine might be. I knew all too well that the bond between a parent and a child is stronger than anything else in the world, no matter what has gone on in the past, or how happy the child has been in foster care. When you added to that the fact that a teenage brain is not fully developed and does not work as rationally as an adult's brain, I knew anything was possible.

Thankfully, Grace said no more about it, and perhaps one of the reasons why was that before long she got herself a boyfriend. His name was Robbie, and she met him at her swimming club. She was totally smitten and wanted to spend all her free time with him.

'Do I have to come on holiday with you?' she said, when half term came around. We'd booked a holiday in Scotland and were going on a coach, as there had been a special offer on at our local travel agent and we fancied a change from Jonathan doing all the driving.

'Yes, Grace, it's all booked now. It's only for a week. You'll love it. Scotland is beautiful.'

'But I'm going to miss Joanna's party, and there's a thing on at the bowling alley and . . .'

I guessed that what she was really bothered about was missing Robbie, which was understandable. I told her that we would give her some holiday spending money and said that she would be able to give Robbie a ring from a phone box if she wanted to, as this was in the days when very few people had a mobile phone.

'I'm not worried about Robbie, it's everything else,' she said, unconvincingly.

'Look, Grace, we're going and that's that. It's all arranged and paid for. Have a look at the brochure. There's loads to do – archery, swimming, we can even go and watch some

Scottish dancing. You'll be so busy you won't have time to think about what you're missing at home, I'm sure.'

'Scottish dancing! Is that when they have those men in kilts playing the bagpipes! I hate all that stuff. It's boring! So boring!'

Grace continued to protest not only up until we left the house, but for the entire coach journey, which I must admit was very long.

'What are we doing here? When are we stopping? Can I go to the toilet? Have you got any more food?'

Grace must have driven the other passengers mad because she didn't stop talking or fidgeting. A girl of a similar age shared her sweets and pop with Grace which didn't help matters at all. She was hyper, taking every opportunity to walk up and down the length of the coach, over and over again.

'Grace, you need to stay in your seat.'

'I can't. I've got to stretch my legs. I've got ants in my pants!'

Jonathan and I tried to engage her in some travel games but she said she wasn't in the mood, and I could see how wired she was.

'I knew this would be long-winded! How long to go? Are we nearly there yet? Can I ask the driver when the next stop is?'

'No, Grace, just sit down, please. Do you want to help me with this word search? How about a crossword or a game of cards?'

'Boring! Boring! Boring!' She tapped her fingers, hummed loudly and jiggled her legs about. The man in the seat in front of her had to ask her several times to stop jolting his seat; I think he'd reached the end of his tether before we'd even clocked up thirty miles!

'See, everyone's fed up on this journey! No wonder! Why did we do this? Why didn't Jonathan drive? I'm never going on a coach again.'

We finally arrived, and the next day I was looking forward to visiting Edinburgh Castle. I tried to drum up some enthusiasm for the guided tour I'd booked. Grace was having none of it. 'Can't I stay in the hotel? I'll be fine on my own.'

'No Grace, you can't.'

'Well I don't want to go.'

We had one of the other girls with us and I explained to Grace that the trip to the castle was one of the highlights of the holiday and that if she refused to go on the castle tour then none of us could go, as we all needed to stay together.

'OK, I'll do it, but you're wasting your money!' she taunted. 'See if I care!'

Thankfully, the day passed without incident in the end, despite the fact Grace was like a coiled spring, which set my nerves on edge. For the rest of the holiday, Jonathan and I decided the best thing was to keep packing in as many activities as we could, to keep Grace entertained and help burn up her energy. It seemed to work, though she was completely underwhelmed by another day trip we went on, to a farm and museum where we tried our hand at some archery. Grace spent the entire day either sulking, dragging her feet or groaning whenever we asked her to do something, or simply keep up.

I was relieved when Grace slept for a lot of the journey home. With her batteries recharged from her long sleep, when we got back she shot straight round to Robbie's house. She said she was very excited to see him again.

'You know what, when I grow up and have kids, I'm going to have a house like Robbie's,' she told me afterwards.

'What's it like?'

'Just, like, normal. You can get peace and quiet.' Robbie was the only child of older, retired parents.

A couple of weeks later, Grace came home with a photo taken in his living room. The house was pin neat and simply furnished. Robbie and Grace were standing together, smiling, and his mum was in the background, wearing an apron and holding a cake on a plate. She looked like a very sweet and homely kind of person.

'What a lovely picture,' I said. 'Perhaps you could put it in a frame in your bedroom? I've got a few spare frames that size, would you like to choose one?'

Grace was pleased with the idea and did it straight away. I thought about the fact she liked the 'peace and quiet' in Robbie's house.

With other children living with us too, our house was always busy, but I hoped it was still a haven for Grace. Whatever we have going on in our lives, above all I always want every child to feel safe, protected and comfortable in our home.

Eventually, several weeks after we got back from Scotland, Grace came and apologised for the way she had behaved on the trip.

'I'm sorry if I was difficult. I just wanted to come home.'

'I know you missed Robbie.'

'It wasn't just that. I love being at home.' She looked around our kitchen admiringly as she spoke.

'I'm pleased to hear that. I love our home too. And I love having you here.'

19

'You won't believe what Grace just said'

Long before she did her GCSEs – for which she was now on track to achieve A–C grades in nine subjects – Grace started looking into local college courses and apprenticeships, with the help of a fantastic careers teacher at school. Needless to say, I was always encouraging her to work hard at school, keep her options open and aim for the best. She was adamant she wanted to leave school at sixteen, and she was still interested in doing something in the advertising or marketing industry, thanks to the chat she'd had with one of her modelling contacts.

We'd found Grace a maths tutor as this was a subject she had continued to find difficult, and she'd responded really well to the extra help she received. She worked hard in the sessions and on the homework set by the tutor and was determined to get the best grade she possibly could, which would hopefully be at least a C, and possibly a B.

'I'll do it, you know,' she told me many times. 'I'm going to do it, you'll see! I'll make sure you get your money's worth!'

'I'm very happy to pay for the tutor because you're working hard. I'm proud of you, Grace. As long as you do your best, that's what matters. You're a hard worker and you deserve to do well.'

'Thanks, Angela. I don't think I would have stood any chance of passing maths without the tutor, or you. I know I can do it now. Thanks.'

She said this to me out of the blue, as she went out the door one morning. It made my day, as I'm sure Grace knew. She had such a good heart, and occasional kind words like that were so wonderful to hear and gave me a great boost.

As well as supporting her school work, I was giving Grace constant support in terms of her ADHD. It had become second nature to prompt her to organise her desk, her books and her school and sports bags. I still made sure she set reminders when she needed to hit homework and coursework deadlines, and I sat with her for hours when she needed to revise, understanding that she worked best in short bursts, and when topics were broken down into manageable chunks. Of course, I was also still vigilant about her diet and made sure she ate healthily, got enough sleep and generally looked after herself well. Those things were a given.

Grace arranged to visit her family on a weekend when Robbie was away playing rugby. She told me she was looking forward to seeing Harley, who was walking by now.

I hadn't seen a picture of Harley since he was a newborn, and I asked Grace if she could bring one home this time.

'It would be lovely to see how he's grown,' I said. 'Maybe we could put some pictures of him in your life story book, or up in your bedroom?'

'OK,' she smiled. 'That's a good idea.'

I'd have liked to have seen Lily and met the baby, but this was not really on the agenda. Colette and the family still never ventured our way, and we were never invited to visit. It had been years since I'd seen either Colette or Lily.

'Do you think Grace ever feels she leads a kind of double life?' I said to Jonathan after Barry drove her away this time.

'I know what you mean. I hope not. I think it probably feels more like that to us than it does to her.'

Whatever the truth, we both agreed that it was good to see Grace going back to visit the family with a smile on her face. Harley had had such a positive effect on them, and the problems of the past seemed to have faded away. I couldn't remember the last time Grace had said a bad word about Lee, Cameron or Lily, or her mum for that matter.

When Barry brought Grace home I could see immediately that she was in a good mood, and I was looking forward to hearing all her news.

'How was it?' I beamed, welcoming her in.

'Amazing! Remember Mum said about me moving back? Well she said it again! She said I can move back any time I like!' Grace was almost breathless with excitement as she delivered this news on the doorstep.

Barry caught my eye and gave me a wink. I knew him well enough by now to know this was his way of showing me a bit of support. I appreciated it, as my heart had sunk like a stone.

'Thank you for bringing her back, Barry. Let me know the dates of the next placement meeting?'

'I will.'

I was almost on autopilot when I said this, as Barry and I always referenced the next placement or review meeting whenever he picked Grace up or brought her home. As time went on the meetings had fallen into a fairly predictable routine, which is not unusual when a child has been in a placement for a long time. Typically, the meetings amounted to a summing up of how Grace was doing at school and a discussion of any problems we had relating to her ADHD, or her contact visits or appointments. Occasionally we had an incident to discuss. This year she'd become more accident prone, perhaps due to puberty, and she'd had a few accidents, including falling off a ladder while dressing the stage for a show, and splintering her shin bone coming off a swimming pool slide.

We could cope with things like that, but what now? I suddenly found myself on high alert, panicking about what might be on the agenda at the next placement meeting. *Will we be talking about Grace moving out?* I shuddered at the thought and tried, unsuccessfully, to push it out of my head.

Barry said his goodbyes and once Grace and I were alone I finally responded to what she'd said.

'Moving back?' I said. 'Did you say your mum said you could move back any time?' I was trying to conceal my alarm and dismay, but I stammered the words and I'm sure I must have looked flustered; I certainly felt it.

'Yeah. I think I should. Not right now! I mean, like, when I finish my exams and leave school and all that. The thing is, I'm fine now! Mum is, too. She can manage. I think it's a great idea, and I'll get to spend more time with Harley.'

Grace said this in a naive, flippant way, in the way only teenagers can, I suppose. She can't have thought through what it would really mean to move back home, away from everything she knew and all her friends, activities and opportunities in our town. *What about Robbie?* I couldn't imagine she would want to live in a different town to her boyfriend. In that moment I felt very glad indeed that she had a boyfriend she was very taken with; Robbie might be the one to keep her here.

I thought that Grace probably didn't have a clue how discussing moving out would affect me. Jonathan and I had given Grace a good home since she was ten years old. She was fourteen going on fifteen now, and it pained me that she could consider giving up her life with us so easily. I wanted her to continue reaching for the stars, as we'd encouraged her to do from when she'd first moved in with us. Despite the positive changes in her family home, I still felt very strongly that staying with us for as long as possible would give Grace the best chance of reaching her potential. I also thought about the other two girls. They had lived with Grace for years and though they were not exactly close, I knew that if they heard her talk so flippantly about moving out they would probably feel hurt too.

Seemingly oblivious to the bombshell she'd just dropped on me, Grace ran up to her room leaving me standing alone in the kitchen. My mind went into overdrive the second she had gone.

What if she went back to her mother's and was exposed to drugs? How would she manage her ADHD if she didn't eat the right foods or get enough sleep? What about her college course or apprenticeship? She was working so hard on her GCSEs, and I was filled with dread that if she lived at home after leaving school her work ethic might change. Lee and Cameron didn't have jobs. To my knowledge Colette had not worked for many years, and Lily had never got onto the job market after falling pregnant as soon as she finished school.

Grace would be sixteen and a half when it was her turn to leave school. At that age she would be eligible to go into supported lodgings, which were a kind of halfway house for kids moving out of care. Nowadays children stay in care for longer, at least until eighteen, and up until the age of twenty-one if they are in education and that is what they and their foster carers want. This 'staying put' policy, as it's called, came into force in 2014, but back in the nineties going into supported lodgings was typically the next step for sixteen- and seventeen-year-olds. We'd seen how supported lodgings worked well for other children leaving care, though we'd also recognised that the teenagers who left us were still very young and impressionable. They needed all the support they could get and we kept in touch with nearly all our children who went into supported flats locally. Though we were in no hurry to rush Grace out, I had imagined this would probably be the next step for her, when she was good and ready, and most probably after she'd worked or studied for at least another year and was seventeen or even older.

As taken aback as I was at what Grace had said, I did manage to keep my counsel. I couldn't tell her what to do. I knew that no matter how a child's natural parents had behaved, they would most likely still hold all the trump cards when it came to loyalty and allegiances. As I've said many times before, a child will forgive their birth parents almost anything, and kids in care nearly always crave a reunion, even after years of disappointment or worse. I'd recognised years ago that Grace had put her mother on a pedestal and, even though there had been ups and downs over the years, deep down this had not changed.

'Cat got your tongue?' Jonathan said, walking in from the shop.

'You won't believe what Grace just said.'

I told him exactly what she'd told me. He said the colour had drained from my face, and he could see how concerned I was.

'Come here,' he said, giving me a big hug. 'We've been down this road before and you know what Grace is like. What was it Barry said all those years ago? "She's a harum-scarum kid." That's as true today as it was then, except now the challenges have become more, well, psychological, I suppose. It's all talk. Her life is here, in this town. I can't see her ever moving back, frankly.'

I let out a long breath. 'God, I hope you're right. I just can't imagine what would happen. It doesn't bear thinking about.'

'Angela, calm down and don't worry. Only last week Grace was talking about her applications for apprenticeships, and she's mad about Robbie, too. And what about the theatre group? She'd never give that up.'

I realised I'd had a nasty shock and got carried away with the worst-case scenario. Besides, it was still quite a while before Grace would start to sit her exams. I'd just have to hope she'd be snapped up by a course or apprenticeship scheme and that the whole idea of going back to her mum would have evaporated by the time she finished school.

I'm very happy to say that after many months of working extremely hard on her revision and putting her heart and soul into her course work, Grace achieved nine GCSEs, including a B in Maths, which was a massive achievement. We were all so thrilled, and we had a very moving moment when we gave Grace a congratulations card.

'I've got a card for you too,' she said unexpectedly, handing us a giant-sized thank you card. She had written some lovely things in it, telling Jonathan and me she could not have got through her exams without us and describing us as 'stars' and 'legends.'

Though there had been no further mention of her going home – I imagined Grace had been too busy during the exam period to give this the thought it deserved – there had been moments when I'd expected, and feared, that the topic might come up again. One was when she filled in applications for her apprenticeship scheme and obviously had to think about where she would be living in order to get to work. This was another.

The thank you card filled me with joy, but I had to push a nagging thought out of my mind. Now that Grace had finished school and got her exam results, what would happen? Was she thanking us like this because she knew she was going to be leaving? I told myself not to fret and to enjoy the moment. I'd been down this road before, and I knew that's what Jonathan would say to me if I voiced my concerns to him yet again, so I kept quiet and focused on drinking in Grace's success.

Shortly after this, Grace heard the exciting news that she had been offered a place on an apprenticeship scheme with a fashionable advertising agency in our area. She accepted it immediately.

'See, you can stop worrying about her leaving us,' Jonathan said.

'I wasn't, honest!' I lied.

'Don't fib! I was too. But this is a fantastic opportunity and it means she's not going anywhere any time soon!'

'At least for twelve months,' I cautioned, as that was how long the scheme would last.

Jonathan was cock-a-hoop and he wasn't going to let doubts creep in.

'Exactly. We can relax. Hasn't she done well?'

'She has. I'm so proud of her.'

I realised I had tears in my eyes and I went to the mirror

in the hallway to check my make-up hadn't smudged. Glancing at the front door, I found myself remembering the slightly dazed and shy-looking little girl who'd arrived on our doorstep some six years earlier.

Grace had come a very long way indeed, and now the world was her oyster.

20

'It's just how my brain works'

Grace began to spend more weekends at home with her mum, Lily and Harley. By now, Lee and Cameron had finally moved out, and at sixteen Grace was old enough to travel home under her own steam, which she enjoyed doing. Mind you, I had to remind her every single time which bus stop to go to, and where to change. If there was any disruption to the timetable, Grace was completely thrown. This led to her making some very convoluted and long-winded journeys, as she never remembered to take the leaflet that contained alternative routes and timetables. I found this incredibly frustrating, but Grace didn't seem to mind. 'I got there in the end,' she'd say. 'It doesn't matter.'

I think this was one of the positives that came from having the ADHD 'label', because when irritating things happened to Grace, or when she created problems for herself that another person may have avoided or been incredibly frustrated by, she took it all in her stride. As she said, she always got there in the end, and usually had a tale to tell about a character she'd met, or a funny encounter she'd had. 'It's just how my brain works' had become another one of Grace's stock phrases. She used it liberally whenever she got her wires crossed and things went wrong. I really admired how she accepted and coped with her ADHD.

In all the years, Grace had never had any further sessions with any kind of therapist or psychologist and she never took any medication. We'd have sought help if we'd felt it was necessary, but knowing she had a name for her disorder was always enough for Grace.

As time went on and information became more readily available, I learned a lot more about ADHD. I devoured all the articles and research I could, while Grace never bothered. She had always been satisfied with what the educational psychologist had told her all those years before and didn't seem to be the least bit curious to find out more. I don't think this was a bad thing; she was doing well for herself and obviously didn't think it necessary. As long as she had her lists and reminders in place, and was vigilant about her general health and lifestyle, she could manage her ADHD very well. We could too. We knew not to overload her with information and to write things down all the time, and we learned to be tolerant of her mood swings and not to be irritated when she interrupted us, lost concentration, did something clumsy or was distracted or overly impulsive.

Grace's apprenticeship started in the September and she had to fill in a medical form and have a meeting with the human resources department at her new company. She wasn't shy about telling the personnel officer, a middle-aged woman called Bev, all about her ADHD.

'Bev is great,' Grace told me. 'Her brother has ADHD too!' Grace said that Bev had listed several well-known brands of sweets that made her brother hyper and said that as long as he avoided those and a few other food products, he could generally keep his hyperactive episodes under control. 'It's never held him back,' Bev told Grace. 'He was a terror when we were kids, but you'd never even know he had it now. All his coping strategies work.'

I was very pleased when Grace told me that. Back then, there was a lot more stigma and mistrust attached to ADHD than there is today. Lack of knowledge and understanding fuelled this, and I'd heard stories of people being unfairly judged because of it. ADHD had also got a bad press for being used as an 'excuse' for unruly behaviour in kids. One article I read talked about the fact it's hard to diagnose and kids don't get statemented when they have it. It quoted a head teacher as saying there had been an influx of parents labelling their kids as having ADHD without the backing of expert opinion.

'What caused my ADHD?' Grace asked out of the blue one day, when the two of us were unpacking the shopping.

'That's a good question,' I said, stopping to consider this.

'Like, what actually is it, and why did I get it?'

'That's not the easiest question to answer. Nobody is sure of the exact cause, but I know it tends to run in families.'

'So it's a dodgy gene?'

'No, they reckon the genes you inherit from your parents

have a bearing on whether you'll develop it, but it's not linked to one single genetic fault.' I added that people with ADHD possibly had differences in the way their brain was structured, and how the neurotransmitters worked. I also told Grace that I'd never heard of ADHD before she was diagnosed, as I wasn't sure if she remembered that. I said that now there was plenty of information available, if she wanted to find out more. I had a book she could borrow, and several websites I could recommend. I'd told her this before, but she had never taken me up on it.

'OK,' she said thoughtfully. 'Thanks, but I don't think I need to know any more. I'm absolutely fine.'

A couple of weeks later she returned to the subject, having had another conversation with Bev at work.

'We talked about coping strategies,' Grace said. 'Bev asked me what mine were and I said I didn't really have any.'

I raised my eyebrows in surprise and Grace started to laugh. 'That's exactly what Bev did. So, how did you know?'

'What do you mean?'

'How did you know about all the strategies, if there was no information available when I was younger?'

She pulled out a leaflet, given to her by Bev, with 'ADHD – HOW TO COPE' written in bold across the front. The literature stated that it could be draining to cope with a child with ADHD and gave tips to counteract the 'impulsive and chaotic behaviours that can make daily life stressful and exhausting for parents and carers.'

Inside, there were sections on the following: how to plan the day, so the child knows what to expect and what equipment they need; setting boundaries, to ensure the child knows the rules and what behaviour is expected; staying positive and giving praise when a child has done a task well; giving simple, clear instructions so there is no doubt what you are asking the child to do; intervening early, when a child becomes frustrated or over-stimulated; monitoring social situations, and making sure the child doesn't become too tired or hungry; encouraging plentiful exercise, a healthy, wholesome diet and a good sleep routine and, finally, speaking to the child's school to make sure they get extra support.

I could identify with all of those pointers. 'We just had to do our best and use common sense,' I told Grace. 'You could say I knew you had ADHD but I just didn't know what it was called. For instance, I worked out even before we'd heard about ADHD that it was best to give you one instruction at a time.'

'But how?'

'Well, it was obvious. If I said go and clean your teeth and put on your pyjamas, and when you come back downstairs, bring your washing, you'd only remember to do one thing. So I'd send you to clean your teeth, and when you'd done that I'd send you back up to put on your pyjamas, and the third time I'd ask you to fetch the washing down. You never minded making three trips up and down the stairs when you could have made one. You ran everywhere all the time.' I added that once we had the diagnosis we simply did more of the same, and it helped enormously that we knew we were on the right track.

'You were on cloud nine,' I told her. 'I've always said it was as if you grew that day. It was so liberating to you to know you had a "thing", as you called it. It explained so much, and it proved you weren't just being naughty!'

'Wow,' Grace said. She looked very moved, and she gave me a hug. 'I can't believe what you've done for me, Angela. You're amazing. I'm very lucky you're my foster mum.'

Grace didn't often say things like this and I was completely taken aback, and thrilled. Moments like that make my job so worthwhile. I told Grace it was an honour, and that I was very proud of the lovely young woman she had become.

A couple of months after she started her apprenticeship, Grace was presented with an 'employee of the month' award. She came home with a little trophy and some gift vouchers for a local shopping centre.

Jonathan and I took her out for a meal to celebrate, and her boyfriend Robbie came too. We invited my mum, on Grace's suggestion, but she had something else on and couldn't make it. Grace was disappointed about this. Like nearly all of the children who lived with us, she was very fond of my mum and got on very well with her. I told Grace I'd invited Mum for lunch on Sunday so at least she'd see her then.

'Great. I'd like to show her my trophy. I think she'll be really pleased.'

'I know she will,' I said. 'We're all very proud of you, Grace.'

On the Saturday, Grace went into town to spend her shopping vouchers. When she came home she ran straight up to her room, trying to hide a red carrier bag behind her back.

'What did you get?' I asked.

'Oh, nothing exciting, nothing really. Just, er, something to wear.'

She normally showed me any clothes she bought before she took them upstairs but I didn't probe. I thought that maybe she'd bought a present for Robbie that she didn't want to show me, as his birthday was coming up.

On Sunday morning, Grace had a rehearsal with the musical theatre group she was still a member of. Many of the teenagers had left school and worked different hours, so they often met on a Sunday, particularly when a show was imminent. Grace only had a minor role this time, but even so she had worked really hard on polishing her performance. Jonathan asked if she needed a lift and she said Robbie was taking her; he'd just passed his test and was glad of any excuse to go out in his new car. She said he would bring her back too.

'Would he like to join us for lunch?'

'No, it's OK. He has to eat with his family, his uncle is visiting.'

I told her to thank him for the lifts. 'I'll have the dinner ready for one o'clock. Jonathan's collecting Mum after she's been to church.'

'Perfect. Can't wait to see her. Are we having apple crumble?'

'Yes, Grace. And custard.' This was her favourite pudding and she could never have enough of it.

'Yum! Looking forward to it already.'

There was a loud beep-beep from outside.

'Sounds like my lift's here. See you!'

Grace grabbed her bag and dashed out of the front door, but a few minutes later I heard her coming back in. I rolled my eyes; Grace rarely managed to leave the house without running back upstairs to fetch something she'd forgotten.

'Bye again!' I shouted from the kitchen, when I heard her opening the front door again.

'See you!'

At one o'clock I called everyone to the table and told them I was about to serve up.

'Grace should be here any minute,' I said, glancing at the clock. Her rehearsal had been due to finish at twelve thirty and the hall where the group gathered was only ten minutes away from our house.

I stalled for time, fetching drinks while I kept everything warm, but the veg was starting to spoil and I decided we'd better start without Grace.

'I'll plate hers up,' I commented. 'I think it's the last full-cast rehearsal before the big day, so I expect they've overrun.'

Everyone was hungry and we all tucked in. I hoped Grace was going to come in at any minute and I was listening for the door. There's nothing I like more than having everyone round the table on a Sunday, and it just wasn't the same when you had to reheat a plated meal. Besides, Grace had been looking forward to seeing Mum and having lunch with her.

'I bet that as soon as you get the apple crumble out she'll appear, as if by magic!' Jonathan joked.

'Oh yes, it's her favourite, isn't it?' Mum said.

I tuned out as Jonathan carried on chatting to my mum. One of the other children who was living with us joined in their conversation, but I stayed quiet. I sat and looked at Grace's empty place and, as the minutes ticked by, I found my heart tightening in my chest. I'd started to worry that they'd had an accident in Robbie's car. He was no boy racer, I told myself. His father had bought him a second-hand 1.4 Ford Escort. Jonathan had looked it over and commented that it was a very sensible choice for a seventeen-year-old boy. Even so, Robbie had only just passed his test and had precious little driving experience.

'Excuse me,' I said. 'I'm just going to check on something.'

In those days people weren't attached to their mobile phones as they are today, but by now Grace did have a small Nokia and I had one too. I checked my mobile, and the home phone, in case I'd missed a message. There was nothing. I called Grace's number and it went straight to answerphone, but this wasn't unusual. She often missed calls as she forgot to switch the volume back on after putting it on silent during rehearsals.

'Everything OK?' Jonathan asked when I returned to the table.

'I just wish Grace would get back, that's all. I can't get

hold of her, I've just tried ringing. You haven't had a text or a missed call, have you?'

Jonathan's phone was in his pocket. He looked at it and said no, he'd had nothing.

'I wish she'd hurry up too,' Mum smiled. 'I'm looking forward to seeing her trophy.'

The conversation went off in a different direction, with one of the other children telling Mum about the trophy cabinet at her school, which contained cups dating back a hundred years.

'Well I never,' Mum said. 'Nearly as old as me!'

I served up the apple crumble and custard but could barely eat mine. Jonathan caught my eye and patted the back of my hand. I told Mum and the two children to go up to the lounge as soon as they'd finished eating and said I'd bring coffee up shortly. 'Just a small one for me, dear,' Mum said, 'and only half a sugar, brown if you have it.' I heard her asking if anyone fancied a game of Chase the Ace. *Good old Mum*, I thought.

Jonathan came through to the kitchen with me.

'You try Grace again and I'll give Robbie's dad a call, make sure everything's OK.'

'Good idea.'

Grace's mobile went straight to answerphone again. Jonathan phoned Robbie's house and thankfully his father picked up the phone immediately.

'I'm just looking for Grace.' There was a pause as Jonathan listened. 'Oh! Right. OK, thank you. Sorry to bother you, Peter. What was that? No, don't worry. Thanks. Bye.'

'What's going on?' I asked.

Jonathan cleared his throat. 'Robbie is away with his rugby team this weekend. He went on the coach, yesterday morning. Peter saw him off.'

I felt sick with worry. We'd looked after lots of children who told lies at the drop of a hat, but Grace was not one of them. If anything, I'd say the impulsiveness that came with her ADHD meant you were more likely to get a raw and unedited stream of consciousness.

'What's going on? Where *is* she then? And who picked her up this morning? I'm ringing Paula's.'

Paula was one of the other members of the theatre group and a former classmate of Grace's. They'd known each other for years and often went to and from rehearsals and shows together. There was no reply at her house and I had no mobile number for her.

'Hopefully they're together,' Jonathan fretted. 'Surely there's a reasonable explanation for this.' I had a mobile number for Paula's mother and I tried that, but she didn't pick up. I immediately started hunting in the phone book for a number for the hall where the rehearsals were held. My hands were starting to tremble as I turned the pages. There was one number listed, for bookings, and I stabbed the digits into the handset of our home phone. It rang out for ages before clicking onto a message advising me to call during office hours.

'I'll drive down there,' Jonathan said, taking his car key off the hook by the kitchen door.

He dashed out.

'Drive carefully!'

I remembered about the coffee and put the kettle on. While it was boiling I started loading up a tray, and then the phone rang.

'Angela? Sorry I missed your call. How can I help?'

It was Paula's mother.

'Thanks for calling. I just wondered if Grace was with Paula. I thought she'd be back from rehearsals by now.'

'No, I'm afraid not. Paula went to her dad's straight from rehearsals, he picked her up.' Though I didn't go into any detail, Paula's mum must have been able to tell I was worried. 'Why don't you give Paula a ring?'

I took Paula's mobile number gratefully from her mum and, to my relief, she answered immediately. However, it wasn't good news.

'Didn't she tell you?' Paula said. 'She's such a scatter-brain! She was going to her mum's this afternoon. I think her sister was picking her up.'

'Oh, thank you, Paula. I'm really sorry to bother you. Enjoy the rest of your day.'

I stared at the phone in disbelief. It was so out of character for Grace to behave like this. If she wanted to visit her mum, why didn't she just say? And why had Lily picked her up, if that was true? Nobody in the family ever collected Grace by car. Barry did all the lifts until Grace became old enough to travel on her own. Since then it had always been up to her to take two or three buses to visit them.

I knew Colette's home number by heart and I dialled it immediately. As I pressed the numbers I told myself to stay calm, whatever news I was about to receive. The phone didn't ring out; all I got was a BT message telling me Colette's landline was temporarily out of service. 'No!' I said out loud. 'No!'

I tried Grace's mobile number again with no joy. Jonathan was still out in the car. I wondered whether to call him to let him know what Paula's mum had said but I decided against it. He'd be driving, and no doubt he'd be back any minute.

I made the coffee and carried the tray into the lounge.

'Any news from Grace? Are you not joining us, dear?'

'No, Mum. I'll be back shortly, there's something I need to do.'

I shut the lounge door behind me and headed up to Grace's bedroom. I remembered her running back into the house after her lift arrived this morning, and the fact she'd hidden her shopping bag from me the previous day. I had no idea what I was about to find, and I was scared she may have packed her bags.

Nervously, I pushed open the door. I can't describe the relief that coursed through me when I saw the usual clutter and chaos of Grace's bedroom. My eyes instinctively flicked up to the top of the wardrobe. Her old suitcase was still there, just as it had been for years. Her cuddly swan was in its usual place too, which was now on the shelf by her bed.

I heard Jonathan come in and I ran downstairs.

'I think she's gone to her mother's,' I said.

He breathed out a sigh of relief and wrapped his arms around me.

'Thank God. But why didn't she tell us?'

'I don't know, I don't know. I think Lily collected her. I spoke to Paula. I can't get hold of Colette, her home phone's not working.'

'OK. We'll just have to keep trying Grace's number, and if we still can't get through we'll have to phone out-of-hours.' The rule was that if a child was missing in daylight, you waited two hours before calling in. After dark, it was one hour. The emergency social worker would log the call and most likely tell us to call the police and report Grace as a missing person. It was nearly two o'clock now. Jonathan and I agreed we'd give it until three before we raised the alarm.

I tried Grace's number again, and then I remembered that she kept her mum's mobile number pinned on the noticeboard in her bedroom. I raced upstairs again, found the number partly hidden under an old concert ticket and dialled it as quickly as possible.

'Hello?'

'Colette, is that you?'

'Yes, who's this?'

'Angela. Angela Hart.'

I hadn't spoken to Colette for quite a long time, but even so I thought she'd have recognised my voice.

'Oh, it's you,' she said rudely.

'I'm looking for Grace. Her friend said Lily picked her up.'

'Yeah, that's right.'

'So she's with you? She's OK?'

'Yeah. What's wrong?'

'I didn't know she was going to your house. I was expecting her in for lunch and I've been worried. Can I talk to her, please?'

Colette sighed loudly, as if this was a huge inconvenience.

'Gracie! Gracie! It's your carer on the phone.'

There was quite a long delay and the line was crackling. I was worried we'd get cut off, but then Grace came on the line.

'I'm really sorry I didn't tell you,' she said. 'But Lily really needs me and I knew you'd go mad if I told you. I was just about to call you.'

'Well we have been worried, Grace. We expected you home by one at the latest. It's three now.'

'Is it? Oh, I had no idea.'

She sounded genuinely surprised by the time. I kept calm and reminded myself that poor time management was one of the symptoms of ADHD.

'I'm sorry,' she went on. 'But, like, Harley needed a nappy change so we had to stop off and the traffic was bad so it took us ages to get here. Anyway, look, I have to help Lily or she'll, like, lose her job. And then how will she feed the baby?'

Breathlessly, Grace explained that Colette was going on holiday to the Canaries for a fortnight and that Lily had asked her to stay and help with Harley. Apparently, the cafe where Lily now worked part time had refused to give her any time off and her boss had told her if she didn't turn up he'd fire her. Lily had told Grace she wouldn't trust Harley with anyone other than her sister, and that it would be great for them to spend two weeks together while their mum was away. The reason Grace had not told me any of this in advance was because she knew I would not approve of her missing a fortnight of her apprenticeship scheme to cover for Lily.

I wanted to scream, I really did. In my opinion, Lily had smooth-talked and emotionally blackmailed Grace, putting her in a really difficult spot. It sounded like incredibly selfish behaviour. For years Lily had bullied Grace and made her feel awkward and inferior for being the one in care while she was allowed to live with her mum. Now, all of a sudden, here she was telling Grace how much she needed her and rated her as a trustworthy person.

'What about your apprenticeship, Grace?'

She was still within her probation period and I knew she didn't have the holiday entitlement to cover this.

'We've worked it out. I'm going to have to call in sick.'

'Grace!'

We hadn't brought her up to behave this way, and she knew exactly what we would have said if she'd told us what she planned to do.

'I'm sorry, Angela. I'll have to go now. Mum wants her phone.'

21

'It's what I've always wanted'

After staying with Lily and the baby for two weeks, Grace announced to me that she had decided she was going to move back into the family home permanently.

'Harley's not going to be a baby forever, is he?' she said. Grace had an unfamiliar swagger about her, and I could just picture Lily saying those same words.

I was standing behind the counter in the shop when Grace delivered this statement. She'd just come back on the bus, on time, which I was pleased about. After her two weeks away I'd been really looking forward to seeing her and getting back to normal, but my heart was beating like a drum now.

'Move home? But how can you, Grace?'

'What do you mean? I can if I want. I'm nearly seventeen.' With that she waltzed off, heading through the back of the shop and into the house. I had no idea if she meant she was planning on moving out now or at the end of her apprenticeship. Surely it would be after she'd done her twelve months at the advertising agency?

Barbara, our shop assistant, was within earshot and she threw me an encouraging look. She'd known Grace for as long as we had, and she also knew me very well. My feelings were hurt and, whether she meant it or not, I was stung by what Grace had said. It must have been obvious to Barbara.

'I can manage here, if you need to take a break,' she said, even though it was a Saturday afternoon and she'd be run off her feet if I left her on her own.

'Thanks, Barbara, that's kind, but I think I'll just let her settle back in. I expect she's tired out after the journey.'

Though Grace had upset me by talking about moving out in such a blunt and insensitive way, I told myself not to stress about it. *I've been down this road before*, I told myself once again, and there was no point in worrying unnecessarily about a 'what if' scenario that may never happen, at least not any time soon.

Grace was only a few months into her apprenticeship. It was a twelve-month scheme with good prospects. All being well, it would lead to a permanent position. She still had a good relationship with Robbie and a very active social life, and she was about to appear in one of her favourite musicals on stage. In short, she'd built up a very good life in our town, and if she left abruptly now she had an awful lot to lose.

Jonathan and I would miss her terribly, of course, but that was not the priority. Grace's happiness, now and in the future, was what mattered. Though Colette and Lily both seemed to have mellowed since Harley was born, I really wasn't convinced that the family home was the best place for her, as both women still seemed to live quite chaotic lives. Grace had told me tales of rows with the neighbours, disagreements with other family members, drunken nights out and run-ins with officials about housing benefit and unpaid bills. I had heard that, because of the baby, Social Services still had the family on their radar.

I didn't underestimate how important it was to Grace to see Harley grow up, but it wasn't as if she'd never see him. She could visit every weekend if she wanted to. When Robbie had passed his driving test we'd talked about booking some lessons for Grace's seventeenth birthday, which was only a few months away. She was very keen on this and had talked about buying a car with the modelling money she had saved, saying how much easier it would be to visit her family when she had her own transport.

'Angela!' a voice called.

I was startled and I jumped out of my skin. 'Angela, are you all right?' It was Barbara, and she was thrusting a tissue at me. I hadn't realised how deep in thought I'd been. 'Take this. Here, let me help you. Are you OK?'

'Fine, yes. Oh!' I looked down and saw blood on my hands. I'd been preparing a bouquet of roses and I must have pricked myself on a thorn while my mind was wandering, thinking everything through about Grace.

There was a lull in the shop now, and Barbara told me again that she could hold the fort, if I wanted her to.

'OK, I think I will take a quick break. I'll bring you a cup of tea when I come back.'

I went into the kitchen and found Grace making a sandwich. She appeared much calmer and more relaxed than she had been when she first came back and made her announcement in the shop.

'Can I get you anything?' she asked politely.

'I was just going to make a cup of tea.'

'Sit down, I'll do it for you.'

'Thanks.'

Grace seemed sheepish, I thought. I guessed she must have been feeling sorry for the way she'd behaved over the last couple of weeks, and in the shop earlier on.

I'd always made an effort to accommodate her impulsiveness and the lack of control she sometimes displayed, as I knew it was down to her ADHD. It must have been very difficult to be in her shoes, and I didn't want to make her suffer. After years of being made to feel like the black sheep of the family, I couldn't blame Grace for the way she'd responded to Lily's dilemma.

I'd learned that Grace was a natural people-pleaser. She always liked to show willing, and for years she'd been looking for any kind of positive endorsement from her family. Unfortunately, her condition sometimes meant that she was over-exuberant and jumped in feet first when really she needed to stop and think. I realised it was for this reason, and not because she was insensitive, that she hadn't been able to help herself from telling me what was on her mind the minute she returned from her mother's. I knew full well that Grace wore her heart on her sleeve, she made rash decisions and her mood could change like the wind. I had to keep trying to be understanding, and I reasoned to myself that her outburst about moving out would no doubt have been an example of her hot-headedness, and that nothing would really come of it.

'I've got you these,' Grace said, handing me a carrier bag. 'Sorry they're not wrapped.'

I opened the bag and lifted out the gift. It was a beautiful pair of woollen gloves, in a shade of blue I loved.

'Grace! They're gorgeous. Thank you so much. You shouldn't have. It's not my birthday, why did you get me a present?'

'I saw them and just thought you'd like them.' She told me which shop they came from and I realised she must have bought them that day she went to the shopping centre with the gift vouchers she received from work. When she'd dashed upstairs that day, hiding something behind her back, it had been this same carrier bag.

'I wanted to say thank you, for helping me get my job and, well, for everything. I'm sorry about all the, like, hassle. I want you to know, I'm not going to do anything stupid. I'm sorry.'

'I'm glad to hear it. As I've always said, Grace, you can talk to me about anything you like. Please come to me and talk to me if there is anything at all you want to have a chat about. There's no need to do anything behind my back. You can always come to me. I have nothing but your best interests at heart.'

'I will. You're the best. My mum still thinks you and Jonathan are only in this for the money, but I know better!'

Grace meant this as a compliment, but it didn't quite come out that way!

*

She returned to work without a problem the following Monday. I never found out the ins and outs, but she told me she had sorted everything out with her employer. I assumed she had continued with the lie about being sick during her two-week absence, but I'm not sure. I'd made it plain I did not approve if that was the case, and I think she got the message that she must never do that again. At last I started to relax about what Grace had said about moving out; clearly she'd blurted this out in the heat of the moment and was not going to do anything rash.

A couple of weeks later, Jonathan and I went to see her performing in the musical she'd been rehearsing for. Despite only having a minor role, Grace stole the show. Her voice was beautiful and, whenever she was on stage, you couldn't take your eyes off her.

'I know I'm biased, but she's absolutely brilliant,' I said to Jonathan.

'Is that your daughter?' the lady sitting next to me said. 'She's got real talent. You must be very proud.'

'We're extremely proud,' Jonathan said. He squeezed my hand and we exchanged a glance. 'She's a star.'

We didn't do it often, but that evening we allowed ourselves a pat on the back. Grace had come such a long way, and we felt privileged to have played a supporting role in her journey.

We had one of our regular Social Services placement meetings the following week. As Grace would soon turn seventeen her social worker, who was a new recruit called Glynn, was focused on her care plan 'going forward'. He talked about

Grace moving into supported lodgings which, as I explained earlier, was the usual procedure in those days.

'We're in no hurry for her to move out,' Jonathan said. Glynn then started talking about money and funding. 'As you know, our policy is to encourage kids to move on at some point during their sixteenth year.' He started to discuss the fact that funding for Grace's foster care place would eventually run out.

Jonathan told Glynn that money was not an issue and we would do whatever was best for Grace. If she wanted to stay with us indefinitely, she was very welcome. This was something we'd discussed and both felt strongly about, and we'd made this plain to Grace too.

Glynn had chatted to Grace privately before he spoke to us. To our relief, she had told him she wanted to stay with us until she had finished her apprenticeship, the following September.

'That's great news,' I said. 'I think that's for the best, and hopefully she'll be kept on at the same firm. She can stay with us until she's good and ready to move on.'

'Agreed,' Jonathan said.

Glynn seemed very happy with this. He thanked us and left. I felt very relieved and pleased about what Grace had told him; this meant she would be with us for at least another nine months, and hopefully longer. Barry, incidentally, had moved to another area and continued working as a social worker until his retirement. We felt he'd done a good job for Grace and were sorry to lose him.

*

Life returned to normal, and the weeks seem to whizz by in the run-up to Christmas. Grace was extremely busy, going to parties, socialising with her work colleagues, keeping up with her old school friends and taking part in a Christmas carol concert put on by the musical theatre group.

She had spent the last six Christmases with us, but this year Grace decided to spend it at home. She was desperate to spend the day with Harley and, though we would miss her, Jonathan and I understood and supported this decision. I enjoyed helping Grace pick out some little clothes for Harley, including a hat with Santa on it.

Jonathan and I gave Grace a present to open on Christmas Day – we'd got her two tickets for a show she wanted to see in the city – and we waved her off at the bus stop, asking her to call us when she arrived at her mum's house. She did, and on Christmas Day we called her on her mobile. She was thrilled with the tickets and said we were 'the best'. She also said she wanted to take me with her to see the show.

'Are you sure? You can take anyone you like.'

'I know. I want to take you.'

I told her I was very touched, as I'd expected her to take Robbie. Jonathan and I both wished Grace a very happy Christmas and asked her to give our best wishes to the family. Very unexpectedly, Colette came on the phone. She told me she was grateful for all we'd done for her daughter over the years. I think she'd had a few drinks, but nevertheless that's what she said and I was grateful for her kind words.

'Grace is such a lovely girl,' I replied. 'I'm so pleased that she's doing so well.'

It wasn't until a week later that I looked back and realised what Colette was actually saying to me on Christmas Day. She was thanking me for everything we'd done over the years because she knew something I didn't. The truth was, she and Lily had finally convinced Grace, once and for all, that it would be a good idea if she moved back in with them permanently, and Grace had agreed.

Grace told me all of this in a breathless, rushed conversation when she returned to our house fleetingly on New Year's Day. We'd been out visiting friends and Jonathan had dropped me home and gone to the garage to fill up the car with petrol. The first sign that something was wrong was when I walked in the front door and saw Grace's luggage stacked up in the hallway. It was an awful shock; it was one of those moments when you feel your blood run cold and your breath catches in your throat.

There was no sign of the old grey suitcase, but several of Grace's holdalls and rucksacks were there, bulging at the seams. She'd obviously helped herself to some bin bags too.

'What's going on?' I gasped as Grace appeared on the stairs.

'I'm going home. I'm moving back home, for good.' She blurted out that her mum and sister really wanted her to move back and she loved being there. 'It's my family, I can't say no. I mean, I want to go. It's what I've always wanted.'

Grace couldn't look me in the eye.

'But Grace, what about your job?'

'I know, but I'll manage. Family is the most important thing. I'm only young.'

Yet again I had the uncomfortable feeling that Grace was regurgitating something that somebody else had dripped into her ear. The doorbell rang as I stood rooted to the spot, trying to take all this in. Grace rushed to answer it and, much to my surprise, Lily appeared. I hadn't seen her for more than six years, but it seemed like yesterday. The curled lip was the same. The rude manner and attitude took me right back. Nothing appeared to have changed, except for the fact her hair was now blonde.

'Ready?' she said to Grace curtly, completely ignoring me as she barged into the hallway uninvited. 'All this to go?'

'Yep,' Grace said. She looked mortified but said nothing to me and started carrying her belongings out to Lily's car.

'Grace, are you sure about this?'

I stood on the pavement outside the house, watching the two sisters load the boot.

'Yes,' she said. 'Like I said, family is important, isn't it? I need to . . . I, like, want to do this. Sorry.'

Lily gave me a valedictory look as they drove off minutes later. I was wiping away my tears in the kitchen when Jonathan came back from the petrol station.

'I can't believe it,' I said. 'I just can't believe it.'

'Nor can I. Are you sure she's serious?'

'Absolutely. You should have seen Lily's face. She thinks she's won.'

'Has Grace taken everything?'

'I don't know, but probably not. I haven't been up to her room, I can't face it. But she took a lot with her.'

I thought about calling Social Services and leaving a message with the duty officer, to let them know the situation, but I decided to leave it until the next day. Though this felt like an emergency to us, it wasn't a situation Social Services needed to respond to urgently. Grace was over the age of sixteen and could have legally moved into a place of her own by now. The fact she was living with her mother and her sister would not give Social Services any cause for concern as, in the eyes of the care system, she was old enough to make her own mind up, and there had never been any restrictions on Grace staying in the family home.

Jonathan made us a cup of tea and we sat at the kitchen table and chatted for a while. The atmosphere was very subdued and we both took it in turns to offer words of comfort to the other: 'She'll come round', 'she'll soon get fed up', 'she'll miss her life here'. Neither of us had a clue if any of these platitudes would turn out to be true; it was wishful thinking.

'It's the apprenticeship I'm really gutted about,' I said. 'She did so well to get on it, and things were going so well.'

'I know. She's made such a bad decision. Why didn't she hang on until September at least? She's already done three months and that went by in a flash.'

'I have a theory about the timing,' I said. 'But I hope I'm wrong.'

I didn't have to spell out to Jonathan what I was thinking.

We'd talked about this before and he knew all too well what was on my mind. Of course, we were all too familiar with the scenario where a parent who has been resistant to caring for their child suddenly wants them back at the point when they are capable of earning money and paying keep.

'I just hope Lily doesn't start bullying her and leaning on her,' Jonathan said.

'I'm afraid it may be too late for that.'

I loaded the dishwasher and went up to Grace's bedroom. It didn't even look like she'd moved out, which was comforting, up to a point. I'd have been devastated if she'd completely cleared her room out, but her posters were still on the walls, there were lots of clothes hanging in the wardrobe and all sorts of belongings scattered around the room. This gave me hope that she'd left the door open and might come back, but I knew there was no guarantee. Perhaps she would simply come back and collect the rest of her things another day, or maybe she just didn't want all this stuff.

I looked to the top of the wardrobe and was surprised that her old grey suitcase was missing. I hadn't seen her take that with her and wondered where it had gone.

The Christmas decorations were still up. Normally I leave everything out until 5 January, but I felt miserable when I looked at the baubles and sprigs of holly and twinkling lights. Suddenly, everything felt so meaningless. I could picture Grace in years gone by, getting out of bed at four in the morning and knocking on our bedroom door, asking if it was too early to open presents. One year we got her a karaoke machine and she sang her heart out for about three days solid. Then there was the Christmas when she bought *herself* a present and wrapped it up and put it under the tree. She'd saved up her pocket money and bought a CD of her favourite band, as she was worried nobody would get it for her!

Our Christmas tree had dropped a lot of its needles and was looking a bit sorry for itself. I used this as an excuse to take it down; I just didn't want to look at it any more. The rest of the decorations could stay. We had two other teenagers in the house, and for their sake I didn't think it was fair to erase Christmas completely, not just yet.

After I'd packed away all the baubles and lights off the tree I asked Jonathan to give me a hand taking it outside. Together, we carried the tree down the stairs and out into the back garden, ready to take it to the tip.

'Let's put it by the wheelie bin.' As I spoke, I glanced over to the shelter where we kept the bins. Wedged down the side was Grace's old, grey suitcase. Jonathan and I both stopped in our tracks and stared at it.

'I wonder why she did that?' he said.

I found myself smiling. 'Do you know what? I don't blame her for throwing that old thing away. In fact, I'm glad she's finally got rid of it. Who knows what will happen next, but at least Grace will never have to go through the ordeal of moving to another foster home.'

Jonathan gave me a smile. 'Now that's a positive spin, if ever I heard one.'

Though Grace's future was uncertain, we both took comfort from the fact that her placement with us had been a success. We had broken the cycle she had been through so many times before, of moving from one foster home to the next. We'd had the honour of raising Grace for six years and, despite the difficulties she'd had to contend with, she had grown into a wonderful young woman.

22

'You are not her foster mum any more'

Grace called me the day after she left. She wanted to say sorry again for moving out in such a hurry, and she asked if we could make arrangements to go to the concert she had the tickets for. I said that, yes, I'd still love to go to the concert.

'Whatever happens, Jonathan and I always want to keep in touch with you, Grace. And if you want to come back, any time, the door will be open for you.'

Though I didn't think Grace had any intention of coming back to live with us I could tell she appreciated the offer. It proved to her that, come what may, we genuinely cared about her and had her best interests at heart.

'Thanks. That's kind, but I think I've kind of made my mind up this time. You've been so good to me, but I'm ready to move on. I think it's all going to work out well – me being at my mum's, I mean.'

I had to face the fact that Social Services would now close her file and, of course, we would no longer be her foster carers. The thought upset me, but at the end of the day

Grace was nearly seventeen, and back then it was normal for children to leave care at that age.

On the afternoon of the concert I took a train and met Grace in the city. She met me at the station and we greeted each other like old friends, which felt bittersweet. I wanted to continue to look after her as a carer, in the way I'd done for so many years, but it was no longer my place to behave in that way. She was wearing a very thin coat despite the bitter cold, but I bit my tongue instead of ticking her off for this, as I would have done in the past. Instead, I told Grace she looked well, which she did.

'Thanks, you do too and it's great to see you,' she said. 'I've missed you!'

'Same here. The house isn't the same without you.'

'No, it's better isn't it?' she joked, laughing loudly.

I laughed too but only out of politeness, as the truth was I missed her a great deal and it felt like there was a huge Grace-shaped hole in the house.

I was happy to see that she seemed quite calm and collected throughout the evening. She chatted openly about her life back with her mum and sister, telling me they were in the process of moving.

'It'll be easier for me to visit you from the new house,' she told me, which was music to my ears. Grace also said she had the chance of a part-time office job, which she was going to look into.

'You don't need to worry about me. And that apprentice-ship wasn't a waste of time, so don't worry about that either.

It was good experience that is going to help me get paid work.'

I didn't argue. It was tough, but I had to accept that our relationship had completely changed. I was not Grace's carer any longer and I realised that if I was seen to be interfering it could cause trouble for her. I imagined her family telling her she didn't have to listen to Jonathan and me any more. It was possible they might even try to stop her seeing us if they thought I was poking my nose in, which of course was the last thing I wanted. Besides, the apprenticeship was past rescuing by now and Grace had clearly bought into the idea that she was ready to get herself an office job.

I told Grace I was pleased her mum's move would make her journey to our house easier and reiterated that she was welcome any time and that we very much wanted to keep in touch.

'Great, I've missed your Sunday lunches. Can I come soon? Maybe next week?'

'Of course you can.'

I didn't hold my breath as I felt Grace had said this in the heat of the moment and might change her mind on reflection, once she was back in the family fold. However, Grace was true to her word, and the following Sunday she came for lunch.

Her relationship with Robbie had survived her move and he collected her from her mum's and drove the two of them to our house. I'd like to say it was just like old times as we sat around the table, but of course it wasn't. Grace went bright red when one of the other teenagers asked her why she'd left.

'I'm sixteen and I can earn a wage and stand on my own two feet now,' she said. I wasn't sure she believed her own publicity; she looked very uncomfortable as she spoke.

'Don't you miss it here? What about all your mates?'

'Yes, but I'm with my family and my nephew is still only little. It's important to see him grow up.'

Before Grace left she took another bag of belongings with her, including her life story books. I told her we would keep her things safe and she could collect the rest of her belongings whenever she wanted to.

From then on Grace kept in touch regularly by phone and visited at least every couple of weeks. She didn't get the office job she wanted and had started to work in the cafe where Lily worked. It sounded like they shared a job and the childcare for Harley while Colette did various 'cash in hand' jobs, as Grace called them, like bar work and helping in her friend's beauty salon.

Grace always told us she loved visiting us, and she never failed to give us a big hug and say how happy she was to see us.

Unfortunately, it wasn't long before we started to see a change in Grace. She put on a great deal of weight. I could sympathise with this as I've struggled with my own weight all my life, but Grace's weight gain was rapid and extreme and made her a very unhealthy size, which worried me. She had started smoking and drinking too, which she made no secret of, and very soon her hair and skin started to look terrible.

A few months after she had moved out Grace broke up with Robbie.

'What happened?' I asked.

I thought the distance must have taken its toll, but that was only part of the story.

'It was just too far and I think we've grown apart,' she said, sounding old beyond her years. 'We'd been together a long time and it happens, you know?'

I was surprised at how unaffected Grace seemed by this break-up. She showed no emotion, even when she confided that he was 'devastated' at what had happened.

'What can I do? The thing is, we're very different. I've changed. He prefers playing sports to going out. He's boring.'

I said I was sorry to hear this and asked if she felt they would stay friends.

'No. What's the point? He's gone so boring, Angela. I've moved on.'

Sadly, Grace had given up all her sports and her musical theatre had gone by the board too. She had vowed to join a theatre company in her new neighbourhood, but nothing ever came of that. She had also lost contact with nearly all of her old friends from our neighbourhood. I was concerned at how disposable her former life seemed to have become.

'How's the job going?' Jonathan asked. 'I expect you'll be busier now the weather's warming up?'

'Oh, you mean that crappy job in the cafe? I'm not doing that any more.'

'What happened?'

Reluctantly, she admitted she'd been sacked, and when we asked her why she was extremely rude about her boss and used language I was very shocked to hear.

'Grace!' I said, afraid others in the house might hear.

'Sorry,' she said moodily. 'I forgot where I was.'

I felt my heart sink. It was obvious she behaved very differently when she was with her family and new friends, and I was growing increasingly worried that all the progress Grace had made when she lived with us was starting to come undone.

Each time I saw her I tried to offer help and advice, such as suggesting ways she could improve her diet, telling her how Jonathan and I used to smoke and how we managed to quit, or talking about starting some form of training to get back on the career ladder. She had an answer for everything, and always knocked every positive suggestion I made. 'Lil needs me to help with Harley so for now I can't do a college course or get a proper job,' 'Mum does the shopping, there's nothing I can do about the food I eat. She buys what she likes and she's no good at cooking,' 'Everyone smokes and drinks and I'd be the odd one out if I didn't.' When I challenged her on this last point she said, 'I've been the odd one out for long enough.'

There were many times when I saw Lily in my mind's eye when Grace spoke. Other times, Grace blamed her ADHD for some of the issues she was now facing in her life, which I found very annoying. She had never used it as an excuse for anything before. Yes, the ADHD was an added hurdle she had to jump, but we had always taught

Grace to look for a way to move forward instead of dwelling on the problem.

'She's going backwards so fast it's frightening,' Jonathan said, after one particularly upsetting visit. Grace had told us, in a very blasé fashion, that Lily had started using drugs again. 'But it's only cannabis, not ecstasy like before,' she said nonchalantly. 'Everyone does dope.' I was horrified, not least because this was the first time I'd been told Lily had taken ecstasy in the past, or any kind of drug for that matter.

Grace was seventeen now. I spoke in confidence to a social worker about the issue of drugs in the family home, asking for advice. She suggested I could report the drug-taking anonymously, focusing on concerns about the baby. I was considering this when Grace told me, out of the blue, that Lily and Harley had been given a council flat of their own and were moving out. I hoped this might prove to be a positive turning point for Grace, but it wasn't.

According to Grace, when Lily and Harley moved out, Colette lost a lot of benefits and could no longer afford the house she had planned to move to. She and Grace ended up in a tiny council house on a rough estate in an area of high unemployment. When they moved in, both of them were jobless and living on meagre benefits. It was incredibly sad to hear how quickly Grace's life had spiralled down-wards. I kept telling her she was welcome back with us at any time, but it seemed that, now Lily had gone, Colette was depending on Grace emotionally and made no secret of this.

'Mum needs me,' Grace told me on many occasions. 'She says she couldn't manage without me. She says she doesn't know what she would do without me, now Lily has gone. I'm her life, you know.'

One day, Grace brought her life story books back to us.

'Mum said she hasn't got room for them.'

By this time Grace had taken everything she wanted from her old bedroom in our house. Though it pained us, Jonathan and I had finally accepted she wasn't coming back and had started to take in other foster children who needed respite care.

'How are things going?' I asked pointedly as I took the life story books off her.

Grace's eyes were flicking around the room, just as they used to when she was a much smaller child. She was distracted, moody, uncommunicative and fidgety.

'What? Hey, everything's cool,' she said. I wasn't convinced.

In my mind's eye I thought of some of the lovely images contained within the life story books. I could see Grace, triumphant on stage in a musical production, collecting the winner's cup at a swimming gala, camping with her primary school friends, grinning as she blew out the candles on a birthday cake, barbecuing with Jonathan on a caravan holiday, beaming as she held aloft her impressive GCSE certificate and posing for the camera in her days as a young catalogue model.

I looked at Grace now. Her bloated cheeks were an angry red and puffed out, she seemed to have a permanent sheen of sweat on her brow and she had taken to dressing in nothing but huge jogging bottoms and sloppy hoodies. Even her speech was different.

'I'm going outside for a fag, OK with you, Angela?' She said this in a confrontational way that made it clear she was not asking a question at all.

As always, I attempted to steer Grace onto the right path while trying not to interfere, for fear of irritating or alienating her. It was an impossible tightrope to tread, and by this time Grace was starting to use that very annoying response 'whatever' to any attempt I made to propel her on to better things.

Jonathan put her life story books in the loft. We both told ourselves that at least she was keeping in touch, and we talked about the fact all was not lost. 'She's still very young. She's still growing up. She'll start thinking for herself before too long. Everything will work out. We've given her a good foundation to build on.' We said those kinds of things often. Fortunately, the other two girls seemed to take Grace's departure in their stride. Both were on the cusp of moving out themselves and had a lot going on in their own lives to distract them. It is sad to say, but even after living together for so many years, the bond between the three girls was not strong. I think their collective problems prevented them from forming the friendships they might have done.

The next time Grace arranged to come over for Sunday lunch she didn't show up. Ever since she'd moved out she had always been punctual for her visits and alarm bells started ringing straight away. I tried her mobile with no luck and left a text message asking her to ring. We told ourselves not to panic, reasoning that she was just running late, or that she'd changed her plans and simply forgotten to tell us. We didn't have her new home phone number and realised we didn't even have her new address, as the move into the new council house was so recent and we hadn't thought to ask her.

Eventually, I tried Colette's old mobile number. It went to answerphone so I left a message, asking if Grace was OK and saying we had been expecting her for lunch. I got a curt text message back which read: 'You are not her foster mum any more. Please leave my daughter alone to get on with her life. Thank you.'

I was staring at the message in shock when I received another text, this time from Grace. It read, 'Sorry Angela. I'll be in touch.' She signed off with a nickname we some-times used, so I was in no doubt the message came from Grace herself.

Jonathan and I were shocked and upset but did our best to try to look on the bright side. It was Colette who had behaved badly. Grace had a mind of her own and would no doubt phone up in a few days' time, we figured. She'd probably start chattering away as if nothing had happened, apologising and asking when she could next visit.

In fact, we didn't hear from Grace that week, or the next, and she didn't respond to any of our subsequent calls or messages, which we made when we started to worry all over again. Eventually, I called Social Services to ask if they could check she was safe. They did this, and said that she was, but they were not at liberty to give us any further details. If

Grace did not want to keep in touch this was her prerogative. As former foster carers, we had no say, and, as our former foster child, Grace had no obligation to maintain contact with us in any way.

As week after week passed, we started to feel extremely disheartened, to say the least. Grace had obviously decided to cut contact after all, no doubt on Colette's advice. When this realisation sunk in it was devastating, although my instincts told me this would still not be the end.

'She'll be back,' I said to Jonathan. 'I don't know when or how, but my gut is telling me this is not the end of our relationship with Grace. We'll just have to be patient.'

'Do you know what? I'm glad you said that. I feel exactly the same. It's strange, isn't it? I know we'll see her again. She's been too much a part of our lives to disappear without trace. We have a bond.'

We sat tight and waited for the day when Grace would finally get back in touch. She was never far from our thoughts, and we never gave up hope, even as the weeks turned to months and the months turned to years.

23

'I've made a lot of mistakes'

It was a very wet, wintery day and we'd just returned from buying our Christmas tree. One of the children had been mucking about at the garden centre and had got herself soaking wet, charging through a puddle. When I heard our doorbell ring, I was on the top floor of the house, my arms full of Chelsea's damp clothes for the wash.

'Jonathan!' I called over the bannisters. 'Can you get that?'

'Yes, will do!'

I heard him asking Finn, the young lad who was also staying with us, to hang on to the Christmas tree. Looking back, Jonathan probably had his hands fuller than I did at that moment, as he was in the middle of fixing the tree into its stand, but thankfully he isn't one to argue! I heard him leave the lounge and head downstairs to answer the door.

We weren't expecting visitors and I wondered who was out in this filthy weather. It was such a dark and bitterly cold afternoon, and rain was lashing down relentlessly.

'I'll put this washing straight on now,' I told Chelsea,

piling the clothes into a laundry bin. 'Enjoy your shower. There's a clean set of clothes on your bed. Come down when you're ready and we'll have a hot drink.'

I started across the landing, carrying the laundry bin with me, but I stopped in my tracks when I heard Jonathan open the front door and exclaim, 'Is that you?' There was a momentary pause before he added incredulously, 'Grace?'

I gasped and dropped the laundry bin at my feet. It had been five years since we'd seen or heard from Grace. I knew without calculating that she would now be a twenty-two-year-old woman.

'It IS you! Grace, well what a surprise this is!'

I ran down the stairs, heart pounding. *Five years! I knew she'd get in touch one day I knew it!* Wide-eyed, Jonathan turned to look at me as I rushed to join him and peered outside. Grace's face was illuminated by our porch light. There was no mistaking her, yet I could scarcely believe what I was seeing.

'Grace!' I exclaimed. 'Is it really you! Come in, come in.'

She smiled shyly but didn't move. In that moment it felt like the years fell away. How many times had I opened our front door to Grace? How long had it been since I'd seen her standing in front of me like this? It seemed like yesterday, yet also a lifetime ago.

The rain was dancing off the pavement. 'What a filthy night. Come in Grace, come on in.' I wanted to rush forward and hug her, but instinctively I stepped back to make way for her. Jonathan did the same.

'OK, but I can't stop,' she said anxiously. Glancing back over her shoulder, she explained, 'Mum's in the car.'

An old but never-forgotten image of Colette shot across my brain. I could see her as clear as day, towering over her slender little daughter. In my memory, Grace had shrunk under her mum's critical gaze. 'I've been good,' she was telling her mother. Grace's voice was squashed to a thin, quiet whisper. But Colette didn't believe her daughter was capable of behaving herself.

'Angela, here, may not be able to keep you if you start getting up to your old tricks, you know that, don't you? Then what? You could find yourself in a children's home.'

I can still recall the anger I felt towards Colette for saying that to Grace. She was just a child. Ten years old and desperate to please her mum, the very person who had shunned her and watched her ricochet from one failed foster placement to the next. I couldn't understand why Colette would say such a thing to her little girl. How could she?

Jonathan's voice brought me back to the present.

'Let me take your coat, Grace.'

'No, honestly. I can only stay a couple of minutes.'

I told her she was welcome to invite her mum in but she said Colette was happy to wait in the car.

Grace was wearing a large shapeless anorak, saggy jogging bottoms and old trainers. I'm afraid I was shocked and saddened by her appearance. You didn't need to be a serial weightwatcher like me to recognise that Grace was dangerously overweight, and she looked scruffy and dishevelled.

'I can't tell you how good it is to see you,' Jonathan said. 'What a terrific surprise!'

'I wasn't sure what you'd say, if you'd even be here or if you wouldn't want to see me . . .'

'Don't be silly,' I said. 'We're so pleased to see you, sweetheart. Come into the kitchen for a minute, it's nice and warm in there.'

'Thanks, Angela.' Unexpectedly, before taking another step, Grace leaned towards me and gave me a gentle little hug. I felt an overpowering surge of compassion for her and experienced the same emotions I'd felt so many years earlier, the first time she arrived at our door, forlorn and insecure after spending years of her childhood in different foster homes, and in disarray. Then and now, I wanted to love her, care for her, protect her and tell her everything would be OK. She was safe. We would offer her support and help her in any way we could.

You couldn't fail to see that Grace's size made it difficult for her to walk and sit with ease. As she wedged herself self-consciously into one of our kitchen chairs my heart went out to her. What on earth had happened these past few years?

Under the kitchen spotlights I could see that Grace's once spectacular mop of strawberry blonde curls had become a frizzy, matted thatch of hair that was a hotchpotch of artificial colours. Two crops of angry spots sat like parenthesis around her mouth. Grace had been overweight the last time we saw her as a teenager, and her hair and skin had not looked good, but she appeared so much worse now. It was heartbreaking.

'What's new then?' Jonathan asked chirpily. 'Tell us your news, Grace.'

'Oh, you know, there's been a lot going on. Look, the reason I came is that I wanted to say sorry for, you know, disappearing like I did. I feel so bad about it. I've wanted to say this for years. And I realised we were driving past the town. I . . . I . . . I'm just so sorry.'

'Grace, sweetheart, you're here now,' I said. 'Thank you for coming, you didn't have to.'

'Don't be so nice! You're too nice! You were always too nice, both of you. I owe you an explanation.'

The sound of a horn beeping made us all jump.

'Look, I'll have to go but I do want to explain it all, if you'll let me?'

'Of course,' Jonathan and I said at the same time.

'You two haven't changed a bit,' Grace smiled. 'Look, I'm so sorry it's taken me this long. I've made a lot of mistakes. Things aren't great. Can I come and see you again?'

'Grace, of course you can. You're welcome here any time.'

She looked visibly relieved and let out a sigh.

'Thank you. Are you still fostering?'

Bang of cue, Finn bellowed down the stairs.

'Jonathan, Jonathan, where are you? My arm's aching.'

'Oh no! I've left the poor little fella propping up the Christmas tree!' Jonathan stepped through the kitchen door and called up, 'Sorry Finn, won't be a minute! Swap arms and you'll get matching muscles!'

Grace laughed. 'What about next week? I could come back on my own. I'd like that.'

We picked a morning when she could come for a coffee, and we swapped mobile numbers.

There was another beep-beep which seemed to put Grace's nerves on edge. Her face reddened and she immediately began to push herself up out of the chair.

'Thank you,' she huffed, lumbering towards the door. 'I wasn't sure . . . thank you for being so nice.'

'Thank *you*,' I said. 'I expect it wasn't at all easy for you to do this.'

'No, but you've made it easy. I should have known you would. I should have done it sooner.'

I have to be honest, I was worried sick about what Grace was going to tell us about her life and what had happened in her 'missing' five years.

I woke very early on the morning she was due to come for coffee. My mind was darting everywhere and I got up at six o'clock and made a cup of tea because I couldn't get back to sleep. It seemed like a very long time until eleven o'clock, when Grace pulled up outside.

I think Jonathan was as anxious as I was, but he tried not to show it.

'Looks like she's got a decent little car,' he said optimistically, looking out the window. 'Good for her!'

We both greeted Grace at the door and welcomed her into the kitchen, where I had a pot of coffee already made.

'I see you're as organised as ever,' she smiled.

Jonathan attempted to make a joke about me being a

'micro manager' and 'wearing the trousers' but it didn't really break the ice. Grace looked self-conscious and nervous.

'I knew we'd see you again,' I said. 'We've both always said it, haven't we?'

Jonathan nodded. 'Definitely. Never had any doubt.'

'And you're really not angry with me?'

'Not one bit,' we said in unison.

Grace finally cracked a smile. 'It's so good to see you two still singing from the same hymn sheet,' she said.

I poured the coffee and Grace took a slow sip before saying, 'A lot's gone on, a lot I'm not proud of.'

'You can tell us anything,' I reassured.

'I'm not sure where to start, but I do want to tell you what's happened. I owe it to you.'

'You don't have to tell us anything you don't want to,' I said. 'And there is no rush either. We're just so pleased to see you.'

There was a long pause and eventually Jonathan filled the silence by asking after her mum and her sister Lily.

'Mum hasn't changed. Lily's got three kids now. She suffers from depression, she doesn't cope well with stuff. She's on her own, and it's not easy for her.'

Grace stared into her coffee cup and let out a long sigh.

'You must have been tearing your hair out when I jacked in my apprenticeship.' We both stayed silent, showing her she had our attention and were not judging her. 'It was such a dumb move,' she added.

Grace started biting her nails and looked extremely

uncomfortable. We told her again to take her time and said she didn't have to tell us everything all at once.

Eventually, over the course of about an hour, Grace offloaded about how her life had spiralled downwards after she moved in with her mum. It was a shocking and very upsetting story, and I had to work very hard not to break down and cry.

Grace had been unemployed for a long time, which made her depressed. She became a heavy smoker and drinker and she got into a lot of debt. Without criticising her mum, Grace explained that Colette had encouraged her to apply for loans and credit cards to help keep them afloat.

'I thought I'd be able to pay everything off when I got a job, but nobody would give me a job, so I borrowed more and got more depressed and started drinking and smoking more. Mum was smoking and drinking a lot too, it was what we did. I started comfort eating. God, you must think I'm such a loser. You must wonder why you bothered doing everything you did for me . . .'

'Stop right there,' Jonathan said. 'We think nothing of the sort. If there's one thing we've learned as foster carers, it's that people aren't bad, well, not unless you're talking *serial killers* . . .' He said this in a theatrical voice and Grace laughed, as he had intended. 'Seriously,' he went on. 'You're not a bad person, Grace. Bad stuff has happened to you, that's all. It's not your fault.'

'Jonathan is right, and you can change things now. I can see you're ready to, and you want to. We can help you, in any way we can.'

Grace began to quietly cry. 'You're saints, both of you.'

'No, we're not. We love you to bits, Grace. We want the best for you, just as we did when you were a child. I can't tell you how pleased we are that you've got back in touch.'

She suddenly looked at her watch and abruptly said she had to go. 'Sorry to rush off. Thanks for the coffee, and everything.'

'OK, Grace. You are very welcome here any time. I admire your courage in telling us about what's gone on. Please phone us whenever you like, or call in. We're here for you. We'll give you as much support as we can, and don't you dare leave it another five years!'

'I promise I won't,' she said, but after she left we really weren't sure when we'd hear from her again. As it turned out, we need not have worried one bit. Grace phoned the next day, and the next. Gradually, she started to ask our advice about this and that, and we did our best to steer her towards her GP, the job centre, and various other support systems we thought could help her.

Over the next few months barely a day went by when Grace didn't phone us, even if just to touch base and say a brief hello. In one call, she told us she'd realised she'd hit rock bottom when she started talking to us. She said hearing herself describe her life had been an eye-opener and, from that point on, she had been trying very hard to make positive changes.

Her GP was excellent and helped her cut down on her smoking and drinking, as well as giving her good advice on her diet and general health. The changes didn't happen overnight of course, but Grace started to make good progress. She told us that one thing that motivated her was the fact she wanted to show Jonathan and me what she could do.

'You told me the world was my oyster and I believed you, but I stopped believing that after I moved out,' she said. 'That was such a big mistake.'

A breakthrough came when Grace managed to get herself a job in a department store. It seemed to give her the boost she needed to keep up the hard work. She told us she was planning on paying off her debts before saving for her own car (it turned out the nice little car she had arrived in when she came to visit belonged to a friend) and she said the job was keeping her focused on improving her health and well-being.

After another few months, Grace told us she'd met a man called Steve, at her local slimming club.

'I'd like you to meet him.'

'We'd love to.'

'Good. I want him to meet all my family.'

We were very pleased about this and it was also very touching to be described as Grace's 'family'.

We invited her and Steve over one Saturday afternoon. Even though we'd spoken on the phone almost every day, by now it had been about eight months since we'd actually seen Grace in person. She was bathed in August sunshine when I saw her standing on our doorstep, and I felt a wave of positivity wash over me. Grace had lost weight and looked so much healthier than she had done the last time she visited. I was also a member of a slimming club and I knew how hard she must have worked and was so proud of her. Steve, who was well over six-foot tall, looked thrilled to bits to have Grace on his arm. He had a friendly, open face and was a very polite and gentle person.

We sat in the garden and chatted for hours, reminiscing about how Grace used to bounce on her pogo stick, climb trees and play Swingball.

'I had the happiest years of my life here,' she announced. Jonathan and I looked at one another and smiled. It was a very gratifying moment.

Grace confided in me that it was only when she met Steve that she'd started to realise just what a negative influence her mother was on her life. She said that for years she attempted to give Colette the benefit of the doubt, desperately hoping to have the relationship with her mum she had always longed for, but she could now see she had been chasing something that was never going to exist in the way she had dreamed it would. 'It's taken me a long time, but I'm finally accepting that my mum is the way she is, and she's never going to change. I'll never get any answers from her, because she doesn't think she owes me any answers. I get it now. Steve's helped me to see things how they are.'

I had a very good feeling about Steve, and it was a huge relief to see how much Grace's life had improved in such a relatively short space of time.

The next time we saw them, a month or so later, they came over for Sunday lunch. Steve told us that he had wondered how Grace had turned into such a lovely, kind and well-rounded person, given how difficult her childhood had been. 'Now I've met you and Jonathan, I understand,' he said. It was a wonderful and humbling compliment to us, but what was most important to us was that Grace had found a partner who adored her, and clearly brought out the best in her.

'She's found her knight in shining armour,' Jonathan said that night.

'I think she has, but you know what the best thing is? She's made this happen herself. She's chosen her life and she's living the life she wants. Steve has helped her, but Grace is the one who has done the bravest thing. She's taken control, dumped her baggage and moved on.'

'I thought she did that a long time ago,' Jonathan said. I realised he was trying to stay deadpan and not laugh.

'What? Oh! Very funny. You're talking about her throwing her suitcase in the bin shelter all those years ago, aren't you? Dumping her baggage, ha ha, very funny!'

We laughed and laughed, much more from relief than because of Jonathan's little joke, I hasten to add!

Grace had been on an incredibly difficult journey throughout her life. We didn't know what the future held for her, but at long last we felt confident she would have a good, fulfilling life, and that she would look forward, undefined by her past, and make the most of every minute. That is what we wish for every child we foster.

Epilogue

Steve proposed to Grace on her twenty-fifth birthday, and of course we were absolutely delighted. They were such a good match, and Grace was happier than I'd ever known her. By now she'd had a promotion at work, her debts had long since been cleared, her weight was under control and she lived a healthy lifestyle. Shortly after they got engaged, Grace asked if they could call in, as they had something they wanted to talk about.

'I wonder if they're thinking about the flowers,' I said. They wanted a church wedding and Jonathan and I decided that we would offer to supply whatever they needed from the shop, as a gift from us.

In fact, Grace had a far more important question to ask.

'Will you give me away?' she asked Jonathan.

It's not often I've seen my husband dumbstruck, but he really was speechless for a moment before he stuttered, 'It will be an honour.' His voice was breaking with emotion, and I had to bite my lip to stop myself blubbing!

During that same visit Grace mentioned her life story books. She said she was sorry she had dumped them, as she would have liked to show them to Steve.

'Dumped them?' Jonathan said. 'You might have dumped them on us, but we didn't throw them away. Hang on.'

He went up into the loft and reappeared five minutes later, the full set of books in his hands. Grace was completely overwhelmed. It was a delight to see her showing them to Steve and reliving some of the happy memories we'd made together.

Grace had moved into a flat with Steve that was closer to us than her previous home had been. She began to call in regularly, often when Jonathan was in the shop and the two of us could have a chinwag over a cuppa. Other times we met in the out-of-town retail park and did a bit of shopping together, or had a bite to eat. Helping her choose her wedding dress was a treat I thoroughly enjoyed.

Every once in a while our conversations took an upsetting turn, but I understood this was necessary for Grace. She was on the cusp of an important new phase in her life and was clearly at a point where she wanted to make sense of the past. She needed to talk about her childhood and the years she spent growing up with us, and she often struck up a conversation about the past when I was least expecting it. I never minded. These chats sometimes helped me too, because along the way I found answers to questions I'd had hanging in my head for years.

For instance, one day Grace wanted to talk about her dad. She said that in nearly all her memories of being with her father she saw herself as a frightened, hungry little girl. She recalled that he used to hit her and Lily with a wooden ruler, which broke my heart. When he died, nobody told Grace what happened, and she found out about his accidental drug overdose by chance when she eventually overheard a conversation in the family home. She said that for many years she never spoke about it to anyone.

Grace said she remembered the string of foster placements she had before living with us as if they were one big, unhappy memory.

'I couldn't tell you how many placements I had, in what order or who my carers were. I tried to describe that part of my life to a friend recently and it was impossible. It was just a very unhappy time. All I wanted to do was go home, and I couldn't understand why Lily was allowed to be there and I wasn't. I still don't, not really, but it's water under the bridge now as far as I'm concerned.'

One afternoon we were drinking coffee in the kitchen when a 'sounds of the nineties' show came on the radio. Listening to Take That and the Spice Girls triggered childhood memories for Grace, and she started to talk about Lee, and the fact he used to take her clothes. I must admit I was nervous about what she was about to say as I'd always wondered if he had abused her in some way. In fact, to my relief, Grace was very kind about her stepbrother. She said she had not seen him for many years but that she forgave him everything when she learned what he had gone through. Lee had some deep-rooted psychological issues, she said. She didn't share what these were, but she made it clear he had problems that stemmed from early childhood experiences, growing up in a dysfunctional environment. 'I wish I hadn't called him names. I wish I'd known more about him, and what made him act the way he did.' I was pleased by her outlook. She had always looked for the best in people, and it was heartening to see that this quality had endured.

We spoke about her ADHD on several occasions, and we still do. Grace asked me to go over exactly how she was diagnosed and, as I had done when she was a teenager, I described how she saw a child psychologist when she was eleven, and then how a young female educational psychologist identified ADHD after several sessions and signed her off, leaving us to our own devices. I said that, in hindsight, it was amazing that the diagnosis was made so quickly, especially at a time when so little was known about ADHD. We know now that it can be extremely difficult to diagnose, and even though we were given virtually no guidance as to how to deal with Grace's ADHD, we agreed that she had been extremely fortunate to have been assessed by that particular psychologist.

'All I can really remember was that it was like a light-bulb moment,' Grace told me. 'When I had a name for it, I felt a lot happier. Before the diagnosis I thought I was just naughty, I suppose. I remember Mum called me Little Miss Trouble. I couldn't understand it because I didn't ever mean to cause any trouble.' She was controlling her ADHD really well, having improved her diet and lifestyle and continuing to use the techniques we'd learned together, such as list-making and focusing on one thing at a time.

In recent times, I've started to read about the very negative impact multiple placements can have on children. In Grace's day this was never discussed but in hindsight it's clear that it was not only ADHD that affected her behaviour. Going into care is a traumatic event in itself and moving between placements inevitably multiplies the effects of trauma. We know that experiencing trauma can adversely affect a child's behaviour, social interactions and ability to learn. Grace lived in a total of nine foster homes, including ours, and she attended eleven schools in all. Not only that, she was moved miles away from her family. Clearly, even without her ADHD, she had a mountain to climb.

Grace was twenty-six when she married Steve, and she made a stunning and radiant bride. She and Steve had maintained their target weight, which they had worked extremely hard to achieve. I'd been on a diet for the big day and managed to lose a stone, which wasn't easy at all. I took my hat off to them.

The wedding was wonderful and unforgettable – a day to remember. Seeing Jonathan proudly giving Grace away will be etched at the forefront of my mind forever. It was a priceless, heart-stopping moment.

The only member of Grace's family who attended the wedding was Lily, who by then was the mother of four children. The sisters had become closer in recent years, while their relationship with their mother had deteriorated to the point where they barely spoke to her.

A few years into their marriage, I was sorry to hear that Grace and Steve were not able to have children of their own.

They decided to adopt and had just been passed as adoptive parents when Lily had her latest baby – her fifth – removed by Social Services.

As I write, Grace and Steve are applying for an SGO, which is a special guardianship order, so they can care for Lily's child. SGOs give the guardians parental responsibility over the child until they reach eighteen, but the child does not officially stop being a member of their birth family in the same way as they do when they are adopted. Once the SGO is granted, Grace and Steve will be able to raise Lily's child as if he were their own, without intervention from Social Services. Lily is not only fully supportive of the plans, but extremely grateful to her sister.

Grace is in her early thirties now and no longer in contact with her mum. It's taken a long time but she told me she made the decision to cut ties for the sake of her own mental health and wellbeing. Going through the gruelling process of applying to adopt made her see what an enormous responsibility it is to care for a child, and it brought back a lot of unhappy memories from her childhood. Grace said seeing her mum always triggered anxiety, and as she got older she felt a lot of anger and resentment too. The image of her old, grey suitcase would come into her mind. It made her heart rate increase and brought on feelings of panic and insecurity.

'It's been a very long road,' Grace said. 'And I couldn't have done it without you.'

I have told Grace many times that I am incredibly proud of her, and I truly am. She has a huge heart and has triumphed against the odds.

If you met her today you would have no idea of her struggle with ADHD, of her difficult childhood and journey through the care system, or of the depths she fell to when she was missing from our lives. You'd simply see a healthy, positive and wonderfully kind young woman who is eagerly looking forward to the next exciting stage in her life. It's incredibly rewarding to watch her thrive and it's an absolute privilege to have Grace back in our lives. She's a remarkable woman, and we love her to bits.

The Girl Who Wanted to Belong

The true story of a devastated little girl
and the foster carer who healed her broken heart.

I'll be very, very good,' she told me. 'I won't make Wendy cross with me.'

'I'm pleased to hear you're going to be well behaved, sweetheart. By the way, have you remembered she prefers you not to call her Wendy?'

'Yes. I need to call her Mum. I don't like calling her Mum, but I will. Mum, Mum, Mum.'

Lucy is eight years old and ends up in foster care after being abandoned by her mum and kicked out by her dad's new partner, Wendy. Two aunties and then her elderly grandmother take her in, but it seems nobody can cope with Lucy's disruptive behaviour. Social Services hope a stay with experienced foster carer Angela will help Lucy settle down. Lucy is desperate for a fresh start back home, but will she ever be able to live in harmony with her stepmother and her stepsister – a girl who was once her best friend at school?

Available now in paperback and ebook.

The Girl With Two Lives

A shocking childhood. A foster carer who understood.
A young girl's life forever changed.

As I stepped back into the kitchen, Danielle looked very proud as she held her notepad up for me to see.

'Finished!' she declared cheerfully. I was surprised to see that the surname Danielle had printed wasn't the one I'd seen on her paperwork from Social Services, and so I asked her casually if she used two different names, which often happens when children come from broken homes.

'Yes,' she said. 'But this is the surname I'm going to use from now on, because it's the name of my forever family.'

Danielle has been excluded from school and her former foster family can no longer cope. She arrives as an emergency placement at the home of foster carer Angela Hart, who soon suspects that there is more to the young girl's disruptive behaviour than meets the eye. Can Angela's specialist training unlock the horrors of Danielle's past and help her start a brave new life?

Available now in paperback and ebook.

The Girl and the Ghosts

The true story of a haunted little girl and the
foster carer who rescued her from the past.

*'So, is it a girl or a boy, and how old?'
Jonathan asked as soon as we were alone
in the shop.*

*My husband knew from the animated
look on my face, and the way I was itching
to talk to him, that our social worker had
been asking us to look after another child.*

*I filled Jonathan in as quickly as I could
and he gave a thin, sad smile.*

*'Bruises?' he said. 'And a moody temperament? Poor little
girl. Of course we can manage a few days.'*

*I gave Jonathan a kiss on the cheek. 'I knew you'd say that.
It's exactly what I thought.'*

*We were well aware that the few days could run into weeks
or even longer, but we didn't need to discuss this. We'd looked
after dozens of children who had arrived like Maria, emotionally or physically damaged, or both. We'd do whatever it took
to make her feel loved and cared for while she was in our home.*

Seven-year-old Maria holds lots of secrets. Why won't she
tell how she got the bruises on her body? Why does she run
and hide? And why does she so want to please her sinister
stepfather?

It takes years for devoted foster carer Angela Hart to
uncover the truth as she helps Maria leave the ghosts of her
past behind.

Available now in paperback and ebook.

The Girl Who Just Wanted to be Loved

A damaged little girl and a foster carer
who wouldn't give up.

The first time we ever saw Keeley was in a Pizza Hut. She was having lunch with her social worker.

'Unfortunately Keeley's current placement is breaking down,' our support social worker, Sandy, had explained. 'We'd like to move her as soon as possible.'

We'd looked after more than thirty youngsters over the years, yet I never failed to feel a surge of excitement at the prospect of caring for another one.

Sandy began by explaining that Keeley was eight years old and had stayed with four sets of carers and been in full-time care with two different families.

'Why have the placements not worked out?' I asked.

'All the foster carers tell similar stories. Keeley's bad behaviour got worse instead of better as time went on. That's why we're keen for you to take her on, Angela. I'm sure you'll do a brilliant job.'

Eight-year-old Keeley looks like the sweetest little girl you could wish to meet, but demons from the past make her behaviour far from angelic. She takes foster carer Angela on a rocky and very demanding emotional ride as she fights daily battles against her deep-rooted psychological problems. Can the love and specialist care Angela and husband Jonathan provide help Keeley triumph against the odds?

Available now in paperback and ebook.

Terrified

The heartbreaking true story of a girl
nobody loved and the woman who saved her.

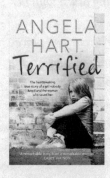

*Vicky stared through the windscreen, her
eyeballs glazed like marbles. She was sitting
completely rigid in her seat, frozen with
fear.*

*I took a deep breath and then asked
Vicky as gently as possible, if she was all
right.*

*'I'm here, right beside you, Vicky. Can
you hear me? I'm here and I can help you.'*

*She still didn't respond in any way at all. Her normally rosy
cheeks had turned ivory white and the expression of terror on
her face was like nothing I'd seen before: I had never seen a
child look so scared in all my life.*

*'Take a deep breath, love. That's what I've just done. Just
breathe and try to calm yourself down. You're with me, Angela,
and you're safe.'*

Vicky seemed all self-assurance and swagger when she came
to live with Angela and Jonathan as a temporary foster placement. As Vicky's mask of bravado began to slip, she was
overtaken with episodes of complete terror. Will the trust and
love Angela and her husband Jonathan provide enable Vicky
to finally overcome her shocking past?

Available now in paperback and ebook.